"Have immoral entertainers in music and cinema become idols you seek out and admire? This soul-searching question is just one of many raised in this excellent book that leverages the author's decades of senior military leadership to establish connections between physical war and spiritual warfare. Irrespective of where you are in your spiritual journey, this book will help you, encourage you, and set you on the right path."
—SIMON GONCHARENKO, author of
Church Government according to the Bible

"As a former member of the Joint Staff in Counterterrorism, I recognize the pattern Jonathan Corrado so adeptly highlights: the ability for the enemy to use partial truths to distort, deceive, and unduly influence believers to compromise their standards. Corrado succinctly identifies the enemies strategies and how we as believers can properly fight in the spiritual world."
—RICHARD DIDDAMS, retired lieutenant colonel, US Marine Corps

"In his new book, Jonathan Corrado exposes the sinister and often subtle schemes (PSYOPS) Satan uses against us. Using a wealth of biblical knowledge and over two decades of military experience, Corrado guides us like a spiritual 'Navy Seal' to help us not only know who and what we are up against, but also how we can win the war and live in victory every day."
—BARRY L. CAMERON, author of *The ABC's of Financial Freedom*

"This book is a great reminder to Christians that we are in a spiritual battle. Satan is the great deceiver who is constantly on the attack. We need to be aware of these methods and take precautions to counter them. Deception can be defeated by using the truth of God's word."

—TIMOTHY CLAREY, director of research,
Institute for Creation Research

"Jonathan Corrado provides a masterful training manual for Christians to combat the deceptive tactics of Satan. Using his military experiences regarding PSYOP and deep biblical wisdom, Corrado helps Christians to overcome spiritual deception and fight the good fight! Prepare yourself for the spiritual battle against the Enemy!"

—JAMIE TRASCRITTI, lead pastor, The Village Church

"An invaluable clear and concise view of Satan's playbook! Jonathan Corrado's *Defying Deception* presents the signals and plans of the Enemy and deftly follows through with the battle plan to strengthen the Christian walk. For the young and seasoned Christian alike, Corrado points out to all of us who are in the battle the tactics and strategies of Satan while also pointing forward to the Bible and Jesus Christ, the one source of true truth and salvation for all."

—CHRIS BERGE, director, EXSEL Discipleship Program,
Officers' Christian Fellowship

Defying Deception

Defying Deception

A Field Guide to Understanding and Countering
Satan's Strategy of Deception

JONATHAN K. CORRADO

RESOURCE *Publications* • Eugene, Oregon

DEFYING DECEPTION
A Field Guide to Understanding and Countering Satan's Strategy of Deception

Copyright © 2024 Jonathan K. Corrado. All rights reserved. Except for brief quotations in critical publications or reviews, no part of this book may be reproduced in any manner without prior written permission from the publisher. Write: Permissions, Wipf and Stock Publishers, 199 W. 8th Ave., Suite 3, Eugene, OR 97401.

Resource Publications
An Imprint of Wipf and Stock Publishers
199 W. 8th Ave., Suite 3
Eugene, OR 97401

www.wipfandstock.com

PAPERBACK ISBN: 978-1-6667-8964-5
HARDCOVER ISBN: 978-1-6667-8965-2
EBOOK ISBN: 978-1-6667-8966-9

02/23/24

This book is dedicated to Earth's Creator.

For by Him all things were created that are in heaven and that are on earth, visible and invisible, whether thrones or dominions or principalities or powers. All things were created through Him and for Him. And He is before all things, and in Him all things consist.

—Col 1:16–17 (NKJV)

Contents

Preface | ix

List of Abbreviations | xiii

1　Deception: An Introduction | 1

2　Satan's Fall, His Ambitions, and His Power | 17

3　Military Deception and PSYOP | 29

4　A Catalog of Deceptive PSYOP as Discussed in Scripture | 39

5　Counter-PSYOP Methods to Guard against Deception: Conditioning, Indirect, and Direct Refutation | 69

6　Counter-PSYOP Methods to Guard against Deception: Forestalling and Restrictive Measures | 96

7　A Final Word on Satan's Tactic of Deception: Viewed through the Lens of Military PSYOP | 121

Appendix A: Absolute (or Universal) Truth | 131

Appendix B: The Foundation of the Gospel | 146

Appendix C: Why God's Word Is True | 165

Appendix D: The Bible: The Sole Authority for Faith and Practice | 184

Bibliography | 191

Subject Index | 201

Scripture Index | 215

Preface

Penn Jillette, the verbal half of the magician duo Penn and Teller and an outspoken atheist . . . posted a YouTube video exhorting Christians to share their faith. Penn and Teller are headliners in Las Vegas, and their shows generally are marked by foul language and shock appeal. Penn Jillette, though, used no coarse language in telling about an audience member who gave him a New Testament.

. . . "If you believe that there's a heaven and hell and people could be going to hell or not getting eternal life or whatever, and you think that it's not really worth telling them this because it would make it socially awkward, and atheists who think that people shouldn't proselytize—'Just leave me alone, keep your religion to yourself.' How much do you have to hate somebody to not proselytize?" Jillette asked. "How much do you have to hate somebody to believe that everlasting life is possible and not tell them that? If I believed beyond a shadow of a doubt that a truck was coming at you and you didn't believe it, and that truck was bearing down on you, there's a certain point where I tackle you. And this is more important than that."[1]

MATT 28:19–20 CONTAINS WHAT is called "the Great Commission": "Go therefore and make disciples of all the nations, baptizing them in the name of the Father and of the Son and of the Holy

---

1. Erin Roach, "ATHEISM: Penn Jillette Urges Evangelism," *Baptist Press* (February 12, 2009). https://www.baptistpress.com/resource-library/news/atheism-penn-jillette-urges-evangelism

Spirit, teaching them to observe all things that I have commanded you; and lo, I am with you always, even to the end of the age." Christ's charge to Christians in this passage is unambiguously clear; however, as conveyed by Penn Jillette above, Christians find themselves stumbling to execute it. This stumbling is in part a result of Satan and his strategy to thwart the plan of God using his most prominent tool: deception.

Having served two decades as an officer in the US Navy in a breadth of operational assignments both at sea and in a ground combat theater, including five deployments, attended war college, and having worked as an engineer and manager at a Department of Defense laboratory and in the defense industry on sensitive programs dealing with clandestine systems, I have firsthand experience of military deception and military psychological operations (PSYOP). Additionally, as a Bible scholar, my experience in both the military and defense industry has provided me with a unique perspective to glean commonalities between Satan's deceptive strategy and PSYOP, and hence formulate a strategy using counter-PSYOP methods to aid Christians in avoiding Satan's deceptive stratagems so that they can live out the life God has intended for them while engaging in spiritual battle, "for we wrestle not against flesh and blood, but against principalities, against powers, against the rulers of the darkness of this world, against spiritual wickedness in high places" (Eph 6:12). Speaking to Penn Jillette's point above and based on my own experience, I believe that it is important to warn Christians of Satan's deceptive strategies and provide tools to equip Christians to overcome them. In doing so, the *real* Christian faith can be earnestly contended, for as Jude asserts in Jude 1:3, "Beloved, while I was very diligent to write to you concerning our common salvation, I found it necessary to write to you exhorting you to contend earnestly for the faith which was once for all delivered to the saints."

This field guide is written in the spirit of military field manuals in that it contains detailed information and how-tos for procedures important to military personnel serving in the field. It contains concise entries and can be conveniently carried for quick reference while traveling, working, or studying. Additionally, this guide opens like an accordion in that it provides layered, in-depth information available should you have questions, want to know more, or dig deeper. You can (1) read the chapter content only, (2) expand in specific areas by engaging with the litany of notes provided, and/or (3) further expand in four foundational Christian topics by reading the appendices. Additionally, this guide addresses many of the common apologetics arguments confronting Christianity by providing a quick reference in order to "always be ready to give a defense to everyone who asks you a reason for the hope that is in you" (1 Pet 3:15).

List of Abbreviations

1–2 Chr	1–2 Chronicles
1–2 Cor	1–2 Corinthians
1–2 Kgs	1–2 Kings
1–2 Macc	1–2 Maccabees
1–2 Pet	1–2 Peter
1–2 Sam	1–2 Samuel
1–2 Thess	1–2 Thessalonians
1–2 Tim	1–2 Timothy
1–2–3 John	1–2–3 John
Acts	Acts
AD	Anno Domini
Amos	Amos
BC	Before Christ
Col	Colossians
Dan	Daniel
Deut	Deuteronomy
Eccl	Ecclesiastes
Eph	Ephesians
Esth	Esther

LIST OF ABBREVIATIONS

ESV	English Standard Version
Exod	Exodus
Ezek	Ezekiel
Ezra	Ezra
FUSAG	First US Army Group
Gal	Galatians
Gen	Genesis
Hab	Habakkuk
Hag	Haggai
Heb	Hebrews
Hos	Hosea
Isa	Isaiah
Jas	James
Jer	Jeremiah
Job	Job
Joel	Joel
John	John
Jonah	Jonah
Josh	Joshua
Jude	Jude
Judg	Judges
KJV	King James Version
Lam	Lamentations
LDS	Latter-day Saints
Lev	Leviticus
Luke	Luke
Mal	Malachi
Mark	Mark

LIST OF ABBREVIATIONS

Matt	Matthew
Mic	Micah
MILDEC	Military Deception
Nah	Nahum
Neh	Nehemiah
NIV	New International Version
Num	Numbers
NWT	New World Translation
Obad	Obadiah
Phil	Philippians
Phlm	Philemon
Prov	Proverbs
Ps	Psalms
PSYOP	Psychological Operations
Rev	Revelation
Rom	Romans
Ruth	Ruth
Song	Song of Solomon
Titus	Titus
UK	United Kingdom
US	United States
Zech	Zechariah

1

Deception: An Introduction

United States F-16 aircraft mockups on a fake runway.[1]

> Propaganda more than ever is an instrument of aggression, a new means for rendering a country defenseless in the face of an invading army.
> —ALFRED MCCLUNG LEE AND ELIZABETH BRIANT LEE, *THE FINE ART OF PROPAGANDA*, 1939

1. *F-16 Mockups on Fake Runway Spangdahlem AB 1985*, Public Domain.

Defying Deception

COMPREHENSIVE TRAINING AND DISCIPLINE are the hallmarks of any robust military training program. Well-instructed soldiers can think clearly and make wise choices under stressful situations. Similarly, Christians must train to be prepared to make biblically sound choices while facing spiritual obstacles—specifically, deception.[2]

Merriam-Webster's Collegiate Dictionary defines "deception" as "the act of causing someone to accept as true or valid what is false or invalid." The scriptures often reference Satan's use of deception as a tactic in spiritual warfare.[3] Curiously, military psychological operations (PSYOP) can reasonably reflect the methods Satan uses to deceive humans.[4] PSYOP are "planned operations to convey selected [false] information and indicators to foreign audiences to influence their emotions, motives, and objective reasoning, and ultimately the behavior of foreign governments, organizations, groups, and individuals."[5] I would contend that military PSYOP define how Satan wages his campaign of deception, and with this understanding Christians can be better equipped to deter deception. This is important because deception will continue to be compounded, as Paul warns Timothy in 2 Tim 3:13: "But evil men and impostors will grow worse and worse, deceiving and being deceived."[6]

The Bible clearly states that deception is Satan's main tool to sway humankind. The warning "do not be deceived" appears many times in the New Testament.[7] Likewise, it discusses deception, false doctrine, and false prophets over forty times.[8] Although material and technological advantages might appear to dominate the battle

---

2. Corrado, "Be Not Deceived."

3. Grudem, *Systematic Theology*, 888–89.

4. PSYOP is pronounced ˈsī-ˌäp (*Merriam-Webster's Collegiate Dictionary*).

5. Department of the Army, *Army Support to Military Deception*, 2–21.

6. Unless otherwise noted, all biblical passages referenced are in the New King James Version.

7. See, for example, 1 Cor 6:9–10, Jas 1:13–18, and Gal 6:7.

8. Strong and Kohlenberger, *New Strong's Expanded Exhaustive Concordance*, 1417.

landscape and shape the outcome, "we wrestle not against flesh and blood, but against principalities, against powers, against the rulers of the darkness of this world, against spiritual wickedness in high places" (Eph 6:12). As Satan's deceptive agenda continues to distort truth, an understanding of his tactics in the context of PSYOP will assist Christians in overcoming spiritual deception by aiding in the development of defensive strategies.

Satan and his demon army are engaged in spiritual warfare with God and humanity, which manifests, in part, in an elaborate campaign of deception. Like the use of PSYOP in military campaigns across the centuries, these tactics are nothing new and derive from Satan's cache of deception tactics. He initially showcased this weapon in the Garden of Eden, where he deceived Eve, thus initiating a cascading series of deceptions that still sway humankind today, and Christians are in the crosshairs. Understanding Satan's deceptive schemes is of vital importance for overcoming them. Accordingly, this guide presents Satan's strategy of deception through the lens of military PSYOP in order to equip Christians to overcome deception in a world that embraces it.

World War II brought with it the beginning of a new emphasis on psychological warfare. War was no longer merely a measure of superior weaponry and armed forces. It was suddenly a mental battle for the minds and spirits of both civilians and soldiers.[9] World War II offers a vivid example of how psychological warfare was employed to target the morale and sentiment not only of soldiers but also of civilians. One fascinating means of dissemination of psychological material took the form of leaflets that were dropped from bomber aircraft. These messages were intended to dampen the soldiers' motivation and enthusiasm on the battlefield. Some leaflets, for instance, depicted scenes of marital infidelity, a subject that undoubtedly speaks to the sense of insecurity felt by many soldiers deployed for extended periods of time.

The effectiveness of psychological warfare is found in one's inability to resist its effects. One of the most powerful aspects of warfare is psychological manipulation. Although people are

---

9. Welch, *Germany, Propaganda and Total War*, 355.

generally aware of the physical brutality and violence of war, psychological warfare is often ignored. Psychological warfare aims at one's insecurities and desires and uses these means for achieving the opposing force's objectives. War is frequently characterized as a mechanistic approach to human affairs, centered on the creation of a powerful and effective war machine. Psychological warfare seeks to destabilize the war machine by targeting individuals within the system, undermining political ideas by focusing on personal motivations. Psychological warfare focuses on unsettling the opponent by the systematic and scientific use of the most personal parts of human life. Fear, anger, humiliation, and loneliness, which are frequently seen as the darkest and most vulnerable aspects of human nature, are relentlessly exploited until the opponent is seemingly too demoralized to fight.

In the context of contemporary military doctrine, psychological warfare is a well-defined and well-established concept that can be employed to support varied operations at the strategic, operational, and tactical levels. According to the US Joint Chiefs of Staff, psychological modes of warfare often form a critical aspect of planning that can be used to gain a decisive battlefield advantage over an enemy force.[10] The military uses PSYOP to confuse or redirect enemy forces prior to critical operations. In the US military context, highly developed PSYOP primarily emerged out of the national experience of World War II, the Cold War, and the Vietnam War. The broader philosophy that undergirds PSYOP, however, has its roots in antiquity. The influential writings of Sun Tzu (544–496 BC) in his book, *The Art of War*, Old Testament depictions of battle planning and operations, and recorded and archeological evidence from the classical world all reference military forces seeking to achieve an operational advantage through the employment of psychologically-based strategic and tactical principles. To this point, Carl von Clausewitz (1780–1831), a renowned Prussian general and military theorist, in his book, *On War* (1827), considered a seminal treatise on military strategy and science, writes that "all military action is intertwined with psychological forces

---

10. Joint Chiefs of Staff, *Psychological Operations*, I-4.

DECEPTION: AN INTRODUCTION

and effects." As with other dimensions of combat, the theories and capabilities related to the concept evolved in various ways after the introduction of firearms, supportive battlefield technologies, and strategic planning concepts that would ultimately inform the development of modern warfare.

Given that Satan and his demon army are engaged in spiritual warfare with God and humanity, warfare that manifests in part as a campaign of deception, this guide establishes a parallel between Satan's deceptive tactics and military PSYOP because both seek to lead people into falsehood. PSYOP are designed to convey a misleading notion of reality to an audience so they will react as the enemy desires. Our enemy, Satan, wants humans separated from God—and sin does just that. Jas 1:14–15 says, "but each one is tempted when he is drawn away by his own desires and enticed. Then, when desire has conceived, it gives birth to sin; and sin, when it is full-grown, brings forth death." Humans are naturally inclined to sin, and Satan, the tempter, as he "prowls around like a roaring lion" (1 Pet 5:8, NIV), via his deceptive PSYOP, nudges us toward sin's seductive grip.

The sin nature is the aspect of humans that makes us hostile toward God. When we refer to the sin nature, we are referring to the fact that we have a natural propensity to sin; if given the option to do God's will or our own, we will choose to do our own will. Ample evidence of the sin nature exists. No one is required to teach a child to lie or be self-centered; instead, we go to great lengths to teach children to tell the truth and place others before themselves. Sinful behavior is inherent. The news is replete with tragic examples of human behavior. Wherever there are people, there is conflict and the Bible explains the cause of the conflict. Humanity is sinful by nature, not just in theory or in practice. Sin is a fundamental component of our being. Rom 8:3 mentions "sinful flesh"; the list of sins in Col 3:5 is derived from our "earthly nature"; and Rom 6:6 speaks of "the body ruled by sin." Our sinful, corrupt essence shapes our physical existence on this Earth. The sin nature is innate to all humans and our sinful essence permeates every aspect of our being. As Satan cannot force humans to sin, his aim is merely to tap into our sin nature in order to tempt us to commit sin (to separate us from God)—and deception is a fundamental way he can do so.

This guide can help equip Christians to detect deception in their everyday lives. The guide discusses the background of Satan's fall, his ambitions, his power, and his deceptive strategies in the context of PSYOP. Using this information, defensive strategies are outlined to help Christians confidently engage in spiritual warfare and "be able to stand against the wiles of the devil" (Eph 6:11).

STRATEGIC DECEPTION AND PROPAGANDA OPTIMIZED BY NAZI GERMANY

Deception, whether exercised in an international context or in individual cases in terms of the human struggle with sin, has permeated human existence since the Garden of Eden. Beginning almost a century ago, the Nazi regime cast upon the German people a spell that was so devastatingly potent that it transformed an entire nation into a mass of individuals enthralled by myths and intoxicated with iconography.

Adolf Hitler, a formerly failed landscape artist who transformed into a powerful, charismatic dictator, has long been considered a master of strategic deception and propaganda.[11] Nazi propaganda, which was often based on pre-existing traditional German values, culture, religion, and mindset, was used to distract the people from the brutal, antisemitic actions being taken in

---

11. "'Propaganda' is a broad term that means management of collective attitudes through communications and symbols, for the purpose of promoting or damaging a cause. Among its non-PSYOP applications are commercial advertising, political campaigning, and religious exhortation. (The term was invented by the Roman Catholic Church in its seventeenth-century campaigns against Protestantism.) But in the contemporary public understanding, those aspects have been overshadowed by the widespread political uses of propaganda in the twentieth century. Although the term had become associated with untruth, propaganda in the PSYOP context must contain large amounts of true information, because of the primary requirement that the audience believe the message." (Federal Research Division, *An Overview of Psychological Operations (PSYOP)*)

order to reinstitute those values and to explain previous and present world events by focusing on emotional manipulation and national political support for restoring ideological German culture.[12] Modern techniques of opinion formation that the Nazis employed to generate a "truly religio-psychological phenomenon"[13] lent particular potency to their propaganda. The operational strategy of the Third Reich, which promoted Nazi ideology, was propaganda. Albert Speer, the primary architect of Hitler's regime, stated before the Nuremberg Tribunal that "what distinguished the Third Reich from all previous dictatorships was its use of all the means of communication to sustain itself and to deprive its objects of the power of independent thought."[14]

Cultural historian Piers Brendon has characterized Nazi propaganda as the "gospel" and remarked that Joseph Goebbels, head of the Ministry of Public Enlightenment and Propaganda, "liked to say that Jesus Christ [was] a master of propaganda and that the propagandist must be the man with the greatest knowledge of souls." Although it also facilitated the recruitment of new members for the movement, the objective of Nazi propaganda was not to brainwash average Germans or mislead the populace. Historian Neil Gregor has asserted that the primary aim was "to absorb the individual into a mass of like-minded people, and the purpose of the 'suggestion' was not to deceive but to articulate that which the crowd already believed."[15] Thus, a fundamental component of the Nazi grand strategy was the overthrow of reason and the exaltation of emotion.

As Nazism appealed to emotions rather than the intellect, its propaganda appealed to feelings rather than thought. The orchestration of sentiments formed the foundation of all Nazi actions;

---

12. Kallis, *Nazi Propaganda*, 301. To exhibit the evil extent of Nazi deception, the phrase, *Arbeit macht frei* (work sets you free), inscribed on the entrance of many Nazi concentration camps, expressed a cruel and misleading false hope to the millions of "undesirables" and "enemies of the Third Reich" who ultimately met their undeserved, brutal demise.

13. Bracher, *The German Dictatorship*, 48.

14. Rutherford, *Hitler's Propaganda Machine*, 32.

15. Gregor, *How to Read Hitler*, 54.

it was the operational formula of their propaganda. For Goebbels, the role of the propagandist was to verbalize the emotions that his audience felt in their hearts.[16] Therefore, propaganda had to be primitive, appealing to what Hitler described as man's inner *Schweinehund* ("pig dog," a derogatory idiom for one's inner self).[17] The propaganda typically demonstrated a cruel "either/or" perspective and appealed to the audience's primitive desire for simplification, as in the following example: "There are ... only two possibilities: either the victory of the Aryan side or its annihilation and the victory of the Jews."[18] The Nazis believed that a formulaic propaganda methodology must be applied even at the cost of alienating sophisticated members of its audience.

The essence of the Nazi propaganda method was repetition. The Nazis' ideological message saturated the barriers of inattention through its overwhelming insistence on its replication. Goebbels advocated for the "repeated exposure effect." Ideas had to be continually re-seeded to germinate, as the Nazis believed the collective mind was dull and sluggish, thus, repetition could facilitate the phases of the cognitive process that comprise the mass mind: recognition, comprehension, retention, and conviction. Hence, it is critical to bear in mind that Nazi propaganda additionally provided the dubious advantage of sensory exhaustion. The citizen was not so much an object to be convinced as a victim to be subdued and even devoured.

In addition to external compliance, the Nazi party desired internal commitment. Goebbels asserted that the Nazis were distinguished by "the ability to see into the soul of the people and to speak the language of the man in the street."[19] The propagandist was an artist who "sensed the secret vibrations of the people."[20] European fascism was primarily distinguished by its development of novel approaches, a methodology to communicate with the

---

16. Paxton, *The Anatomy of Fascism*, 78–82.
17. Newcourt-Nowodworski, *Black Propaganda in the Second World War*, 154.
18. Bracher, *The German Dictatorship*, 85.
19. Spotts, *Hitler and the Power of Aesthetics*, 98–101.
20. Rutherford, *Hitler's Propaganda Machine*, 64.

working class. The fascists were not ashamed of mass media and marketing; they comprehended the culture of consumerism and acknowledged the pervasive influence of these phenomena on the lives of the general public. The media had become a new language with which the masses were acquainted, including its styles, forms, and assumptions. Fascists were comfortable in this exciting new world and understood that it could be utilized for political gain, both as a source of method and as a novel culture based on an alternative set of governing assumptions.

Nazism did not ask for belief but for surrender; this was primarily accomplished through an assault on consciousness rather than through coercion. The fundamental objective was to eradicate independent thought through the use of images that would think for people. Yet the seeming ease with which Germans "went along" with, or apparently ignored, the true frauds continues to astonish.[21]

While this deception and propaganda focused on restoring Germany to a state of supremacy and traditional values, Hitler's plan included the control and annexation of many countries and cultures. Nazi Germany's annexation of the Sudetenland in the prelude to World War II is an example of well-executed deception and showcases the extent to which deception can be used to wield significant influence. The annexation of the Sudetenland, which was then a part of Czechoslovakia and was inhabited primarily by Sudeten Germans, involved clever propaganda and strategic deception aimed at many groups to further the Nazi cause, including residents of the Sudetenland as well as the German people.[22]

Czechoslovakia was strategically located, and its subjugation was central to Hitler's plans for European conquest, as it had one of the strongest armies in Europe and an ample arms industry. Additionally, it included the Sudeten Mountains, a militarized, fortified barrier deterring Hitler's plans to sweep across Europe. As an outright military campaign to seize this land seemed impossible, given Czech military strength in the area and the guarantee by Western

21. O'Shaughnessy, *Selling Hitler*, 32–87.
22. Shirer, *Rise and Fall*, 448.

powers to resist aggressive attack via the Treaty of Versailles, Hitler instigated an unparalleled crusade to politically coerce the Czechs to surrender their land. He was able to do this by pushing the narrative that the Sudetenland's inhabitants were predominantly of German origin and deserved the right of self-determination—this despite the fact that Sudeten Germans already enjoyed full civil rights and economic prosperity under the democratic government of Czechoslovakia. To bolster this false narrative, Hitler backed the formation of the *Sudetendeutsches Freikorps* (Sudeten German Free Corps), a liberation movement, and he prompted a sequence of well-organized and vicious uprisings that the Czechs were obliged to suppress by force. Additionally, Hitler commissioned Goebbels to orchestrate a disinformation crusade about "Czech terror" and Sudeten German oppression.[23]

Hitler asserted that the Czech government's refusal to return the Sudeten territories to their "rightful" German owners was an impediment to regional peace. Moreover, the Czechs were trying to hasten a European crisis in order to prevent the breakup of their state. The choice between war and peace in Europe rested in Czech hands. Hitler graciously offered a simple solution: the Western powers could force Czechoslovakia to relinquish these "rightfully" German territories.[24]

On September 18, 1938, under the pressure of a September 28 deadline set by Hitler, a consensus was reached between the British and French that Czechoslovakia must accede to Hitler's demands. Despite the Versailles agreement that the West would go to war to defend the Czech borders, it agreed that the Sudetenland must be relinquished to maintain peace and protect its vital interests. In exchange, Britain and France would provide an additional international guarantee to defend the new borders against unprovoked foreign aggression.[25] If the Czechs chose not to accept this plan, they would be left to face Germany alone. However, British Prime Minister Neville Chamberlain knew, as the world

23. Shirer, *Rise and Fall*, 524–26.
24. Shirer, *Rise and Fall*, 490, 519, 538.
25. Shirer, *Rise and Fall*, 489.

closely watched, that if the Czechs chose to fight, France and Britain would very likely be forced to fight also.[26] Chamberlain became progressively more desperate to deter war by buying off Hitler, and moments before the looming September 28 deadline pleaded with Hitler to participate in an international peace conference starting the following day, to which Hitler eventually "agreed."

At the Munich peace conference, after eleven hours of pleading, Britain and France convinced Hitler to "compromise" and take the Sudetenland peacefully. The Sudetenland was duly annexed to Germany without a single shot fired. Hitler had succeeded in elevating propaganda over reality. The speed and readiness with which this transparent ruse was received, digested, and adopted by the West are astonishing. As the Western leaders returned home in supposed victory, Chamberlain declared, "I believe it is peace for our time"—which turned out to be far from the truth.[27]

As demonstrated in this example, well-executed deception can have a tremendous effect: advantageous to the entity inflicting the deception and deleterious to the recipient. Similarly, Satan's well-executed deception can have a profound consequence: advantageous to his campaign to deter people from God and to bolster his pride and deleterious to those that fall for his deceptions, which distort their understanding of God and the truth of Scripture, thus affecting salvation and eternal life.

THE FALL OF MAN

Propaganda has the capacity to incorporate any information, ranging from unadulterated truth to flagrant deceit. To assist in classifying (in order to appropriately counter), propaganda is

26. Shirer, *Rise and Fall*, 535.

27. This example just scratches the surface of propaganda-driven dictatorship deception. There are many examples of truth-manipulating tyrants that institutionalized propaganda to sway the public to their agenda—Idi Amin of Uganda, Muammar Gaddafi of Libia, Fidel Castro of Cuba, Joeseph Stalin of the Soviet Union, Saddam Hussein of Iraq, among many others—all of which employed propaganda from the same playbook. Unsurprisingly, this same playbook is in use today in spiritual warfare waged by Satan and his demon army.

categorized into three distinct domains—white, gray, or black—on the basis of the veracity of the information disseminated and the recognition of its source. White propaganda originates from a properly designated source and disseminates accurate information. For instance, the information presented on *Voice of America* may be deemed reasonably accurate by its audience, albeit with a slight bias towards democratic principles. The source may or may not be accurately identified in gray propaganda, rendering the information's veracity uncertain. An instance of this category of propaganda was a Russian television documentary concerning the Afghanistan War, which posited that the conflict had been instigated by external forces. Additionally, an individual, identified as a Turkish national, testified that he had been sent to carry out a mission for the Central Intelligence Agency. Lastly, black propaganda provides a fabricated source and intentionally disseminates falsehoods, fabrications, and deceptions. A more precise term for this form of propaganda, as modernly redefined, is "disinformation."[28]

Interestingly, the use of propaganda by the US military dates back to the American Revolution, which is regarded as the first people's war. Thus, even before the war began, it was a struggle for the "hearts and minds" of the people, according to John Adams. America's architects might not have been able to accomplish their objectives without the assistance of the press and an effective propaganda campaign that embellished successes and softened setbacks. It is possible that Benjamin Franklin was the first American to employ black propaganda; he composed a number of letters and documents under aliases in an attempt to incite other nations to oppose the British government. George Washington employed the press as a tool of disinformation to maintain public morale by disseminating fabricated accounts of enemy casualties. In 1777 he wrote, "It is in our interest, however much our characters may suffer by it, to make small numbers appear large."[29] The inference that can be drawn from this earliest example of the use of propaganda employed during wartime is that our forefathers, who

---

28. Crumm, "Information Warfare," 15.
29. Crumm, "Information Warfare," 17.

established the foundations of our democratic system, utilized every variety of propaganda.[30]

Similar to the Sudetenland's annexation, Eve's temptation in Gen 3:1–6 was a well-executed, propaganda-stimulated deception with monumental effects. The story is rich in detail for a good reason: this is where everything goes wrong for God's creation as a result of human sin. From this point forward, creation is subject to futility and decay;[31] henceforth, man suffers because of sin, following in Adam and Eve's footsteps.[32] It is therefore not surprising that the author of Genesis places considerable emphasis on the conversation between the serpent and Eve. The first temptation is as much a model for unfortunate future behavior as is the first sin itself. Details provided later in the Bible have colored our understanding of this event. John identifies Satan as the serpent in Rev 12:9; Jesus labels Satan as the "father of lies" and declares that he has no truth in him (John 8:44).

Gen 3:4 says, "Then the serpent said to the woman, 'You will not surely die.'" And Gen 3:5 continues, "For God knows that in the day you eat of it your eyes will be opened, and you will be like God, knowing good and evil." In this passage, Satan transforms the truth into a lie by stating 80 percent of God's words in Gen 3:4 (employing white propaganda) and adding only one word—20 percent—as the lie (employing black propaganda; that which is devised with the intent of subversion). On the surface, however, everything the serpent says in Gen 3:5 is true: God knows that on the day Adam and Eve eat the fruit of the tree of the knowledge of good and evil, they will be as God in terms of knowing good and evil. However, according to Jesus, Satan has nothing to do with the truth and is the father of lies. How is this possible?

Satan does not lie by what he says in Gen 3:5; it is what is left unsaid that deceives—in a sense, employing gray propaganda, or information of questionable origin, by allowing Eve to source what is left unsaid. He has a deep understanding of the human condition

---

30. Crumm, "Information Warfare," 16–17.
31. See Rom 8:20–23.
32. See Rom 5:12–18.

and the frailties of the human spirit. His temptation is an attempt to shake Eve's faith in God's goodness toward her. His sole purpose is to cast doubt on God's nature and intentions toward his creation. He is successful in persuading Eve to question God about what knowledge he is hiding from us. Why does God not want us to know good and evil? Is he concerned that we will become like him and thus too powerful? It all appeals to human vanity: the desire to know more, the desire for independence.

The serpent did not say much: he is more subtle than that. He simply left Eve to her own devices and allowed her to derive the conclusions he desired. In doing so, he deceived Eve: she believed the serpent was more trustworthy than God and was willing to question and challenge God's goodness and character, and the sin had already been committed before she ate the fruit.[33]

Satan (the serpent) knew better. God cared for his creation; God sought to preserve the man and the woman's innocence and was truly looking out for their best interests. Eve had no valid reason to question God: he had created her and provided her with

---

33. See 1 Tim 2:14. Eve's plunge into sin is the earliest and most easily identifiable example of the workings of spiritual deception. In Gen 3:1–3, when asked by the serpent (Satan), "Has God indeed said . . . ?" Eve responds by reciting what God had told Adam and her, but she adds to the command that they shouldn't even touch the tree, indicating that she clearly understood God's commandment. In Gen 3:4–5, the serpent then tempts her with the incredible knowledge she would receive by eating of the tree, and in Gen 3:6 she perceives other appealing aspects of the fruit, i.e., that it was "good for food" and "pleasant to the eyes." Per 2 Cor 11:3, Eve was undoubtedly lied to, and the serpent was crafty, but she ultimately chose to disobey God, pursuing gratification and advancement above what God had desired for her. Additionally, when God confronted her regarding the sin she had committed, Eve stated, "The serpent deceived me, and I ate" (Gen 3:13), attempting to pass the buck, so to speak, and propagating her sin. (Storms, *Understanding Spiritual Warfare*, 139)

Not surprisingly, the same deception occurs today. Via his deception, Satan leverages our fleshly desires to tempt us to quench them in ways that disgrace God. Our natural desire to self-satisfy makes Satan's deception even more effective. Because Satan disguises himself as an angel of light (2 Cor 11:14), he presents sin to humankind as desirable; sin appears to be pleasing and beautiful, and he presents false teaching as life-changing, enlightening, and better than what God has to offer.

an abundant supply of food and drink in the Garden of Eden.[34] However, Satan made it all about power and the vanity of being like God; he wanted God's creation to be as he is.

We all face the same difficulty as Eve. Sin is rebellion against God, deliberate rejection of his ways, and thus a declaration of lack of trust in God.[35] He created the universe and everything in it and desires to bless us with every spiritual blessing in Christ;[36] his standards of right and wrong are holy, profitable, and for our own good.[37] God never provides us with a reason to doubt his goodness and affection for us.

Nevertheless, like Eve, we are easily deceived. We frequently find God's standards bothersome, if not in words, then in practice. We struggle with life's difficult questions, pondering how God could allow us to be in whatever difficult condition we find ourselves in, how God can allow things to continue as they do, etc. These temptations erode our faith in God; in any situation in which we stop trusting God and start trusting something else; the sin is already committed before we act on the impulse.[38]

Eve would soon realize the folly of her actions; if she had truly understood the situation and what was at stake, she would not have made the same choice. And, whether we want to admit it or not, we are in a similar situation: if we truly understood our situation in life, the nature of sin, the consequences of sin, etc., we would likely not make the same decisions.

34. See Gen 2:4–25.
35. See Isa 59:1–2; Rom 6:16–23.
36. See Acts 17:24; Eph 1:3.
37. See Gal 5:17–24.

38. The Bible conveys a consistent message about the relationship between sin and deception. From a spiritual vantage point, deception is more than merely being fooled. Because salvation is available to all, one's level of knowledge, intellect, or wisdom has no bearing on God's grace (see Gal 3:28; 1 Cor 1:20, 26). However, an important aspect of spiritual deception is the reality that people frequently believe what they selfishly want to believe instead of the truth of Scripture, even when evidence overflows (Luke 16:31). John 12:37 drives this point home: "But although he had done so many signs before them, they did not believe in him." Note that they made the willful choice not to believe Jesus, despite the miracles he had performed.

Defying Deception

Today, Satan's deceptions continue to plague both Christians and non-Christians alike. Therefore, a firm understanding of his deceptive PSYOP strategy will help deter his agenda and at the same time bolster our defenses.

2

Satan's Fall, His Ambitions, and His Power

US Army soldiers drop PSYOP leaflets, intended to promote the idea of self-government, over a village in Iraq on March 6, 2008.[1]

> It is your attitude, and the suspicion that you are maturing the boldest designs against him, that imposes on your enemy.
>
> —FREDERICK THE GREAT, *INSTRUCTION TO HIS GENERALS*, 1747

---

1. *UH-60 PSYOP Leaflet Drop, near Hawijah, Iraq 06 March 2008*, Public Domain.

Defying Deception

To understand Satan's strategy in relation to PSYOP, it is important to understand why he is the way he is. To this end, John MacArthur, a well-known Christian author, speaker, and Bible expositor, comments on the importance of understanding Satan: "Every military leader devours intelligence reports on the enemy before he enters battle. The intelligence report on Satan is in the Bible. Therefore, ignorance of the enemy will never be a valid excuse for defeat. God has given Christians a decided edge in the contest with advance information on the enemy."[2] Sun Tzu (544–496 BC), the Chinese military general, strategist, philosopher, and writer credited as the author of *The Art of War*, an influential work of military strategy that has affected both Western and East Asian philosophy and military thinking, advises, "If you know the enemy and know yourself, you need not fear the result of a hundred battles." Satan's background, his relationship with God, and his overall motivation are important in framing the deceptive PSYOP strategy Satan employs. Satan's fall, his ambitions, and his power are explored in this chapter in order to "know the enemy."

SATAN'S FALL

Scriptural accounts of Satan's fall from heaven appear throughout the Old and New Testaments. These accounts often depict Satan's fall as having occurred at an unspecified time in the past. For example, Isa 14:12 —"How you are fallen from heaven, O Lucifer, son of the morning! How you are cut down to the ground"—can be interpreted as describing a primordial historical event.[3] These accounts also share a tendency to connect Satan's fall from heaven and his degeneration into a fallen being with other corresponding

---

2. MacArthur and Mayhue, *Biblical Doctrine*, 685–86.

3. Gathercole, *Jesus' Eschatological Vision*, 145. In colloquial usage, Lucifer is an alternative name for Satan. The usage of the term "Lucifer" in Isa 14:12 is found in the King James Version and the New King James Version of the Bible, whereas alternative translations, such as the New International Version, use "morning star," the English Standard Version uses "Day Star," and the New English Translation uses "shining one."

events that biblical authors examine and address. A key example occurs in 1 Tim 3:6, where Paul admonishes the young pastor to avoid placing new converts in the role of deacons within his church. The principal threat that Paul identifies is that an undisciplined deacon may become accustomed to holding power, develop a prideful spirit, and engage in the types of rebellion attributable to Satan in the court of heaven.[4]

Scholars have discussed the New Testament's depiction of Satan, illustrating how various themes from the Old Testament carry over into the Gospels and other New Testament books. According to William G. Bellshaw, John's description of Satan in Rev 12:10 as an accuser of the brethren reflects a Jewish tradition that linked the figure to his role in accusing righteous individuals of hidden sins.[5] A similar motif can be seen in Job 1, as Satan's appearance in heaven represents disruption and serves the fallen angel's purpose of accusing Job of exhibiting a superficial commitment to following the Lord. In Luke 10:18, Jesus obliquely references the fall of Satan when he says, "I saw Satan fall like lightning from heaven." He says this to the seventy-two followers after they deliver people from demonic possession and similar afflictions.[6] Jesus' reference to Satan's fall can be read as a critique of his followers' implicit pride. Just as Satan once served in heaven and fell due to his pride, followers of Jesus could also become subject to similar temptations.

The connection between the events discussed in Luke 10:18 and Satan's fall relies on an approach that appears in other scriptures, including Old Testament passages such as Isaiah 14 and Ezekiel 28. In both cases, Israel's prophets proclaim judgments against antagonistic foreign rulers who mock the laws of God and who threaten Israel's existence with military invasion and subjugation.[7] Specifically, these scriptures address the kings of Babylon and Tyre, respectively.

---

4. MacArthur, *1 Timothy*, 72.
5. Bellshaw, "New Testament Doctrine of Satan," 25.
6. Löfstedt, "Satan's Fall," 98.
7. Grudem, *Systematic Theology*, 413.

According to Harold Wilmington, Ezekiel 28 indicts the king of Tyre for his cruelty, pride, and rebellion against God's laws, while also indirectly attributing similar crimes to Satan.[8] This approach alludes to Satan's fall in order to highlight ideas of rebellion, spiritual usurpation, and forthcoming divine judgment. One of the passage's most notable references to Satan's fall occurs in vv. 13–19. Here, Ezekiel explicitly describes Satan's fall and degeneration.[9] As part of the prophet's descriptions, he attributes Satan's pre-fallen state to his beauty, adornment with jewels, and musical abilities. In both cases, the targeted figures allow themselves to develop pride in their abilities; later, they will face God's judgment.

The prophet's indictments against the king of Babylon in Isa 14:13–15 similarly link that earthly ruler's pride and transgression to Satan's rebellion.[10] In vv. 13–14, Isaiah states, "For you have said in your heart: 'I will ascend into heaven, I will exalt my throne above the stars of God; I will also sit on the mount of the congregation on the farthest sides of the north; I will ascend above the heights of the clouds, I will be like the Most High.'" The judgments identified in v. 15—that Satan will be brought to Sheol (hades or hell)—are thus prophesied at least twice: first, in the context of Isaiah's own period, and second, at the end of the age when God judges Satan and his works. The passage's allusion to Satan's fall thus reaffirms this event's significance and draws explicit parallels between Satan's initial rebellion and instances in which a worldly ruler engages in similar transgressions. Isaiah's statements effectively mix his indictment of the king of Babylon with Satan's lapse into pride while he served in heaven. The prophet's accusation identifies the king's primary sin as his desire to exert his authority over the people of Israel and to transform himself into a God-like earthly king. Isaiah's allusions to Satan's fall thus reinforce this claim by connecting the two events. The description in both Isaiah

---

8. Wilmington, *Doctrine of Satan*, 4.
9. Henry, "Commentary on Ezekiel 28," 719–23.
10. Henry, "Commentary on Isaiah 14," 65–71.

SATAN'S FALL, HIS AMBITIONS, AND HIS POWER

14 and Ezekiel 28 allude not only to the earthly king, but also to Satan, who is the real power behind the throne.[11]

Isaiah 14 identifies transgressive pride as the sin that motivated Satan's rebellion and that continues to tempt human beings. Most importantly, pride is the sin that led to Satan's expulsion from heaven and is the trait he continues to exhibit today. He will do anything, including deceive, to divert people from God to satisfy his prideful desires in his quest to "be like the Most High" (Isa 14:14).

SATAN'S AMBITIONS AND CAMPAIGN

After the Japanese bombing of Pearl Harbor on December 7, 1941, that "day of infamy," the United States declared war on Japan.[12] The Joint Resolution declaring a state of war with Japan stated, "be it Resolved by the Senate and House of Representatives of the United States of America in Congress assembled, That the state of war between the United States and the Imperial Government of Japan which has thus been thrust upon the United States is hereby formally declared." Similarly, in Gen 3:15, following the temptation and *the fall of man*, God declares war on Satan, saying "I will put enmity between you and the woman, and between your seed and her seed; He shall bruise your head and you shall bruise His heel."[13] Spiritual warfare has been raging ever since. Therefore, it is

---

11. Some scholars disagree that these two passages refer to Satan; however, the explanations go beyond those describing a man and fit Satan accurately.

12. The "Day of Infamy" speech was delivered by Franklin D. Roosevelt, the 32nd president of the United States, to a joint session of Congress on December 8, 1941. The speech is known for its first line: "Yesterday, December 7, 1941—a date which will live in infamy..."

13. This verse is known as the *protoevangelium*. This is a compound of two Greek words, *protos* meaning "first" and *evangelion* meaning "good news" or "gospel" (Liddell and Scott, *Greek-English Lexicon*). Thus, the verse is commonly referred to as the first mention in the Bible of the "good news" of salvation. The verse presents two elements up to that time unknown in the Garden of Eden, elements that form the foundation of Christianity: the curse on humanity as a result of Adam's sin and God's provision of a Savior from sin who would bear the curse. Verse 14 makes it clear that God is addressing the serpent, whom he curses to "eat dust" for the rest of his days. In v. 15,

important to maintain a military mindset, and this necessitates a comprehensive understanding of adversary tactics. According to Eph 5:11, "have no fellowship with the unfruitful works of darkness, but rather expose them." Christianity stands or falls with the reality of Satan and demons. Why? Jesus committed his ministry to opposing them. Since man has inhabited Earth, Satan has attempted to sabotage God's plan as God incrementally revealed it via a targeted approach aimed at five primary objectives.

Objective 1: The Human Race. When God created humanity, he did so in his own image and likeness.[14] Adam and Eve were

---

God shifts from condemning the serpent to condemning Satan, its possessor. He curses Satan to eternally wage war against humanity, represented as the woman's offspring. In a general sense, the woman in question is Eve herself, whose descendants would eternally be harassed by Satan and his demons. Sin enters the human race at this time, and its ravages and consequences continue to affect us to this day. We inherited sin and the sin nature from Adam, and we continue to suffer as a result. Here begins the hostility and animosity between humans and demons, between whom the conflict continues. Evil angels and also wicked men are termed serpents, and even, as per Matt 3:7, a "brood of vipers," and they wage war against the people of God, the church, whom they despise and persecute, and have done so since the Garden of Eden incident. The woman's offspring refers specifically to Jesus Christ, who was conceived of a woman. The "enmity" or hostility and animosity between Satan and Christ is referred to here. When the Pharisees, Judas, and the Romans plotted to condemn Jesus to crucifixion, malevolent men and demonic forces struck at the heel of the Messiah. His wound, however, was not the decisive act. He rose on the third day, having paid the price for the sins of every believer who would ever exist. The ultimate victory was his, and he crushed Satan's head, ending Satan's dominion over mankind forever. Christ's power would destroy Satan and all of his principalities and powers, thwart all of his schemes, and demolish all of his works. The power of the cross would destroy Satan's entire empire, strip him of his authority (especially over death), and end his oppression over the bodies and spirits of men. All of this was accomplished by the incarnate Christ when he suffered and ultimately died for the salvation of humanity (Heb 2:14–15). Because of what he did on the cross, Jesus "crushed" Satan's head, eternally defeating him.

The protoevangelium demonstrates that God always had a plan for our salvation in mind, and that he informed us of that plan as soon as sin entered the world. "For this purpose the Son of God was manifested, that He might destroy the works of the devil" (1 John 3:8). (Pettus, "Reading a Protoevangelium in the Context of Genesis")

14. See Eph 2:10. The immaterial aspect of humanity is referred to as the

created "very good" and set in a "good" environment.[15] Nevertheless, Satan tempted them to sin, and they yielded to this temptation. The race that was created perfectly would now be subjected to judgment. Further, Satan attempted to corrupt the entire human race to the point that God would destroy everything he had created—and Satan nearly succeeded. From Gen 6:5–6: "Then the Lord saw that the wickedness of man was great in the Earth, and that every intent of the thoughts of his heart was only evil continually. And the Lord was sorry that He had made man on the Earth, and He was grieved in His heart." God sent the flood to destroy the entire world, with the exception of eight individuals whom he preserved, thus thwarting Satan's plan to exterminate the human race, which ultimately failed.

Objective 2: The Nation Israel. 4,000 years ago, God made a number of promises to a man named Abram.[16] God promised, among other things, that the descendants of Abraham would exist forever. God's Word would be rendered false if Israel, the nation descended from Abraham's progeny, were ever eliminated. Because of this, Satan has given Abraham's descendants special attention. In the book of Esther, for instance, the attempted annihilation of an entire nation is detailed. An order was issued to exterminate all Jews;[17] however, the nation was spared by God's providential

---

image of God (Latin, *imago Dei*). It distinguishes human beings from animals, prepares them for the authority that God designed for them to have dominion over the earth (Gen 1:28), and facilitates their ability to communicate with their Creator. It is a moral, social, and mental likeness. God commanded, "Let Us make man in Our image, according to Our likeness" (Gen 1:26) on the final day of creation. Therefore, he concluded his labor by adding a "personal touch." Adam was created by God from the dust, and he breathed life into him (Gen 2:7). As a result, humanity is distinct from all other creations of God in that it possesses both a material body and an immaterial spirit/soul.

15. Throughout Gen 1, as God created, he saw that "it was *good.*" In Gen 1:31, on the sixth day, "God saw everything that He had made, and indeed it was *very good.*" (Emphases added)

16. See Gen 12:1–3.

17. See Esth 3:12–14.

intervention. God's promises would have been untrue if Satan had been able to destroy the nation of Israel.[18]

Objective 3: The Line of the Messiah. Satan has endeavored since the beginning to eliminate the Messiah's selected lineage, as God's plan would be thwarted if the selected line were destroyed. God has vowed to judge Satan through the Messiah (Gen 3:15). From the very beginning, Satan has persisted in this endeavor. For instance, Cain, the firstborn son of Adam and Eve, killed his brother Abel compelled by anger and envy over the Lord finding Abel's offering more favorable.[19] First John 3:12 (NIV) instructs to "not be like Cain, who belonged to the evil one and murdered his brother," indicating Satan was an accomplice to this murder. However, after Abel's death, Adam and Eve had another son named Seth who became part of the line of Jesus, thus resuming the Messianic line.[20] Throughout history, Satan has never been successful in his attempts to eliminate the promised line.[21]

---

18. Wishart, "The Preservation of the Messianic Line—Part 1," 19.

19. See 1 John 3:12.

20. There are many examples throughout the Bible where Satan has attempted to obstruct the Messianic line. One such example is the curse of Jeconiah (also referred to as Jehoiachin and Coniah) found in Jer 22. Jeconiah's curse is found in the passage where God pronounced judgment on many of the evil kings of that day. These kings had rebelled against God and led God's people to do the same. Jer 22:30 reads, "thus says the Lord: 'Write this man down as childless, A man who shall not prosper in his days; For none of his descendants shall prosper, Sitting on the throne of David, And ruling anymore in Judah.'" The issue is that the curse of Jeconiah appears to negate Jesus' claim to the Davidic throne. The Davidic Covenant guaranteed that the Messiah, the "Son of David," would rule eternally on Jerusalem's throne (see 1 Chr 17:11–14). If Jesus is a Jeconiah descendent, how can he be the Messiah when the curse prevents any of Jeconiah's descendants from claiming David's throne? The solution is Jesus' virgin birth. Mary was Jesus' only human parent. His mother was descended from David, but not from Jeconiah (Luke 3:31). Although Joseph was Jesus' legal father, he was not his biological father. Thus, Jesus was of royal blood through Mary, but the curse of Jeconiah ended with Joseph and was not passed on to Jesus (Jeconiah is listed in the genealogy of Jesus, in Joseph's family line found in Matt 1:12). This is yet another example of God divinely intervening against Satan's opposition to ensure his own purposes and plans are fulfilled.

21. Wishart, "The Preservation of the Messianic Line—Part 1," 18.

Objective 4: Jesus Christ. Satan sought to prevent Jesus from fulfilling his destiny to sacrifice himself to save the world. For instance, Satan stood behind Herod in the massacre of the innocent children of Bethlehem, where baby Jesus was at the time. At the temptation of Jesus, Satan attempted to thwart God's plan by having Jesus worship him.[22] Jesus of course refused. Lastly, Satan entered Judas in a final feat to ensure the betrayal of Jesus occurred.[23] Consequently, the mission that Jesus set out to do was indeed accomplished, as he declared right before his death, "It is finished!" (John 19:30).[24]

Objective 5: The Church. In Matt 16:18 (ESV), Jesus says ". . . I will build My church, and the gates of hell shall not prevail against it." The true followers of Jesus, the church, are carrying out his plan to disseminate his message throughout the world. Matt 28:19–20 contains what is called "the Great Commission": "Go therefore and make disciples of all the nations, baptizing them in the name of the Father and of the Son and of the Holy Spirit, teaching them to observe all things that I have commanded you; and lo, I am with you always, even to the end of the age." We have been given a priceless gift: "the faith which was once for all delivered to the saints" (Jude 1:3). The words of Jesus in the Great Commission reveal God's heart, "who desires all men to be saved and to come to the knowledge of the truth" (1 Tim 2:4). The imperative of the Great Commission requires the dissemination of the gospel message until it reaches the ears of all individuals. Similar to the servants mentioned in Jesus' parable, it is the church's responsibility to actively engage in the affairs of the kingdom, making disciples of all nations. As stated in Luke 19:13 (KJV), the church is to ". . . Occupy till I come." However, from the very first mention of the church by Jesus, a warning was given that it would be opposed by Satan.[25] For example, Satan has attempted to destroy the church from within via false teaching: "Now the Spirit expressly says that

---

22. See Matt 4:9.
23. See Luke 22:3; John 13:27.
24. Wishart, "The Preservation of the Messianic Line—Part 2," 14.
25. See Matt 13.

in latter times some will depart from the faith, giving heed to deceiving spirits and doctrines of demons" (1 Tim 4:1); with his ministers: "Therefore it is no great thing if his ministers also transform themselves into ministers of righteousness, whose end will be according to their works" (2 Cor 11:15); by persecution: "Indeed, the devil is about to throw some of you into prison, that you may be tested" (Rev 2:10); and he has been successful in getting Christians to sin: "But Peter said, 'Ananias, why has Satan filled your heart to lie to the Holy Spirit and keep back part of the price of the land for yourself?'" (Acts 5:3). The book of Acts and two thousand years of church history attest to the fact that Satan has attempted to thwart the church's mission and that he will continue to do so until Christ's return.[26]

While the time and opportunity have passed for Satan to target objectives one through four, he is currently and actively targeting objective five—the church. Satan, however, has failed and continues to fail in his attempts to obstruct God's plan. Nonetheless, Satan does continue to take casualties in his mission to thwart God's plan; hence the remainder of this guide is dedicated to equipping Christians to resist Satan's attempts to sway the church.[27]

---

26. See Rev 12:17. Ressa, "Satanic Influences in the American Christian Church in a Post-Modern Consumer Society," 116–38.

27. It is no secret that Christianity is declining in the US and Europe (while in the rest of the world it is on the rise). In fact, Pew research predicts that if the current trend continues, less than half of Americans will identify as Christian within the next fifty years (Pew Research Center, "Modeling the Future of Religion in America"). The situation is even worse in the UK, where just 28 percent of respondents agreed to the statement that they believe in God or a higher power (Field, "Counting Religion in Britain, December 2016"). Additionally, according to a recent study, UK church membership has declined from 10.6 million in 1930 to just 5.5 million in 2010, or, as a percentage of the population, from about 30 percent to 11.2 percent. By 2013, this had declined even further to 5.4 million or just 10.3 percent. According to the study, if the current trend continues, membership will fall to 8.4 percent of the population by 2025 (Brierley, *UK Church Statistics*, 1–7). Needless to say, Satan has been effective in taking casualties in his mission to thwart God's plan.

THE STRENGTH OF THE OPPOSING FORCE

While they are not as powerful as God, Satan and his demon army are real beings of the spiritual dominion and are an obstructive evil force. Paul refers to Satan as "the prince of the power of the air" in Eph 2:2 and as "the god of this world" in 2 Cor 4:4. In John 12:31 and 14:30, Christ calls Satan the "ruler of this world." In John 8:44, Jesus says that Satan is a murderer, a liar, and the father of lies. According to Rev 12:9–10, he "deceives the whole world" and "accused them [brethren] before our God day and night." The title Satan means "adversary," while the name Devil means "accuser" or "slanderer."[28] In Gen 3, Satan emerges as the serpent that deceived Eve and prompted humanity's fall into sin. Satan is our enemy, our adversary, and our nemesis—and deception is his primary means of waging war.

Paul asserts in Eph 6:12 that our spiritual opposition is not "flesh and blood," and it resides "in heavenly places," which means that it is not physical, as humans are; rather, it consists of spiritual entities that inhabit the spiritual world around us. However, they can interact with and have an influence on humans. As expressed in many passages in the Bible, demons can possess humans and create disease and unusual behavior.[29] While these are certainly ways Satan and his demonic followers can interact with humans, their typical method of interface is to employ deception through non-Christians and their religions, societies, and governments, and through the media, as a means of advancing Satan's orchestrated resistance to God and God's mission.[30]

While humans do not possess a thorough capacity to understand how the spiritual world works and how Satan and his demons interact with humankind through it, we do know from Ps 103:20 that angels "excel in strength," and 2 Pet 2:11 tells us

---

28. Storms, *Understanding Spiritual Warfare*, 108.

29. See Mark 1:23–26, 32; 5:1–5; 16:9; 1 Sam 18:9–10; Matt 12:22; 15:22; Luke 22:3; Acts 5:16; 19:13–16.

30. Carson, "God, the Bible, and Spiritual Warfare," 253–54.

that angels are "greater in power and might" than humans.[31] From these verses, it can be inferred that Satan and his demons, all fallen angels, are extremely powerful. However, according to Isa 45:7, they are subject to God's power and purpose; as God says, "I form the light and create darkness, I make peace and create calamity." Contrary to common perceptions, Satan is neither omniscient nor omnipresent, meaning that he does not know everything about us and can only be in one place at a time.[32] However, he has an army of demons to assist him in his deceptive initiatives, and they are more than capable of completing these objectives. In other words, we as humans should not antagonize Satan or believe that by using our human power, we can oppose him.[33]

The spiritual influence of this satanic force is revealed in Daniel 10, when, after Daniel prays and fasts for three weeks, an angel appears to him. The angel explains that he was dispatched in response to Daniel's prayer, but it took him three weeks to arrive because "the prince of the kingdom of Persia" (v. 13) resisted him. He further explains that Michael, one of the named archangels of God, had to help him break through the spiritual obstruction in his journey to Daniel, thus exhibiting the power of the opposition.[34] This story briefly discusses the unseen world of angelic engagement, thus highlighting the potential strength and breadth of the adversary.[35]

---

31. Specifically, Peter says that the angels are far more powerful than the false teachers mentioned in 2 Pet 2:10.

32. The devil is not, nor can he be, omniscient. If he were omniscient, he would be God. A passage pertinent to this discussion is 1 Cor 2:6–8: "However, we speak wisdom among those who are mature, yet not the wisdom of this age, nor of the rulers of this age, who are coming to nothing. But we speak the wisdom of God in a mystery, the hidden wisdom which God ordained before the ages for our glory, which none of the rulers of this age knew; for had they known, they would not have crucified the Lord of glory." Additionally, nowhere in Scripture is it indicated that Satan possesses any sort of omnipresence. Although he has a firm grip on this world, he cannot be in all places at all times.

33. Grudem, *Systematic Theology*, 412–15.

34. Also see 2 Kgs 6:17 for the reality of the unseen spiritual world.

35. Longman and Garland, *Expositor's Bible Commentary* vol. 8, 178–83.

3

Military Deception and PSYOP

"Quaker guns," logs used as ruses to imitate cannons, in former Confederate fortifications at Manassas Junction in March 1862.[1]

> To seduce the enemy's soldiers from their allegiance and encourage them to surrender is of especial service, for an adversary is more hurt by desertion than by slaughter.
>
> —FLAVIUS VEGETIUS RENATUS, *THE MILITARY INSTITUTIONS OF THE ROMANS*, CA. 378 AD

---

1. Cuerden, *Centreville, VA, Quaker Guns in the Fort on the Heights*, Public Domain.

Defying Deception

During World War II, the Western Allies formulated an elaborate strategy prior to the D-Day landings in Normandy with the intention of misleading the Germans regarding the precise moment and whereabouts of their 1944 invasion of Europe. The purpose of the deception was to obscure the precise time and date of the invasion, dissuade the Germans that the bulk of the invasion would be concentrated in the Pas de Calais, France (175 miles from Normandy), and prevent them from relocating forces from the Pas de Calais to Normandy, France. In order to accomplish this, they sought to persuade them that the Normandy landings were a diversionary maneuver designed to distract defenders from the Pas de Calais and thereby weaken it in preparation for the main invasion.

Operation Fortitude South, which established a fictitious "First US Army Group" (FUSAG) in southeast England opposite the Pas de Calais under the command of General George S. Patton, was a significant component of the deception. Through the use of fabricated radio traffic between fictitious FUSAG units, Allied intelligence informed the Germans of the existence of the fake army group. German air reconnaissance was granted permission to fly over and photograph concentrations of FUSAG transports and tanks, which were in fact, inflatable dummies. Additionally, German intelligence was provided with false reports regarding FUSAG's intentions to invade the Pas de Calais through the use of double agents and turned spies. For the purpose of tying down German divisions in Norway, a subsidiary, Fortitude North, established a fictitious Fourth British Army in Scotland and managed to persuade the Germans that the army intended to invade the country.

The Allied deception strategy effectively thwarted the Germans' complete recommitment to a counteroffensive following D-Day by persuading them that the Normandy landings were merely the initial phase of a series of landings. Instead of deploying them to reinforce the Normandy defenders, the German high command was swayed to maintain units guarding other potential landing sites, primarily the Pas de Calais, which was threatened by the fictitious FUSAG led by Patton.

MILITARY DECEPTION AND PSYOP

The success of the deception surpassed the highest expectations of the Allies. After D-Day, intelligence planners had intended to persuade the Germans to remain in the Pas de Calais for two weeks before relocating reinforcement units to Normandy. Instead, the deception worked so well that the Germans stayed put in the Pas de Calais not just for the hoped-for two weeks, but for seven. The Allies utilized the breathing room to fortify their Normandy beachhead in order to not only endure German counteroffensives but also to storm through France in July and swiftly conquer the country. France had been largely liberated by September when the advancing Allied armies stopped at the German border, marking the conclusion of their campaign.[2]

As expressed in this example, deception in a military strategic context can be defined as an approach that enables a friendly force to confuse, delay, or divert likely enemy forces away from a potential primary objective. Current US Army doctrine identifies the functions of deception as the following: causing surprise or delay on the part of an enemy force; causing an enemy force's misallocation of personnel or critical resources; causing an enemy force to reveal its position either intentionally or unintentionally; and causing an enemy force to waste critical resources by attacking or defending against feints of the friendly force.[3]

Deception is one of the world's oldest strategies for warfare. Sun Tzu, in roughly the 5th century BC, advocates the use of strategic deception to achieve military advantage, while biblical accounts of Joshua's campaigns in Canaan, in roughly the 13th century BC, highlight the ancient general's reliance on similar concepts to achieve strategic and tactical victories. In the context of modern and contemporary warfare, deception took on an increasingly sophisticated role beginning with the Napoleonic Wars, 1799–1815 AD. The subsequent development of military technology and the incorporation of operational concepts into strategic planning additionally enabled planners to cultivate complex schemes aimed at delaying, diverting, or wasting the enemy's critical resources. US

2. Howard, *Strategic Deception in the Second World War*, 103–34.
3. Department of the Army, *Army Support to Military Deception*, 1–1.

military experiences during the two decades in the Global War on Terrorism, 2001–2021, have reaffirmed deception's value as a critical theoretical and tactical approach as forces engage in highly complex theaters. Deception may provide additional value as the nation's forces prepare to face potential cyber, conventional, or hybrid attacks in the near and distant future.

Under the umbrella of military information operations, military deception (MILDEC) is "intended to deter hostile actions, [to] increase the success of friendly defensive actions, or to improve the success of any potential friendly offensive action."[4] As the name implies, MILDEC is the manipulation of information to achieve an intended, specific result. According to US Joint Publication 3-13.4, *Military Deception*, the functions of MILDEC include:

- Causing ambiguity, confusion, or misunderstanding in an adversary's perceptions of friendly information.
- Causing the adversary to misallocate personnel, fiscal, and material resources in ways that are advantageous to the friendly force.
- Causing the adversary to reveal strengths, dispositions, and future intentions.
- Conditioning the adversary to particular patterns of friendly behavior to induce adversary perceptions that can be exploited.
- Causing the adversary to waste combat power with inappropriate or delayed actions.[5]

More specifically, PSYOP are "planned operations to convey selected [false] information and indicators to foreign audiences to influence their emotions, motives, [and] objective reasoning."[6] PSYOP, if employed correctly, cause the adversary to make errors and to pursue a path damaging to attaining its objectives.

---

4. Joint Chiefs of Staff, *Military Deception*, vii.
5. Joint Chiefs of Staff, *Military Deception*, I-3–I-4.
6. Joint Chiefs of Staff, *Military Deception*, I-8–I-9.

MILITARY DECEPTION AND PSYOP

In the context of spiritual warfare and Satan's strategy of deceiving humans with the goal of drawing people away from God,[7] if humanity is the "adversary," PSYOP are clearly a powerful tool for Satan's campaign of deceit. It is no surprise that this tactic has been in the arsenal of militaries for millennia, as the "father of lies" (John 8:44) has effectively and consistently employed it against humanity since humans first walked the Earth.[8]

UNDERSTANDING SATAN'S STRATEGIES IN THE CONTEXT OF PSYOP

In John 8:44, Jesus condemns those who turn away from God, stating, "You belong to your father, the devil, and you want to carry out your father's desires. From the beginning, he was a murderer, not holding to the truth, for there is no truth in him. When he lies, he speaks his native language, for he is a liar and the father of lies." Satan is first and foremost known as a deceiver,[9] which means that an analysis of Satan could prove fruitful for other contexts in which deception is central. One such context, as mentioned above, is PSYOP in military strategies, which consist of warfare based on the control and manipulation of information to alter perceptions to the aggressor's advantage. Therefore, PSYOP should help to reveal the nature of Satan. More to the point, there are similarities between how PSYOP are intended to deceive people and how Satan attempts to deceive people.

PSYOP take several forms, but the differences between them are perhaps less relevant for the present purposes than their basic unity.[10] Sunil Narula writes, "The psychological dimension of conflict is as important as its physical dimension, and Psychological Operations (PSYOP) have become even more relevant in this age of information, especially for a nation-state where the threat in

---

7. Bubeck, *Preparing for Battle*, 54.
8. See Gen 3:1–5.
9. See Gen 3; 2 Cor 4:4; Rev 20:3, among others.
10. Joint Chiefs of Staff, *Psychological Operations*, IV-2

the socio-psychological domain is more pronounced."[11] PSYOP are designed to convey a notion of reality that is biased so that the audience will react in a way that is favorable to the aggressor. PSYOP generally involve the distortion or outright falsification of truth; there is thus a clear connection between PSYOP and Satan's deceptive strategy. PSYOP are intended to keep the target audience in a state of confusion and falsehood, ultimately distracting it from the pursuit of its objective;[12] it is the charge of Satan, meanwhile, to distort our understanding of God and the truth of Scripture. Satan's objective is to ensure that people remain confused and in a state of falsehood, such that he can more easily steer people away from God.[13]

SATAN'S CHARACTER, THE USE OF DECEPTIVE PSYOP, AND THE EXPANSION OF THAT USE

The scriptures often reference Satan's use of deception as an aspect of his character; for example, in John 8:44, 2 Cor 11:3, and Rev 12:9. Satan's fall from the status of archangel to the leader of a rebellion coincided with his adopting deceit as a primary tactic.[14] He used deception to lure one-third of the angels in heaven to his side at the time of his fall from righteousness;[15] he has used the same

    11. Narula, "Psychological Operations (PSYOP)," 178.
    12. Joint Chiefs of Staff, *Psychological Operations*, I-2.
    13. Storms, *Understanding Spiritual Warfare*, 24.
    14. "Receipt and deceit come from two important words in the Bible: receive and deceive. The second half of these words is the same. '–Cieve' means to grasp, or take. What makes these two words significantly different is how they begin: 're–' and 'de–'. In words like receive, 're–' means, back to the original place. In words like deceive, 'de–' means, down from, off, and away from. Put it all together and to receive is to grasp back, or to get something back. Makes sense, right? A receipt is proof you got something back. But to deceive, is to take something away from, or down from, where it was. A receipt puts everything in the open. Deceit pulls everything into the dark. Why focus on these two words? Because one of them describes our response to God, and the other describes the devil's. Don't miss this. We receive. The devil deceives." (YouVersion, "When the Devil Knocks")
    15. While it is not unanimous among theologians, the "stars" discussed in

approach against humankind since Adam and Eve, and deception will represent a prominent aspect of the Antichrist's rise to power in the end times.[16] Throughout Scripture, references to light and truth are used to describe God's character, to describe the power of the Word to unshackle the powers of darkness, and to describe Jesus' earthly ministry and role as an intercessor for humankind. The Bible unambiguously communicates that Jesus is the way and the truth, and the Gospel includes the concept of truth as a central feature. A Christian's sanctification (the process of growing as a Christian) gradually aligns with and is imparted by God's wisdom; it works to unshackle the burdens of sin and deception.[17] The need for this unshackling is proof, in part, of Satan's influence on Earth and evidence of his status as the "prince of the power of the air" (Eph 2:2).[18]

Scriptures that reference Satan's character frequently identify deceit as a primary characteristic. According to Ezek 28:15, Satan, before his fall, was recognized for his beauty and perfection at the time of his creation. These traits remained until iniquity was found within him. Second Cor 11:14 presents the idea of Satan masquerading as an angel of light. Even in his fallen condition, he remains, via disguise, beautiful and appealing on the surface as he exploits our love of the light in his quest to deceive. He wants us to believe that he is loving, upright, and honest—all the characteristics God possesses.[19] In some contexts, Satan's appeal enhances

---

Rev 12:4 can be interpreted as a figurative allusion to Satan's "angels" discussed in v. 9 and, thus, as a reference to the angels that were cast out for joining Satan's rebellion. See Grudem, *Systematic Theology*, 412–13.

16. Penn-Lewis, *War on the Saints*, 23.

17. Penn-Lewis, *War on the Saints*, 120.

18. It is necessary to highlight that humans are plagued by sin and deception without it necessarily being the result of Satan's actions. God did not create sin, but he did create free-willed beings with the ability to sin. These include Satan, fallen angels (demons), and humanity. Humans have inherited Adam's spiritual depravity and ever since have been born with a sin nature. As per Rom 6–7 and Jas 1:13–15, we are predisposed to sin.

19. King, *Is It of God?*, 108.

his ability to use deceptive PSYOP to deceive both Christians and non-Christians worldwide.

Satan's appeal and use of deceptive PSYOP is found throughout Scripture.[20] For example, Satan used PSYOP to tempt Jesus to throw himself from the temple in order to "force" God to make good on his promises. In this temptation, Satan used distorted Scripture as the basis for his deception.[21] Satan quotes Ps 91:11–12 in Luke 4:10–11 in an attempt to convince Jesus to act in the flesh rather than obey the Spirit.[22] But Satan failed to conclude the psalm's thought: the next verse, Ps 91:13, states, "You shall tread upon the lion and the cobra, the young lion and the serpent you shall trample underfoot." These animal references are metaphors for fierce and dangerous adversaries; the Bible compares Satan to both a lion and a serpent.[23] The real meaning of Ps 91 is that God will both protect and empower his servants as they defeat Satan, their adversary. As conveyed in this example, one of Satan's methods of deception is to omit crucial portions of the Bible in order to twist its meaning to suit his agenda.[24] Regardless, Jesus was able to refute this attempt with the correct use of Scripture, despite Satan's willingness to use deceptive PSYOP to manipulate Jesus to his will.[25]

---

20. *Wiles* are manipulations or ruses intended to deceive. The wiles of the devil are Satan's cunning strategies to trap us through temptation, threat, or intimidation. Eph 6:11 warns, "Put on the whole armor of God, that you may be able to stand against the wiles of the devil." The Bible gives us insight into the enemy's strategies so that "we are not ignorant of his devices" (2 Cor 2:11); therefore, it is prudent to consider its warnings. (MacArthur, *Ephesians*, 37–50).

21. Also see Matt 4:1–11 and Mark 1:12–13 for parallel accounts of Jesus' temptation in the wilderness.

22. See Gal 5:16, 25.

23. See Gen 3:15; Rev 20:2; 1 Pet 5:8, and compare to Rom 16:20.

24. Today, prosperity teachers and false prophets quote Scripture in self-serving and deceitful ways, demonstrating Satan's wiles. They use enough of God's Word to appear authoritative, but they distort it to serve their own agendas. Most participants are unaware they have fallen victim to one of Satan's snares when they cherry-pick the Bible for verses that affirm whatever they want to believe or do.

25. Bubeck, *Preparing for Battle*, 158.

Jesus' temptation also highlights a theme that appears in other scriptures: Satan's deceptive PSYOP potentially impact both the righteous and the unrighteous.[26] Christ was without sin, yet Satan tempted him through manipulation of Scripture and targeted appeals to Jesus' earthly desires for food, recognition, and appeals to worldly power and authority. Accordingly, believers are not immune to the power of deception. In Eph 2:13, Paul observes that believers no longer live under Satan's authority after they accept the gift of Christ's atonement. In the same passage, Paul argues that this process enlightens a person's spirituality and renews the mind, enabling him or her to see past deception and Satan's ability to blind people to the world of his schemes.[27] Despite this transformation, Christians are still at risk of deceptive PSYOP by false ministers and prophets.[28] Paul's admonition to the Corinthian Church in 2 Cor 11:3–4 and vv. 13–15 warns believers of the possibility of being deceived by false teachers. Additionally, religious deception is earmarked as a major characteristic of the end times as presented in Rev 12:9.

The prophetic scriptures indicate that deceptive PSYOP will play a dominant role during the ascension and the reign of the Antichrist. Jesus warns his disciples in Matt 24:24 that a great falling away will occur through false prophets as history nears its end. The specific warning in this passage indicates that "the elect," or saved, followers of Christ, are at risk of being deceived. Paul's warning about the Antichrist's rise in 2 Thess 2:3–8 presents

26. King, *Is It of God?*, 54.

27. MacArthur, *Ephesians*, 93.

28. Prophets were New Testament believers whose messages came immediately from God via the Holy Spirit. Their ministry was to edify, encourage, and comfort (1 Cor 14:3). Their messages were tested by the listeners to determine whether they were truly from God (1 Cor 14:29; 1 Thess 5:19–21). Eph 2:20 makes it clear that apostles and prophets worked together to lay the foundation of the church, and we may assume that they were no longer needed once that foundation was completed. Conversely, false prophets are individuals who spread false doctrines or messages while professing to speak God's Word. They also spoke on behalf of false gods in the Bible. False prophets performed their prophetic duties illicitly or with intent to deceive. The Bible condemns false prophets for misleading people. (Wiersbe, *Wiersbe Bible Commentary*, 1688)

a similar message, indicating that the "lawless one" or "the man of sin" will rely on widespread delusion to achieve and maintain political power and spiritual authority. As indicated in Rev 12:9, Satan's fall at the end of the tribulation shows that he will be the one to deceive the entire world, a role he assumes throughout Scripture and history.

4

A Catalog of Deceptive PSYOP as Discussed in Scripture

An inflatable dummy tank, modeled after the US M4 Sherman.[1]

> In this war, which was total in every sense of the word, we have seen many great changes in military science. It seems to me that not the least of these was the development of psychological warfare as a specific and effective weapon.
>
> —GENERAL OF THE ARMY DWIGHT D. EISENHOWER, 1945

1. *Dummy Sherman Tank*, Public Domain.

Defying Deception

The Nazis established a propaganda system wherein authority flowed top down; and from the people came blind, instant, and unquestioning obedience. This was done utilizing seven common propaganda devices: First, "name-calling" is a device to make the population form a judgment without examining the evidence on which it should be based. Here the propagandist appeals to one's hate and fear. Second, "glittering generalities" is a device by which the propagandist identifies their program with virtue by use of "virtue words." Here they appeal to people's emotions of love, generosity, and brotherhood. In the case of Nazi ideology, a "biological mythology" storyline had to be invented and was then proclaimed by professors appointed to university chairs to lend authority to the contrived theory. Thus, we see the card-stacking and testimonial devices (discussed below) used to strengthen the application of the glittering-generalities device. In doing so, the Nazi regime utilized the word "science" to sanction practices, policies, beliefs, and races for which it sought approval. From "science" it obtained approval for the destruction of all the regime's opposition.

Third, "transfer" is a device by which the propagandist carries over the authority, sanction, and prestige of something one respects and reveres to something they would have one accept. Fourth, the "testimonial" is a device to make one accept anything from a patent medicine or vaccine to a program of national policy. No authority and no adjustment which does not follow from or accord with theirs can be right. No specialist knows better than the propagandist. The propagandist can deny the authority of science. In the case of the Nazis, only the conclusions of "German science" as approved by the Fuehrer could be accepted. When the conclusions of science did not accord with Hitler's wishes, as in genetics, a new science had to be invented (card stacking); its prestige had to be established by the regime's testimonial.

Fifth, "plain folks" is a device used by politicians, labor leaders, businessmen, and even by ministers and educators to win our confidence by appearing to be people like ourselves—"just plain folks among the neighbors." Sixth, "card stacking" is a device in which the propagandist employs all the arts of deception to win

A CATALOG OF DECEPTIVE PSYOP AS DISCUSSED IN SCRIPTURE

one's support for the propagandist, their group, nation, race, policy, practice, belief, or ideal. The propagandist stacks the cards against the truth. The propagandist uses underemphasis and overemphasis to dodge or evade facts. Lastly, the "bandwagon" is a device to make one follow the crowd, to accept the propagandist's program en masse. Here the propagandist's theme is "everybody's doing it." The techniques range from those of touring acts to dramatic spectacles.[2]

The combination of these propaganda devices nearly facilitated the conquest of Europe for Naziism and recorded in history the optimal combination to win over the "hearts and the minds" for pure evil. This history lesson should alert Christians to the power and cunningness of Satan and his deceptive strategy. Given the "issues" of today, politics, crises (foreign, domestic, or fabricated), etc., one can easily see these devices being employed in a modern setting. As per Eccl 1:9, "that which has been is what will be, that which is done is what will be done, and *there is nothing new under the sun*" (emphasis added).

Like the seven devices of Nazi propaganda, Satan has seven tactics, schemes, and methods to deceive—that is, deceptive PSYOP—in his arsenal, and Christians must be aware of them.

Before discussing Satan's "devices" of PSYOP, it is important to understand how Satan sets the stage for his deceptive strategies. Satan's shaping operations, that is, the creation, and preservation of conditions for the success of his deceptive schemes,[3] consist of diverting his targets' attention toward something they do not possess—not pointing out what they do possess, how blessed they are, or how healthy they are. In the Garden of Eden, Adam and Eve had everything, but in Gen 3, Satan brings to Eve's attention the one thing they did not have, and this is the same strategy he uses today. Satan uses it to divert attention from God because he knows these false needs will never satisfy, and people will follow these lies in the pursuit of false happiness and false satisfaction. In addition, Satan chooses his timing carefully to attack people when they

---

2. Yourman, "Propaganda Techniques within Nazi Germany," 148–63.
3. Joint Chiefs of Staff, *Joint Operations*, V-8.

are most vulnerable, such as when they are hungry, angry, lonely, and tired. For instance, Jesus was tempted by Satan forty days into a fast, as Matt 4:1–11 discusses. Once Satan has lured someone toward a false need at a vulnerable time, he creates doubt in God, the scriptures, and God's promises in order to persuade his target to follow him instead of God.

Satan is a thief and a liar and uses deception to rob people of their most valuable possession: eternal life. His deceptive practices vary, but they all aim to steer people from truth.

In order to counter deceptive PSYOP, it is important to know how Satan deceives. Accordingly, what follows is a survey of the specific "devices" of deceptive PSYOP Satan employs[4] to "convey selected [false] information and indicators to . . . audiences to influence their emotions, motives, [and] objective reasoning."[5]

DECEPTIVE PSYOP OF LIES

John 8:44 tells us that Satan is the "father of lies" because he "does not stand in the truth, because there is no truth in him. When he speaks a lie, he speaks from his own resources." In the Garden of Eden, Satan deliberately questioned whether God really said that the fruit from the Tree of Knowledge was forbidden. He sows doubt in people's minds and manipulates the truth. The spiritual deception of humankind results from the rejection of truth, and as per 2 Thess 2:8–10, anyone who rejects God and his truth risks being a victim of Satan's deceptions. Additionally, according to 1 Cor 10:13, all human sin originates with human choice. When humans reject the truth, they make themselves vulnerable to the lie. When God is rejected, humankind has "exchanged the truth of God for a lie" (Rom 6:25), and Satan cheerfully assists in facilitating this exchange by providing a spectrum of lies to choose from. Consequently, the repeated rejection of spiritual truth invites spiritual

---

4. Ingram, *Invisible War*, 59–63.
5. Joint Chiefs of Staff, *Military Deception*, I-3-I-4.

deception.⁶ Satan disregards absolute truth; therefore, truth can very easily be compromised to convey false information to influence emotions, motives, and objective reasoning.⁷ (For more on Absolute (or Universal) Truth, see Appendix A.)

In *The Lies We Believe: Renew Your Mind and Transform Your Life*, Chris Thurman identifies five categories of lies that Satan advocates, perpetuates, and shrouds in deception so that people can eventually be deceived into believing them if they are not equipped to resist them. First, *self-lies* make us and our accomplishments the critical elements of our happiness. Since Scripture points us toward a life of selflessness and grace, these lies position us for defeat. Second, *worldly lies* establish expectations that cannot be fully attained; we pursue their attainment at the cost of our relationship with God and his plans for our lives. Third, *marital lies* manifest when marriages begin to unravel and strain; they are characterized by placing blame on the spouse for supposed unmet needs in an attempt to extract one's needs from the other person rather than giving to one's spouse and engaging in reciprocity. Fourth, *distortion lies* keep us from seeing reality accurately, and we cannot live to our full potential for God if our sight is distorted by lies. Lastly, *religious lies* lead to hopelessness by making people think they are too sinful to be saved or be useful to God's kingdom.⁸

These lies sow doubt in people's minds and manipulate the truth with the goal of drawing them away from God. This deceptive PSYOP of lies is affected by Satan through the many overwhelming modern venues of media and humankind's natural inclination toward self-centeredness and pride.

DECEPTIVE PSYOP OF LUST

As fallen humans, we are naturally prone to greed, jealousy, vanity, and lust, and Satan aims to take advantage of those tendencies and

---

6. Twibell, "Strategic-Level Spiritual Warfare," 88.
7. Wilson, *Gospel According to Satan*, 36.
8. Thurman, *Lies We Believe*, 49–97.

weaknesses. In modern society, impure sexual temptations are difficult to avoid—whether one is married or single, old or young—and they manifest via television, the internet, social media, movies, and magazines. Satan, who deceitfully nudges us toward temptation and lust, knows how to use the brain and human anatomy against us. He establishes an atmosphere that inspires "disobedience" (Eph 2:2). As a former angel in God's heavenly ranks, Satan knows the Bible and knows that God designed the human sexual drive to be enjoyed and shared with a loving spouse within marriage.[9] To distract people from God and true happiness, Satan wants to deny humans the pleasure of a pure, biblically blessed sexual union; therefore, he deceives humans, whether married or single, by advocating for sexual satisfaction via lust that is not accompanied by love.

The most dramatic example of this in the Bible is the story of David and Bathsheba. King David was walking on his roof at night in Jerusalem when he noticed a beautiful woman bathing nearby (2 Sam 11:2). David inquired of his servants regarding her, and they informed him that she was Bathsheba, the wife of Uriah the Hittite, one of David's mighty warriors (2 Sam 23:39). David invited Bathsheba to the palace despite the fact that she was married, and they slept together. David was informed when Bathsheba later discovered she was pregnant (2 Sam 11:5). The king's response was to try to conceal his sin. David ordered Uriah back from the battlefield. Bathsheba's husband obediently responded to David's summons, and David sent him home with the hope that Uriah would lie with Bathsheba and thus conceal the pregnancy. Instead of obeying David's orders, however, Uriah slept in the servants' quarters, declining to enjoy an evening with Bathsheba while his men were still in danger on the battlefield (2 Sam 11:9–11). The following night, Uriah did the same thing, demonstrating integrity in stark contrast to David's lack thereof.

It became clear that David and Bathsheba's infidelity could not be concealed in such a manner. As a result, David enacted a second, more nefarious plan: he ordered his military commander,

---

9. See Gen 2:24; Prov 5:19; 1 Cor 7:2, 5; Song 1:2–4; Heb 13:4.

A CATALOG OF DECEPTIVE PSYOP AS DISCUSSED IN SCRIPTURE

Joab, to position Uriah on the front lines of the battlefield and then purposefully retreat from him, leaving Uriah vulnerable to enemy attack. Joab complied with the order, and Uriah was slain in combat. After her period of mourning, Bathsheba wed David and gave birth to a son. However, 2 Sam 11:27 notes, "the thing David had done displeased the LORD." Consequently, this sin continued to cause problems for David as time went on.[10]

Satan uses lust to fracture marriages (and ultimately families) because he detests the marriage union for many reasons, including the fact that, as per Eph 5:30-32, "we are members of His body, of His flesh and of His bones. 'For this reason a man shall leave his father and mother and be joined to his wife, and the two shall become one flesh.' This is a great mystery, but I speak concerning Christ and the church." Marriage is a type of relationship between God and the church,[11] which Satan actively combats at every opportunity. Additionally, marriage, if implemented according to the Bible, represents stability in life and a platform for the raising of godly children, and Satan targets marriage to destabilize the biblically defined (nuclear) family and, thereby, unravel society. Consequently, he is effective at this. The percentage of children living with two parents in their first marriage decreased from 73 percent in 1960 to 46 percent in 2014; likewise, the percentage of children living with a single parent increased from 9 percent in 1960 to 26 percent in 2014. The emotional fallout impacts adults

---

10. Given the prevalence of the issue of ethical compromise and marital infidelity, the US military conducts ethical training on the "Bathsheba Syndrome," or the ethical failure of successful leaders, in an effort to prevent this from happening among military leaders. (Ludwig and Longenecker, "The Bathsheba Syndrome: The ethical failure of successful leaders," 265-73)

11. Human marriage between a husband and wife was meant to represent Jesus Christ's marriage to the church. Christians are his Bride collectively, presently betrothed or engaged to him and later to join him in a heavenly marriage relationship for all eternity. Several scriptures allude to the church of God as the Body of Christ, with the people who comprise it being compared to the various parts of a body (Rom 12:4-5; 1 Cor 12:12-27; Eph 1:22-23; Eph 4:12; Col 1:24). Furthermore, Jesus is the "head of the body, the church" (Col 1:18). This is why, in an earthly marriage, as per the Bible, the husband is the head of the wife (Eph 5:23).

and children alike and can cause developmental effects in children and physiological effects in adults. Not often discussed are the economic effects resulting from reduced productivity, poverty in some cases, and the developmental impact on some children that result in lower educational attainment. Combined, these result in decreased societal stability over time, among a litany of other negative effects.[12] Ultimately, Satan aims to undermine the family because God uses the family to teach us his most intimate truths.

God uses metaphorical language to explain many aspects of Christian life and teaching, with the concept of family serving as a prevalent metaphor. A comprehensive understanding of many aspects of Christian life and doctrine are better illustrated, signified, and understood with a prior understanding of the concept of family as divinely established and intended by God.

God teaches us about his nature through the family. The relationship between parents and children resembles the godhead's relationships, particularly the relationship of the first person of the Trinity to the second—God the Father to God the Son. We can only define and apprehend God the Father's relationship to God the Son if we apprehend the relationship of earthly dads to earthly sons. If Satan can pervert or destroy a family, he can also pervert and destroy our understanding of God's triune nature.

God teaches us about the Gospel through the family. God says that when we are justified by faith in Jesus Christ, he adopts us as his sons and daughters. As a result, we know that the bond between parents and their children is not merely a byproduct of God's design for his people. Rather, the relationship of children brought into their parents' family is intended to teach us about our relationship with God and the intimacy of that relationship. If Satan can pervert or destroy a family, he may also pervert or destroy our understanding of the Gospel.

God teaches us about his church through the family. The church is referred to as "the family of God" by Peter (1 Pet 4:17) and "God's household" by Paul (1 Tim 3:15). As Christians, we are members of the same family since we have been linked by adoption as sons

---

12. Pew Research Center, "Parenting in America."

and daughters of the same Father.[13] Because we are all sons and daughters of the same Father, Christians call one another "brothers" and "sisters." If Satan can pervert or destroy family, he can pervert or destroy our concept of the church.

To apprehend God's nature, the Gospel, and the church, one must first apprehend the family. The analogies become skewed when a father abandons his family, when there are two fathers and no mothers or two mothers and no fathers in a family, and even when a Christian couple decides not to have children for selfish reasons.[14] A strong family, however, established on the Word of God, provides a compelling representation of God's nature, the Gospel, and the church.

Furthermore, God created the family to be a form of ministry to the church and the world. The local church is served by the family. We learn how to function as a church by turning to the example of healthy families, since the church is fundamentally a spiritual family. This means that developing robust, biblical families is important to the church's life and health. When Paul instructs Timothy on how to connect to others in the church, he instructs him to regard older men as fathers, elder women as mothers, and younger women as sisters. He tells him to think about family and how they behave. When Paul describes church leaders to Timothy, he tells him that he would be able to identify elders in the church

---

13. See Eph 1:5. Adoption is a Roman, not a Jewish, practice; not all offspring were heirs. One does not get into God's family by adoption: one gets into his family by regeneration—the new birth (John 3:1–18; 1 Pet 1:22–25). Adoption is the act of God by which he gives his "born ones" an adult standing in the family so that born-again Christians can immediately begin to claim their inheritance and enjoy their spiritual wealth. An infant cannot legally use this inheritance, but an adult son can and should (Gal 4:1–7).

In regeneration, a Christian receives the nature of a child of God; in adoption, one receives the position of a son of God (John 1:11) the moment one believes (Gal 3:25–26; 4:6; 1 John 3:1–2). The full manifestation of this sonship awaits the resurrection, change, and translation of saints, called the redemption of the body (Rom 8:23; Eph 1:14; 1 Thess 4:14–17; 1 John 3:2).

14. For a more detailed discussion on the problems with same-sex marriage, see Erwin Lutzer, *The Truth About Same-Sex Marriage: 6 Things You Must Know About What's Really at Stake* (Chicago: Moody, 2010). Also see Gen 19:1–13; Lev 18:22; 20:13; Rom 1:26–27; 1 Cor 6:9; 1 Tim 1:10.

by looking for individuals who are good earthly father figures.[15] If a man is capable of overseeing and managing his own household, he may well be capable of overseeing and managing the church, as both require many of the same abilities and skill sets. As a result, family serves the church by teaching its members how to connect to one another (like brothers and sisters); teaching the church how to recognize leaders (faithful fathers); and even teaching about God's attributes (the spiritual parents, but exceedingly more so).

The family ministers to the entire globe. Not only does the family minister to the local church, but also to the whole world. It was God's purpose that everyone be ready to hear the Gospel to some extent. He created the family to be a global model of some of the most profound and priceless truths about who he is and what he is doing in the world: he is a father; he desires to adopt us as his children; Christians are spiritually brothers and sisters in Christ. Healthy, scripturally founded, Gospel-centered families are an essential component of pre-evangelism, which is a method of introducing anyone to the basic concepts through which they might understand Christianity. When we lose or distort the concept of father, when we lose or distort the concept of parents, when we are reckless with the concept of brother and sister, we lose the very conceptions that allow us to describe who God is and what he is doing.

Family educates us about God's nature, the Gospel, and the church, and it ministers to both the church and the world. So, it's no surprise that Satan is constantly assaulting families, and that he'll go to any length to attack yours. If he can ruin the family, he can certainly demolish these tremendous metaphors and ministries. If Satan can pervert or destroy the family, he can obscure the Gospel for those who have not yet been saved.[16]

---

15. See 1 Tim 3:4–5.

16. Satan also perverts the role of men and women in society by blurring the gender lines. Androgyny, the quality of being neither feminine nor masculine, is also a deceptive playground for Satan. A significant proportion of individuals that choose to appear androgynous also contend with gender identity issues, transsexuality, or homosexuality—which in today's culture, the LGBTQ+ movement is disguised under the banner of "diversity," whose

A CATALOG OF DECEPTIVE PSYOP AS DISCUSSED IN SCRIPTURE

According to 1 John 2:16, the sharpest arrows in Satan's quiver against the Godly marriage union, which affects the biblically defined family, are the "lust of the flesh" and "the lust of the eyes."[17] Hence he conveys false information regarding sex, relationships, and marriage to influence emotions, motives, and objective reasoning, corrupting the marriage union, the biblically defined family, and ultimately enticing people away from God.

DECEPTIVE PSYOP OF PRIDE

The last stanza of the poem, "The Kite, or the Fall of Pride," written in 1770 by John Newton, the author of the famous hymn, "Amazing Grace," reads: "'How oft I've wished to break the lines [of a flying kite] thy wisdom for my lot assigns? How oft indulged a vain desire for something more or something higher. And but for grace or love divine, a fall thus dreadful had been mine.'"[18] Pride is an unfortunate manifestation of the fall of humanity, and according to Isa 14:13–14, it is the driving force of Satan's deceptive strategy. Humans are naturally driven to feel important, and Satan is right at our side, bolstering this desire. He deceives us into thinking we are self-sufficient and have no need for anyone but ourselves, our strength, and our abilities to lift ourselves up.[19] Unfortunately, this lifestyle leads to self-destruction and separation from God, as we are instructed in Jas 4:10 to "humble yourselves in the sight of the

---

definition has deceptively morphed and expanded over the last five decades to accommodate it; initially comprising racial inequality to today referring to differences in "human experience" (Fassler, "Theories of Homosexuality as Sources of Bloomsbury's Androgyny," 237–51). God specifically created two distinct genders to fulfill two distinct roles in his creation (Gen 1:27) and he put prohibitions against the blurring of gender (Deut 22:5). People who intentionally reject the gender he assigned them are rejecting him, his design, and his Lordship. And even though gender-confusion, transgenderism, and androgyny are propped up in popularity today, that doesn't make them right, healthy, or natural.

17. Longman and Garland, *Expositor's Bible Commentary* Vol. 13, 445–46.
18. Newton, "The Kite, or the Fall of Pride."
19. Bellshaw, "New Testament Doctrine of Satan," 27–29.

Lord, and He will lift you up." The Bible is full of examples of unchecked pride and the ensuing destruction. For example, in Acts 12:20–23, King Herod allowed himself to be worshipped as a God; "then immediately an angel of the Lord struck him, because he did not give glory to God. And he was eaten by worms and died" (v. 23). The Pharisees and other Jewish leaders were among the most prideful people in the Bible, as evidenced by how they mistreated and degraded those below their social status. Jesus said concerning them in Matt 23:6–12,

> They love the best places at feasts, the best seats in the synagogues, greetings in the marketplaces, and to be called by men, 'Rabbi, Rabbi.' But you, do not be called 'Rabbi'; for One is your Teacher, the Christ, and you are all brethren. Do not call anyone on earth your father; for One is your Father, He who is in heaven. And do not be called teachers; for One is your Teacher, the Christ. But he who is greatest among you shall be your servant. And whoever exalts himself will be humbled, and he who humbles himself will be exalted.

King Uzziah, who ventured to burn incense on the altar of incense and was struck with leprosy as God's punishment, fell because of his pride.[20] Hezekiah was filled with pride after the Lord healed him. His pride brought the vengeance of God not only upon himself but also upon the entirety of Judah and Jerusalem.[21]

Satan aims to amplify pride in our lives by tempting us to elevate ourselves over others by conforming to an image the world identifies as worthy. This creates a fleshly need to be noticed, commended, and revered. As a result, pride and self-centeredness obscure our motives and objective reasoning to draw us inward to ourselves and away from God.

---

20. See 2 Chr 26:16.
21. See 2 Chr 32:25–26.

A CATALOG OF DECEPTIVE PSYOP AS DISCUSSED IN SCRIPTURE

DECEPTIVE PSYOP OF BITTERNESS

Bitterness is an emotion that Satan aims to activate in our lives. It can manifest as a feeling of rage, anger, resentment, or disappointment over treatment one considers unfair. According to Heb 12:15–16, bitterness springs up from a root. It may start small, but if left unchecked, it swells and buttresses itself in both the heart and the mind. The Bible refers to bitterness as a root because it hides deep inside our core; it is thus difficult to dislodge.[22] Bitterness destroys everything in its path, including both the offended and the offender, and it leads to senseless clamor, anger, and eventually malice. In Eph 4:31–32, Heb 12:14–15, and Col 3:13, for example, the Bible warns against this sin because of the damage it can cause. Satan exploits bitterness by creating turmoil to provoke people not to forgive or love each other because he knows that if bitterness is harbored, people will alienate themselves from God's forgiveness of sin. The greatest risk associated with submitting to bitterness and allowing it to rule one's heart is the development of a spirit that refuses reconciliation. As a consequence, bitterness leads to rage, which is the external manifestation of internal emotions. Such unbridled rage and anger frequently result in "brawling," which is the brazen self-absorption of an enraged person who wants everyone to hear his or her complaints. Another negative consequence of bitterness is slander. As used in Eph 4, it does not refer to blasphemy against God or mere slander against men, but rather to any angry speech intended to wound or injure others.

The primary example of bitterness in the Bible is the relationship between Saul and David in 1 Sam 18. The first king of Israel, Saul, was envious of David's popularity and military success. This bitterness drove him to persistently pursue David in an effort to harm him. The story functions as a cautionary tale about the destructive nature of envy and the importance of humility in leadership.[23]

---

22. Longman and Garland, *Expositor's Bible Commentary* Vol. 13, 174.
23. MacArthur, *The MacArthur Bible Commentary*, 320–29.

Satan encourages bitterness in our lives in order to influence our emotions, motives, and objective reasoning to sidetrack and eventually destroy our relationship with God.

DECEPTIVE PSYOP OF LACK OF FAITH

In Eph 6, Paul encourages Christians to put on the "full armor of God that you may be able to stand against the wiles of the devil" (v. 11) and specifically says in v. 16, "above all, [take] the shield of faith with which you will be able to quench all the fiery darts of the wicked one," thus elevating the shield of faith as a prominent tool in spiritual warfare.[24] Accordingly, the strongest defensive component in a soldier's assorted equipment is a soldier's shield. Shields are purposeful tools meant to be employed with awareness and strategy. In fact, the shield protects the rest of a soldier's armor and equipment (as discussed in Eph 6:14–17). The shield of faith, as expressed in Eph 6:16, is what repels the attacks of Satan.[25] Faith is an important element of a Christian's walk and resolve, and this is conveyed by the author of Hebrews, who says that Christians must "not cast away your confidence, which has great reward" (Heb 10:35). By virtue of being in Christ, our faith is threatened at every opportunity. Satan is determined to undermine and destroy our faith because, as in Eph 6:16, if faith is destroyed, we are then exposed to "the fiery darts of the wicked one," and the stronger one's faith is, the fiercer the battle. Nothing presents a greater threat to Satan and his ambitions than a Christian who is unmovable in faith, because faith strengthens God's kingdom and

---

24. The phrase "full armor of God" is found in Eph 6:13–17. Eph 6:12 indicates unequivocally that the conflict with Satan is spiritual; consequently, no physical weapons can be used effectively against him and his minions. Although we are not given a list of Satan's specific strategies, the passage makes it abundantly clear that if we faithfully obey all the instructions, we will be able to stand, and we will win regardless of Satan's strategy. God has equipped us with the full armor of God—truth, righteousness, the gospel, faith, salvation, the Word of God, and prayer—with which we can achieve spiritual victory. Satan, consequently, is a defeated adversary.

25. Longman and Garland, *Expositor's Bible Commentary* Vol. 12, 166–67.

subdues Satan's. By faith, righteousness is born, and Satan's power and influence are quelled. Satan aims to chip away at people's faith and have them question every aspect of it in an effort to shake its foundation to influence emotions, motives, and objective reasoning, and thus to draw people away from God and his plans for them.[26]

Further, Paul exhorts believers to "walk by faith, not by sight" (2 Cor 5:7). Here, we see a contrast between truth and perception, or between what we know and believe to be true and what we perceive to be true. This is the origin of the Christian struggle with a lack of faith. We follow our perceptions of what is true rather than what we know to be true by faith. Christians find it difficult to believe the biblical account because it contradicts our perception of reality. We may believe that Jesus was a real person, that he was crucified by the Romans, and that he lived a perfect life according to God's Law, but we do not "see" how faith in Christ renders us righteous before God. We cannot "see" Jesus offering atonement for our sins. Because we cannot "see" or "perceive" any of the major Christian truths, we struggle with a lack of faith. Due to this lack of perception, our lives frequently do not reflect what we claim to believe in reality.

Many factors contribute to this phenomenon among Christians. We struggle with faith primarily because we do not genuinely know the God in whom we profess faith. The world, our flesh, and Satan are frequent sources of distraction. By "the world" is meant the conventional "wisdom" of the unbelieving world, enabled by Satan's deceptions, and the culture in which we reside (e.g., naturalism, atheism, materialism, and skepticism). The phrase "the flesh" refers to the sinful nature that adheres to Christians and with which we struggle daily. Lastly, Satan and his demon army excite and entice us via the world and our senses. All of these factors cause us to struggle with our faith. Consider the Old Testament example of the Israelites. The Pillar of Smoke and Fire, the Ten Plagues, and the Crossing of the Red Sea were the major miracles God performed to free his chosen people from slavery in Egypt.

26. Wiersbe, *Wiersbe Bible Commentary*, 1804.

God brings his people to the base of Mount Sinai, where he gives them the Law and enters into a covenant with them. The moment he does so, the people begin to grumble and abandon their faith. As Moses ascends the mountain, the people persuade Aaron, Moses' brother, to construct an idol for them to worship (Exod 32:1–6)—despite God's explicit prohibition. They no longer walked by faith but rather by sight. In spite of all the obvious miracles God performed during their redemption, they lost faith and began to rely on their own perceptions.[27]

DECEPTIVE PSYOP OF FALSE OCCULT PRACTICES

The occult has appeared in many forms throughout history, and in every manifestation it has appealed to humans. Whether through the desire to communicate with deceased relatives via a medium, the attractiveness of witchcraft and sorcery in modern media, or acting on dreams and visions, Satan uses dreams, visions, and "miracles" to deceive as many people as possible. With respect to miracles, Satan has the power—albeit limited compared to God's—to perform miracles. For instance, God conducted miraculous signs through Moses to prove that Moses was indeed his messenger when he sent Moses to deliver the Israelites from slavery in Egypt. However, Exod 7:22 states, "Then the magicians of Egypt did so with their enchantments; and Pharaoh's heart grew hard, and he did not heed them...."[28] Later, God demonstrated his superiority by performing miracles that the magicians, or more precisely the demons who empowered the magicians, were unable to replicate.[29] The fact remains, however, that Pharaoh's magicians could perform miracles. The prime example is the rise of the Antichrist, who, according to Rev 13:11–14, will essentially act as a counterfeit Christ and will perform great "signs, and lying wonders" (2 Thess 2:9) to deceive those on Earth to follow him. In this

---

27. MacArthur, *2 Corinthians*, 159–70.
28. Also see Exod 7:11; 8:7
29. See Exod 8:18; 9:11.

A CATALOG OF DECEPTIVE PSYOP AS DISCUSSED IN SCRIPTURE

context, these "miracles" and associated spirits, if tested, according to 1 John 4:1, will reveal that the miracle worker is teaching something contrary to God's Word, and subsequently the miracles, no matter how compelling, will be revealed as a Satanically generated illusion. Fueled by Satan, false religious leaders have performed and will perform great signs and miracles to influence emotions, motives, and objective reasoning to deceive humans to fall away from God.[30]

DECEPTIVE PSYOP OF FALSE DOCTRINE

In several places, the Bible warns people not to yield to the deception of false doctrine.[31] False doctrine is any belief that adds to, subtracts from, contradicts, or nullifies biblical doctrine. In some cases, this takes the form of "religious" leaders preaching what people want to hear (e.g., the prosperity gospel,[32] progressive Christianity,[33] etc.) rather than scriptural truths; in other cases, it

---

30. Martin, *Kingdom of the Cults*, 35–40.

31. See 1 John 4:1; 2 Cor 11:13–15; Gal 1:8–9; 2 John 1:7; Rom 16:17–18; 1 Tim 6:3–5, etc.

32. Thomas Carlyle (1795–1881), a Scottish essayist, historian, and philosopher, said, "Adversity is sometimes hard upon a man; but for one man who can stand prosperity, there are a hundred that will stand adversity" (Carlyle, "The Hero as Man of Letters," 160). To that end, instead of emphasizing the value of wealth, the Bible cautions against seeking it. Heb 13:5 instructs believers, notably church leaders (1 Tim 3:3), to be free from the love of money. The passion for money leads to all manner of evil (1 Tim 6:10). Jesus warned, "Beware! Be on guard against all forms of covetousness, for a man's life does not consist of the abundance of his possessions" (Luke 12:15). Jesus said, in stark contrast to the prosperity gospel's emphasis on acquiring wealth and possessions in this life, "Take heed and beware of covetousness, for one's life does not consist in the abundance of the things he possesses" (Matt 6:19). The contradictions between prosperity teaching and the gospel of Jesus Christ are best summarized in Matt 6:24 (NIV), where Jesus says, "You cannot serve both God and money."

33. Progressive Christianity is a recent Protestant movement with a variety of beliefs and perspectives on various topics but most prominently a strong emphasis on social justice and environmentalism and a frequently revisionist (or non-traditional) interpretation of the Bible. The Bible is replete with

relates to "religious" teachings that are completely contrary to the truth of the Scripture (e.g., Mormonism and Jehovah's Witnesses, among many others). In Gal 1:6–9, Paul addresses directly those who accepted the Gospel of Jesus during his first missionary journey to their region. They heard the simple truth that they could be saved from their sin through faith in Christ. No additional works were necessary to ensure their place in God's family. Jesus had made complete payment with his life. According to this passage, Paul is frustrated, if not furious, with his readers. He is actually "astonished" (NIV) that they are abandoning the simple truth so rapidly. Paul writes more specifically that they are deserting Christ himself by believing a different idea, a different "gospel," than the one Paul presented. How did this happen? A group of "religious" people had infiltrated the Galatian Christians after Paul's departure, distorting what Paul had taught. In brief, they stated that specific works or actions were required for salvation. Faith in Christ

---

commands "to visit orphans and widows in their trouble" (Jas 1:27) and to safeguard the Earth that God has entrusted us to have "dominion" over (Gen 1:28). Progressive Christianity, insofar as it is a movement that strives to emphasize and honor these principles, is consistent with the Bible. However, some aspects of Progressive Christianity are incompatible with a biblical worldview. In general, adherents of this movement reject the biblical doctrine of scriptural inerrancy and do not consider the Bible to be God's literal Word. Additionally, Progressive Christianity tends to emphasize "collective salvation" over the biblical concept of individual salvation. The Bible makes it plain that God redeems those who accept Jesus Christ as their Savior and rescues them from an eternity of separation from him. Collective salvation, in contrast, emphasizes the restoration of entire cultures and societies to the socioeconomic structure that Progressive Christians consider to be the correct one, namely Marxism. Marxism is an economic and political theory devised by an atheist (Karl Marx) and is based on nonbiblical assumptions. Therefore, the views of many Progressive Christians are incompatible with biblical principles in this regard. In the end, however, discretion is required when evaluating a specific claim or belief in light of the Bible; the entire continuum of beliefs identified by the term "Progressive Christianity" is too broad to permit a definitive conclusion as to whether or not it can be deemed unbiblical. As with all ambiguous issues, Christians would do well to compare the claims of the Progressive Christianity movement with the Bible and pray for discernment and wisdom to separate truth from error (Jas 1:5). (Got Questions Ministries, "What is Progressive Christianity, and is it Biblical?" and Thompson, "Progressive Christianity," 1–12)

alone was insufficient. From this example, one can easily see how false doctrine arises in the church.

As Paul witnessed and foretold such events, he encouraged Timothy, in 2 Tim 4:2-4, to "preach the word! Be ready in season and out of season. Convince, rebuke, exhort, with all longsuffering and teaching. For the time will come when they will not endure sound doctrine, but according to their own desires, because they have itching ears, they will heap up for themselves teachers; and they will turn their ears away from the truth and be turned aside to fables."[34] This passage conveys the necessity not to deviate from scriptural truth; however, the day is coming where people will seek after and succumb to false doctrine.

Further, as discussed in Matt 24:4-5, Jesus foretold that there would be imposter Christs: "And Jesus answered and said to them: 'Take heed that no one deceives you. For many will come in My name, saying, "I am the Christ," and will deceive many.'" Additionally, in Matt 24:24, Jesus goes on to say that "false Christs and false prophets will rise and show great signs and wonders to deceive, if possible, even the elect." Satan will work to deceive the whole world, and, according to 2 Tim 2:26, those deceived have "been taken captive by him to do his will."[35] Clearly, false doctrine conveys false information, influencing emotions, motives, and objective reasoning to draw people away from God.[36]

---

34. While the Bible was still being written, false doctrine was an emerging issue in the church. Accordingly, several of the New Testament epistles (or parts thereof) were composed to respond to these errors (e.g., Col 2:20-23; Gal 1:6-9; Titus 1:10-11).

35. Martin, *Kingdom of the Cults*, 474-77.

36. It is necessary to point out the difference between false doctrine and denominational disagreements. Various congregational groups view secondary, non-essential, biblical issues differently. These differences are not always the result of false doctrine. Since they are not specifically addressed in the Bible, church policies, governmental decisions, devotional styles, etc. are all subject to discussion. Even issues addressed in the Bible are frequently debated by equally sincere Christ-followers. Differences in interpretation or practice do not inherently constitute false doctrine, nor should they cause division within the Body of Christ (1 Cor 1:10-11).

SATAN'S GRAND PSYOP STRATEGY CULMINATING IN RELIGIOUS DECEPTION

While the previous section on the deceptive PSYOP of false doctrine discusses the topic generally, because false doctrine spread by false prophets (as per Matt 24:11) is an indicator of the end of the age and, to an extent, characterizes the end times, a more in-depth discussion is necessary to provide some additional clarity on the employment of this PSYOP.[37]

If salvation were summarized in a single phrase, it would be "running to the open arms of Jesus Christ"; as Isa 45:22 says, "Look to Me, and be saved, all you ends of the earth! For I am God, and there is no other." In other words, God invites us to come to him. Accordingly, the discipline of truth guards the one and only Gospel of salvation from the "demon doctrines"—in other words, running to the incorrect "Jesus." First Tim 4:1 discusses this specifically: "Now the Spirit expressly says that in latter times some will depart from the faith, giving heed to deceiving spirits and doctrines of demons." This prompts the question: What are the doctrines of demons?

Fueled by self-delusion that he can defeat God, Satan wants to thwart the message of the Gospel of the true Jesus Christ; thus, in 1 Tim 4:1, Paul warns that some people "will depart from the faith," albeit willfully. They will give heed to deceiving spirits. They will believe these doctrines of demons, and that is the history of the enduring battle for the truth that began in the Garden of Eden. Eve was deceived by choosing to believe that she would not die because of her sin, and that she could be like God if she followed Satan. That lie is the doctrine of demons, and it has been woven into every false teaching and every cult religion throughout the history of humankind. Contrary to Matt 7:13, the world promotes

---

37. Hunt, *Woman Rides the Beast*, 15.

A CATALOG OF DECEPTIVE PSYOP AS DISCUSSED IN SCRIPTURE

a wide road or many paths to God.[38] Accordingly, humans are warned in 1 Tim 4:1 to be aware of doctrines of demons.[39]

Satan is so efficient at deceptive PSYOP, Jesus says in Matt 24:24, that if it were possible, even the elect would be deceived; for this reason, Christians must be vitally concerned about the discipline of truth. Satan's true work is not carried out in drug houses or prostitution rings; human flesh perpetuates the wickedness in those areas. Additionally, Satan only needs to devote minimal attention to the deceptive PSYOP of lies, lust, bitterness, pride, and lack of faith, as he merely needs to nudge people in the wrong direction, and human flesh will take over. Subsequently, Satan's main focus is on religious deception by confusing people and distracting them from truth.[40] Second John 1:7–11 says:

> For many deceivers have gone out into the world who do not confess Jesus Christ as coming in the flesh. This is a deceiver and an antichrist. Look to yourselves, that we do not lose those things we worked for, but that we may receive a full reward. Whoever transgresses and does not abide in the doctrine of Christ does not have God. He who abides in the doctrine of Christ has both the Father and the Son. If anyone comes to you and does not bring this doctrine, do not receive him into your house nor greet him; for he who greets him shares in his evil deeds.

As this passage conveys, Christians must abide in the doctrine of Christ. Accordingly, Jesus repeatedly warns followers to beware of spiritual deception. This is a consistent message from the beginning to the end of his ministry.[41] This warning rises above all other warnings Jesus gave; he repeats over and over the importance of not being spiritually deceived. Further, to counter all the false teachers, Jesus Christ told his disciples on the night before his death that there was one thing they had to remember: To trust in

---

38. It is important to note that some other religions also promote a narrow way; it just isn't the same narrow way as the Bible conveys.
39. Bubeck, *Adversary*, 82.
40. Bubeck, *Adversary*, 27.
41. As seen, for example, in Matt 7:15; 24:4–5, 11, 24.

the real Lord Jesus Christ. Trusting in the Jesus of the Bible is an immense step in harboring truth and deterring deceptive PSYOP.

Jesus provides a method in 1 John 4:1–6 to determine whether deception is occurring. The truth this verse presents is that the divine God, the Son Lord Jesus Christ, is the only way of salvation; that is the central, most important point of all life. To know who a spirit is, John says one must ask two questions: (1) as per 1 John 4:1–3, does it confess that Jesus is the only divine Son of God, and (2) as per 1 John 4:4–6, does what it says agree with what God has already said in the Bible? If the answer to these two questions is "no," the spirit is a demon spreading demonic doctrines.

Interestingly, two characteristics of most false religions are that they confuse the essence of Jesus Christ and they postulate a substitute scripture or an addition to the Bible. Simply put, they have a different Christ, and they have a substitute for or an addendum to Scripture because they assert that the Bible is not sufficient, not authoritative, and not final, which is antithetical to what the Bible actually says. For instance, in Mormonism, Jesus is understood to be a created being, only one of an infinite number of finite gods, and the brother of Adam and Satan, and the Book of Mormon is said to be "Another Testament of Jesus Christ."[42] The Bible says in John 1 that the real Jesus is infinite and not only exists eternally with the other members of the trinity, but also created everything.[43] Additionally, Rev 22:18 sharply warns against dis-

---

42. Martin, *Kingdom of the Cults*, 193–260.

43. The doctrine of the Trinity means that there is one God who eternally exists as three distinct Persons — the Father, Son, and Holy Spirit. Stated differently, God is one in essence and three in person. Please understand that this does not imply the existence of three distinct Gods. (1) The Bible teaches that there is only one God (see Deut 6:4; 1 Cor 8:4; 1 Tim 2:5: Gal 3:20). (2) There are three Persons that comprise the Trinity (see Gen 1:1, 26; 3:22; 11:7; Isa 6:8, 48:16, 61:1; 2 Cor 13:14; Matt 3:16–17, 28:19). (3) The Trinity's members are distinguished from one another in numerous Bible passages. (4) Each Trinity member is God. The Father is God (see John 6:27; Rom 1:7; 1 Pet 1:2). The Son is God (John 1:1, 14; Rom 9:5; Col 2:9; Heb 1:8; 1 John 5:20). The Holy Spirit is God (see Acts 5:3–4; 1 Cor 3:16). (5) Within the Trinity, there is subordination (called the Doctrine of Eternal Functional Subordination). The Holy Spirit is subordinate to the Father and the Son, while the Son is subordinate

torting its message: "If anyone adds to these things, God will add on him the plagues that have been written in this book."[44] Most false religions do not have a commitment to the divine Lord, nor do they have a commitment to the divine Word. Eastern religions of today and almost all other religions, even Islam, consider Christ to be a great teacher (like Confucius, Muhammad, or Buddha), but they do not consider him God in human flesh.[45] It has always been Satan's strategy to affirm the wrong, defective doctrine of Christ and to subtly deceive people by redefining Jesus. Demon doctrines about Jesus will come through false teachers who will go against Christ's deity and will subtly misrepresent him.[46] Thus, this is a deceptive PSYOP of Satan that, unfortunately, impacts many subscribing to false doctrine.

As an example, Jehovah's Witnesses (and the Watchtower and Tract Society) believe that Jesus is the archangel Michael, the highest created being. This contradicts numerous biblical passages that declare Jesus to be God (John 1:1, 14; 8:58; 10:30). Jehovah's Witnesses believe that salvation is achieved through a combination of faith, good actions, and obedience. This contradicts the Bible, which states that salvation is received through grace and faith (John 3:16; Eph 2:8–9; Titus 3:5). Jehovah's Witnesses reject the Doctrine of the Trinity, believing that Jesus is a created being and the Holy Spirit is fundamentally God's inanimate power. Jehovah's Witnesses deny the concept of Christ's substitutionary atonement in favor of the ransom theory, according to which Jesus'

---

to the Father, according to Scripture. This is an internal relationship that does not negate the divinity of any of the Trinity's members. This is just something that our finite minds cannot apprehend about the infinite God. (6) The Trinity's members have different duties and responsibilities. (Got Questions Ministries, "What Does the Bible Teach About the Trinity?")

44. While the caution in Rev 22:18–19 refers specifically to adding to or distorting the book of Revelation, logically, the rule applies to anyone who pursues the deliberate distortion of Scripture to mislead. Parallel cautions are conveyed in Deut 4:1–2 and Prov 30:5–6.

45. When a distinction is made between "Western" and "Eastern" religions, Islam falls on the "Western" side (even though, like Judaism and Christianity, it originated in the Middle East).

46. Martin, *The Kingdom of the Cults*, 41.

death was a ransom payment for Adam's sin. Jehovah's Witnesses defend these unbiblical doctrines by asserting that the church has corrupted the Bible over the centuries; consequently, they have retranslated the Bible to reflect their distinctive doctrines, resulting in the New World Translation. As Jehovah's Witnesses discover more and more passages in the Bible that contradict their doctrines, it is not surprising that their New World Translation has undergone numerous revisions. Jehovah's Witnesses are arguably the most devoted religious group when it comes to spreading their message—one that unfortunately contains many distortions, deceptions, and false doctrine.[47]

In Matt 7:13-14, Jesus discloses that (1) the way [to salvation] is narrow, (2) the way is difficult, and (3) the way leads to life. In this passage, Jesus says that salvation is a small target, and in Matt 7:15-19, he indicates that Satan and his false prophets want to obscure salvation. This is why salvation's narrow path must be declared as the only real Jesus Christ; in John 14:6, we read "Jesus said to him, 'I am the way, the truth, and the life. No one comes to the Father except through Me.'"[48] According to John 17:3, salvation is a person; it is not a prayer, baptism, circumcision, joining a church, an experience, or a feeling. Jesus Christ is the creator of everything, the only savior able to save, God the Son, the second person of the Trinity; he is also the final judge of humanity. Jesus did not begin to exist in Bethlehem. According to John 1, he eternally

---

47. Martin, *The Kingdom of the Cults*, 49-148.

48. 1 Tim 2:5 says, "For there is one God and one Mediator between God and men, the Man Christ Jesus." A mediator is someone who facilitates an agreement between disputing parties. The perfection of a mediator is determined by his influence with the parties he must reconcile, and this influence derives from his connection with both parties: the mediator would attain the utmost level of perfection if he were substantially one with both parties. The hypostatic union (the combination of divine and human natures in the single person of Christ) makes him the Head of humanity and, consequently, its natural representative. By his human origin, Christ is a member of the human family and a partaker of our flesh and blood (Heb 2:11-15); by virtue of his Divine Personality, he is "the image and likeness of God" in a way that neither man nor angel can approach. Therefore, no one other than Jesus Christ is qualified to mediate between men and God, including priests, saints, Mary, or the Pope.

existed as God, and he came in human form as God the Son. If one does not know the real Jesus Christ, following Matthew 7, one is not saved. Humans' eternal souls are tied to trusting the right person. It is not a matter of saying the right words; rather, what matters is making sure that the words we say are properly defined biblically. This is because many false religions today say similar words, but what they mean by them is absolutely, categorically different.[49] This is the danger of the deception of false doctrine, one of Satan's most successful PSYOP.

As Christians, we are supposed to be aware of, but not afraid of, everything Satan is doing, and we are supposed to resist it. So, what is Satan doing? Initially, as discussed in Mark 4:15, the famous parable of the sower, Satan snatches away the seed before it can take root. In other words, he snatches the Gospel away before it can save lives. Secondly, and much more deceptively, he is sowing tares in the church. Not everybody who goes to church, not everybody who says they belong to Christ, actually does. That's part of Satan's plan. In fact, Satan is far more active in churches than anywhere else, transforming and masquerading in religion, and the primary place Satan works today is in the religious realm.[50] If he can just get people to believe something slightly off about the Lord, he wins.[51] For instance, he can get people to believe that

---

49. For instance, when a Christian refers to God, they mean God who was always God, unchanging, spirit, always omnipotent, always perfect, and always all-knowing (Isa 44:6, 8, among others). When a Mormon refers to God (Heavenly Father), they are referring to a God who is not eternal, used to be a man, has a body of flesh and bones, started as a man, lived and died, was resurrected, and became a God, gained all the "God" attributes progressively, and has a wife (Mormon Doctrine and Covenants 130:22–23, among others). Another example is when a Christian refers to exaltation, they mean being with God forever, in glorified human bodies. When a Mormon refers to exaltation, they mean becoming a God and populating their own heaven with spirit children. These are just two of many examples of saying similar words but with completely different meanings.

50. MacArthur, *Mark*, 189–208.

51. For instance, that the righteousness of Jesus (justification) is infused—where righteousness comes gradually to the believer through obedience, confession, penance, and the other sacraments—rather than imputed as the Bible clearly teaches (Rom 3:28; 4:3, 22; Gal 3:6).

Jesus is a great prophet but not God, especially not God the Son, or that Jesus is a great moral teacher but not the Risen and reigning Son of God, or that Jesus was not virgin-born but was just like everybody else.[52] If you misunderstand who Jesus is, what the reality is, you are not a follower of Christ[53]—and that is precisely Satan's deceptive PSYOP strategy.

Matt 13:25 implies that Satan is dangerous because he multiplies evildoers: "while men slept, his enemy came and sowed tares among the wheat." In this parabolic teaching, the wheat—the ones that bear fruit—are the believers. Tares, in contrast, look like wheat, but they are toxic.[54] They have grown alongside the church throughout the ages.[55] Matt 13:38 says, "The field is the world,

---

52. Today, there are numerous variations of Jesus. For instance, Jesus is an angel (Jehovah's Witnesses); he is Satan's brother (Mormons); he is a great prophet (Muslims); and he is a great moral teacher (Buddhists, Confucians, Taoists). All of these examples are antithetical to the real Jesus as described in the Bible.

53. As an example, the core teachings of Mormonism are not only dissimilar to Christianity, but they are also contradictory (e.g., who Jesus is, polytheism, etc.). By embracing Mormon teaching, one is actually required to reject Christian teaching regarding Jesus, therefore Mormonism cannot be Christian, and adherents are not followers of the true and living Christ. Similarly, a core doctrine of Islam is that God has no son therefore Jesus is not God. So, if one embraces Islam, the core truths of Jesus must be rejected. Thus, the consequence of subscribing to Satan's deceptions results in an unfortunate, damning reality as salvation is only possible through the Jesus described in the Bible.

54. "Tares" refer to the plant now called darnel. It *does* have "fruit" (i.e., seeds), just as wheat does, but darnel seeds can be toxic in large enough doses.

55. Satan, in opposition to Jesus Christ, attempts to destroy Christ's work by introducing false believers and false teachers who lead many astray. One need only consider the litany of televangelist scandals to realize that the world is full of professing "Christians" whose ungodly actions bring disgrace to the name of Christ. However, we are not to pursue such individuals in an attempt to eliminate them. One reason is that we do not know if immature and innocent believers will be harmed by our efforts. Moreover, one need only consider the Crusades, the Spanish Inquisition, and "Bloody Mary's" reign in England to see the consequences of men assuming the task of separating true believers from false ones, which is God's alone. Christ allows these false believers to remain in the world until his return, rather than requiring that they be uprooted and possibly harm immature believers in the process. Moreover, because the distinction between true and false believers is not always clear, we are not to take it

the good seeds are the sons of the kingdom [the true believers, the born-again ones], but the tares are the sons of the wicked one. The enemy who sowed them is the devil."[56] So where is Satan at work? Is he sowing crack houses, new methods of murdering and extorting money, and new ways of sexual immortality? No! He's sowing in the field of religion and trying to promote a religion that does not acknowledge God, his Word, Jesus Christ, and his all-sufficient work on the cross.

Religious Deception Demonstrated

As an expanded modern case study of Satan's grand PSYOP strategy, Mormonism provides a textbook illustration of false doctrine resulting in religious deception. Unfortunately, there are many who fall victim to this deception as Mormon membership surpassed 17 million members worldwide in 2022, lending credence to the effectiveness of the PSYOP of False Doctrine.[57] Regardless, its theological foundation is severely flawed, and it fails to stand up to even rudimentary interrogation.

Joseph Smith founded the Mormon religion (Mormonism), whose adherents are known as Mormons and Latter-day Saints

---

upon ourselves to remove unbelievers. As tares resemble wheat, a false believer may also resemble a genuine believer. Jesus warned in Matt 7:22 that many profess faith but do not know him. Therefore, each individual should evaluate his or her own relationship with Christ (2 Cor 13:5). Accordingly, 1 John serves as an outstanding litmus test for salvation. (MacArthur, *Mark*, 189–208)

56. To quote John 8:44, "You are of your father the devil, and the desires of your father you want to do. He was a murderer from the beginning, and does not stand in the truth, because there is no truth in him. When he speaks a lie, he speaks from his own resources, for he is a liar and the father of it." In this verse, Jesus is talking to the religious leaders of the temple in Jerusalem. He says that these leaders are hanging around the temple but are not real. They are tares. They are false. They do not have the fruit of the spirit inside of them. They are sons of the devil!

57. The Church of Jesus Christ of Latter-day Saints, *2022 Statistical Report for the April 2023 Conference*.

(or LDS), less than two centuries ago. He claimed to have received a personal revelation from God the Father and Jesus Christ (*Articles of Faith*, 35), who instructed him that all churches and their doctrines were abominations (1 Nephi 13:28; *Pearl of Great Price, Joseph Smith—History* 1:18, 19). Joseph Smith then endeavored to "restore true Christianity" and asserted that his church was the "only true church on earth" (*Mormon Doctrine*, 670; 1 Nephi 14:10). Mormonism is problematic because it contradicts, modifies, and expands the Bible. Christians have no reason to believe the Bible is false or insufficient. To genuinely trust and believe in God is to believe in his Word, for all Scripture is inspired by God, which means it originates with him (2 Tim 3:16).

Mormons believe that there are not just one but four sources of divinely inspired words: (1) the Bible, "as far as it is translated correctly" (8th Article of Faith). However, not always is it made clear which verses are considered to be mistranslated. (2) *The Book of Mormon*, which Smith "translated" and released in 1830. Smith asserted that it is the "most correct book" on Earth and that observing its precepts brings one closer to God "than by any other book" (*History of the Church*, 4:461). (3) *The Doctrine and Covenants*, a compilation of modern revelations concerning the "Church of Jesus Christ as it has been restored." (4) *The Pearl of Great Price*, which Mormons consider to "clarify" lost Bible doctrines and teachings (*Articles of Faith*, 182–85) and adds its own information about the Earth's creation.

Mormons believe that God did not always exist as the Supreme Being of the universe (*Mormon Doctrine*, 321), but attained that position through righteous living and perseverance (*Teachings of the Prophet Joseph Smith*, 345). They believe that God the Father has a "body of flesh and bones as tangible as man's" (*Doctrine and Covenants* 130:22). Additionally, Brigham Young, the second LDS President, taught that Adam was literally God and the father of Jesus Christ, but modern Mormon leaders have abandoned this belief.

Christians, in contrast, recognize that there is only one true God (Deut 6:4; Isa 43:10; 44:6–8). He has existed eternally and will continue to exist eternally (Deut 33:27; Ps 90:2; 1 Tim 1:17). He was not created, but is the Creator (Gen 1; Ps 24:1; Isa 37:16). He is perfect, and no one is equal to him (Ps 86:8; Isa 40:25). God the Father was never a man (Num 23:19; 1 Sam 15:29; Hos 11:9). He is Spirit (John 4:24), and Luke 24:39 states that Spirit is not composed of flesh and bone.

Mormon leaders have taught that the incarnation of Jesus Christ was the result of a physical relationship between God the Father and Mary (*Journal of Discourses*, vol. 8, 115; *Mormon Doctrine*, 547). Mormons believe that Jesus is a deity, but that anyone can become a god as well (*Doctrine and Covenants* 132:20; *Teachings of the Prophet Joseph Smith*, 345–54). In the King Follet Discourse, Joseph Smith said, "God himself was once as we are now, and is an exalted man." In June of 1840, the fifth LDS President, Lorenzo Snow, declared, "As man is, God once was; as God is, man may become." Additionally, Mormonism teaches that salvation can be earned through both faith and good works (*LDS Bible Dictionary*, 697).

In contrast, Christians have traditionally taught that no one can attain the status of God; only God is holy (1 Sam 2:2). Only through faith in God can we be made holy in God's sight (1 Cor 1:2). Jesus is the only-begotten Son of God (John 3:16), the only person to have ever lived a sinless life, and the current occupant of heaven's highest place of honor (Heb 7:26). Jesus, who is the same in essence with God, is the only man to have existed prior to his physical birth (John 1:1–8; 8:56). In the end, everyone will confess that Jesus Christ is Lord because he died as a sacrifice for our sins and was resurrected from the dead (Phil 2:6–11). Jesus tells us (Matt 19:26) that it is impossible to reach heaven through our own efforts and that it is only possible through faith in him.[58] For our transgressions, we all deserve eternal punishment, but God's infinite love and grace have provided us with a way out. "For the

---

58. Receiving salvation is accomplished via faith rather than works (Rom 1:17; 3:28). This gift is available to us regardless of who we are or what we have done (Rom 3:22). Knowing God and his Son, Jesus (John 17:3) is the only true path to salvation "and there is salvation in no one else, for there is no other name under heaven given among men by which we must be saved" (Acts 4:12).

wages of sin is death, but the gift of God is eternal life in Christ Jesus our Lord" (Rom 6:23).[59]

Despite referring to themselves as Christian and the generally friendly, compassionate, and caring demeanor of Mormons, they are deceived by a religious belief system that is false, as it misrepresents the essence of God and the Person of Jesus Christ, and distorts the Bible and the means by which salvation is attained.[60]

---

59. With the exception of biblical references, the references are from Mormon publications and passages from the Book of Mormon.

60. Got Questions Ministries, "What is Mormonism?," Martin, *Kingdom of the Cults*, 193–260, and www.lds.org.

5

Counter-PSYOP Methods to Guard against Deception

Conditioning, Indirect, and Direct Refutation

British "sunshields" used to disguise tanks as trucks, used during World War II.[1]

> Your first job is to build the credibility and the authenticity of your propaganda, and persuade the enemy to trust you, although you are his enemy.
>
> —*A Psychological Warfare Casebook*, Operations Research Office, Johns Hopkins University, 1958

---

1. WO201-2841 *Middle East Command Camouflage Development and Training Centre, Helwan 'Sunshield'*, Public Domain.

GERMAN POLITICAL AND MILITARY leaders ascribe a portion of Germany's defeat in World War I to the ineffective countering against Allied propaganda campaigns.[2] By the spring of 1917, propaganda efforts in Germany had devastated the country. In fact, senior German officials convened in May 1917 to devise a strategy to counter the demoralizing effects of the Allied propaganda campaign.[3] The proposal encompassed the creation of a centralized agency operating within the Foreign Office with the responsibility of gathering Allied propaganda and press releases, devising initiatives to boost the morale of German troops, and formulating policies to direct propaganda endeavors against the Allies.[4] The Germans' strategic choice to allocate resources at such a strategic level signifies the criticality they attributed to countering propaganda. Unfortunately, their endeavor commenced too late and was futile in altering the course of the war.[5]

There are numerous instances in history that illustrate the consequences of employing or neglecting counterpropaganda strategies. Among the earliest documented occurred throughout the Peloponnesian Wars. Propagandists on both sides of the Athenian and Spartan Archidamian War (431–404 BC) counterasserted each other's statements without openly refuting them or acknowledging the propaganda itself.[6]

Thucydides (c.460–c.400 BC), an Athenian historian and general, observed that the counterassertions were always more severe than the original, concluding it was a necessity for effective counterpropaganda.[7] Using this rational, Italian counterpropaganda operations against Austro-Hungarian soldiers were carried out

2. Bruntz, "Allied Propaganda and the Collapse of German Morale in 1918," 61.

3. Bruntz, "Allied Propaganda and the Collapse of German Morale in 1918," 67.

4. Bruntz, "Allied Propaganda and the Collapse of German Morale in 1918," 68.

5. Bruntz, "Allied Propaganda and the Collapse of German Morale in 1918," 68.

6. Pearson, "Propaganda in the Archidamian War," 36–52.

7. Pearson, "Propaganda in the Archidamian War," 52.

during World War I through the alteration of trench newsletters by the Austro-Hungarians to include propaganda messages.[8]

History also demonstrates, however, that counterpropaganda campaigns must be skillfully executed to avoid backfiring. An intriguing counterpropaganda leaflet was produced by German propaganda practitioners in the midst of the Battle of Anzio in World War II.[9] German propagandists attempted to refute the assertions made in an Allied leaflet, which detailed Allied victories against German positions along the Cassino Front, by making statements that mirrored a reversal of the Allies' battlefield fortunes. The German leaflets ultimately failed in their objective of undermining the credibility of the Allied leaflet among American soldiers and, due to their exceptionally absurd claims, inadvertently boosted the soldier's morale.[10]

When skillfully implemented, counterpropaganda can exert a formidable and conclusive impact on an ideological opponent. In 1987, for instance, President Ronald Reagan disseminated arguably one of the most effective instances of effective counterpropaganda, which had an unprecedented global impact. Throughout the 1980s, the Soviet Union effectively employed propaganda to cultivate the notion in Europe that Mikhail Gorbachev, the then President of the Soviet Union, spearheaded peace initiatives.[11] Reagan exploited this perception during a speech near the Berlin Wall by undermining it with an explicit and flagrant challenge:

> There is one sign the Soviets can make that would be unmistakable, that would advance dramatically the cause of freedom and peace... Secretary General Gorbachev, if you seek peace—if you seek prosperity for the Soviet Union and Eastern Europe—if you seek prosperity:

---

8. Row, "Mobilizing the Nation: Italian Propaganda in the Great War," 151.

9. Herz, "Some Psychological Lessons from Leaflet Propaganda in World War II," 486.

10. Herz, "Some Psychological Lessons from Leaflet Propaganda in World War II," 486.

11. Boyd, "Raze Berlin Wall, Reagan Urges Soviets."

come here, to this gate. Mister Gorbachev, open this gate. Mister Gorbachev, tear down this wall.[12]

This challenge, which exposed the Soviet Union's public declarations of hypocrisy in a straightforward and glaring manner, induced tremendous international political and public pressure on the Soviet Union. Twenty months later, in reaction to increasing public unrest stemming in large measure from Reagan's open challenge, East Germany opened the Berlin Wall.[13]

As these examples convey, deception (or propaganda as expressed above) *should* be countered, and with well-executed counter-deception (or counterpropaganda) methods, deception *can* be countered successfully.

Now that deception and the employment of PSYOP have been explored, the question becomes: How does one defend against these tactics? PSYOP tactics and their employment shed light on Satanic deceptive tactics and, therefore, can help Christians construct defenses to avoid their harmful effects. This chapter and the next describe practices that can be used to counter deceptive PSYOP, noting the type of deception against which each is best used. Where this chapter discusses the more foundational counter-PSYOP methods, the next chapter discusses the more subtle but equally important methods.

While there is a wide variety of practices to counter PSYOP, there is no "best fit" method. The practices must be employed based on the situation and type of deception Satan is employing, and one or more practices may be used in counter-PSYOP defense (see Chapter 4 for a catalog of deceptive PSYOP Satan employs).[14] The techniques discussed in this chapter and the next are several of the "Counterpropaganda Techniques" presented in the manual published by the Department of the Army titled *Psychological Operations Tactics*. The following methods can identify, amplify, and reinforce truth so that deceptive PSYOP can be detected and

12. Boyd, "Raze Berlin Wall, Reagan Urges Soviets."
13. McIntrye, "To Respond or Not to Respond," 62–69.
14. Department of the Army, *Psychological Operations Tactics*, 11–22.

defeated. It should be noted that employing these defenses takes time and discipline; thus, the solution to immediate problems may involve a lifelong armament process.

CONDITIONING

The counter-PSYOP defense strategy called conditioning is described by the US Army as "a nonspecific means of eliminating potential vulnerabilities in the target audience before they can be exploited."[15] Conditioning is a preemptive and preventative measure that can be used against *all* of Satan's deceptive PSYOP, and can be used specifically against a *lack of faith*. "This technique does not specifically address potential themes that the opponent may use in a propaganda program against the force, but seeks to remove or reduce potential vulnerabilities before they can be exploited."[16] In a military sense, conditioning can be accomplished in a number of ways, such as visual, auditory, and audiovisual media, in order to convey messages. At the tactical level, conditioning can be conducted via loudspeaker and face-to-face communication. Pamphlets, radio, or television can be used for more deliberate campaigns. Social media, radio or television broadcasts, various publications, airdropped leaflets, and, as part of a covert operation, material inserted in foreign news media, may all be utilized to condition in order to communicate correct, truthful information to remove probable weaknesses in the target audience before they can be manipulated by the enemy.[17] Conditioning oneself as a

---

15. Department of the Army, *Psychological Operations Tactics*, 11–24–11–25.

16. Department of the Army, *Psychological Operations Tactics*, 11–25.

17. Interestingly, the *Psychological Operations Tactics* manual says that, "when using this technique [conditioning], PSYOP personnel must avoid the use of specific end dates for operations." For example, when the US entered Bosnia in 1995, PSYOP personnel and the Implementation Force (IFOR) stated the conditions that must exist in Bosnia for IFOR to depart instead of giving a departure date (Department of the Army, *Psychological Operations Tactics*, 11–25). Similarly, regarding the return of Christ, Jesus said in Matt 24:36, "But of that day and hour no one knows, not even the angels of heaven, but My Father only," and in Matt 24:5–8, 1 Tim 4:1, 2 Tim 3:1–9, and 2 Thess 2:3, clues are

Christian simply involves knowing, applying, and reinforcing the truth of Scripture and, thus, living a pure life reflective of God's holiness, mercy, love, faithfulness, forgiveness, graciousness, and justice.[18] However, the vital first step—the *sine qua non*—in conditioning oneself is to apprehend the real Gospel to grasp lifesaving truth and then to grow (condition) from this truth.

The Gospel is the "good news" that Jesus Christ paid the penalty for human sin by dying on the cross so that humankind can be saved by God through *sola fide* (faith alone), *sola gratia* (grace alone), and in *solus Christus* (Christ alone).[19] Concisely, "the Gospel," which appears 101 times in the King James Version of the Bible,[20] is the entirety of the truth that saves, as it is dis-

---

given for discerning the approach of the end times, thus, in a sense, establishing conditions (also, depending on one's view of eschatology, Gen 17:8, Ezek 37, Dan 10:14; 11:41, and Rev 11:8, could provide conditions for the end times). Not "setting a date" not only encourages Christians to live their lives by faith, for God's glory, before an unbelieving world, but, because he is not omniscient, also keeps Satan on his toes and in a disadvantaged position. Not a surprising tactic coming from the Creator and premier military Strategist, our Lord!

18. Christians do not need an organization, a religious hierarchy, a priest, the magisterium, or a higher authority to interpret Scripture for them. John 16:13-14 says, "However, when He, the Spirit of truth, has come, He will guide you into all truth; for He will not speak on His own authority, but whatever He hears He will speak; and He will tell you things to come. He will glorify Me, for He will take of what is Mine and declare it to you." If you are saved, as per Eph 1:13-14, you are sealed with the Holy Spirit (referred to as the Spirit of truth in John 16:13) and he will guide you toward truth in Scripture. Also see Deut 30:11-14; John 14:16-17; 15:26; 2 Cor 4:2; 1 John 2:19-21, 27.

19. For completeness of the five *solae*—five Latin phrases propagated during the Protestant Reformation (1517-1648) that emphasized the differences between the early Reformers and the Roman Catholic Church—also *sola scriptura* (by Scripture alone) and *soli Deo gloria* (glory to God alone). The doctrine of *Sola Scriptura*, affirms that Scripture is the only source of normative, apostolic, infallible revelation and that "all things necessary for salvation and about faith and life are taught in the Bible with sufficient clarity so that the ordinary believer can find it there and understand it" (*Reformed Dogmatics*, 2:209-10) *Soli Deo gloria* is the teaching that all glory is to be given to God alone, because salvation is accomplished solely through his will and action— not only the gift of Jesus' all-sufficient atonement on the cross, but also the gift of faith in that atonement, which the Holy Spirit creates in the heart of the believer.

20. Strong and Kohlenberger, *New Strong's Exhaustive Concordance*, 545.

closed in the person of his Son and in writing through the Bible. The recognition and acceptance of the Gospel is the first line of defense and conditions one against deceptive PSYOP. *The Wycliffe Bible Encyclopedia* encapsulates the Gospel quite simply as follows:

> The central truth of the gospel is that God has provided a way of salvation for men through the gift of His Son to the world. He suffered as a sacrifice for sin, overcame death, and now offers a share in His triumph to all who will accept it. The gospel is good news because it is a gift of God, not something that must be earned by penance or by self-improvement. (John 3:16; Rom 5:8–11; 2 Cor. 5:14–19; Titus 2:11–14)[21]

In its most real and most straightforward form, Paul summarizes the primary elements of the Gospel in 1 Cor 15:1–8, specifically the death, burial, and resurrection of Jesus Christ:

> Moreover, brethren, I declare to you the *gospel* which I preached to you, which also you received and in which you stand, by which also you are *saved*, if you hold fast that word which I preached to you—unless you believed in vain. For I delivered to you first of all that which I also received: *that Christ died for our sins according to the Scriptures, and that He was buried, and that He rose again the third day according to the Scriptures*, and that He was seen by Cephas, then by the twelve. After that He was seen by over five hundred brethren at once, of whom the greater part remain to the present, but some have fallen asleep. After that He was seen by James, then by all the apostles. Then last of all He was seen by me also, as by one born out of due time. (Emphases added)

These verses give us the kernel of the Gospel, which is a double acknowledgment: Christ died on the cross for our sins and he was resurrected from the dead on the third day. The scriptures can verify the reality of these two elements in several places, including Ps 16:10 and Isa 53:8–10, and by historical accounts and evidence such as the empty tomb and eyewitness accounts. Accordingly, the

---

21. Pfeiffer, *Wycliffe Bible Encyclopedia*.

other two elements mentioned in 1 Cor 15:1–8 confirm two other important facts concerning the Gospel: that he was buried confirms the fact that he died, and his post-resurrection appearances to eyewitnesses authenticate his resurrection.[22]

The Gospel is not only clearly and eloquently presented in the Bible, but, as we read in 1 Thess 1:5, it also comes "with power." It is not merely a message consisting of words in a book, but a message that is active, living, authoritative, and capable of bringing humanity into a saving union with the one and only living God. Paul adds "and in the Holy Spirit" because the Holy Spirit dwells within Christians when they accept the Gospel. The Holy Spirit, the third person of the Trinity, is called "the Spirit of Truth"[23] because of his charge to reveal the truth of the Bible to humanity.[24] According to Rom 3:11, due to the innate hardness of the human heart, we are incapable on our own of apprehension of the life-giving truth provided by the Gospel, but we can do so by the powerful service of the Spirit who, as per Acts 16:14, prepares hearts and convicts and attracts humankind to God.[25] (For more on the Gospel, see Appendix B.)

In addition to the power that comes with the Gospel, as expressed in Acts 20:24, one of the Gospel's most attractive aspects is the component of grace. Salvation is a free gift from God to be

---

22. In these passages, Paul reminds the believers in Corinth of three proofs to assure his readers that Jesus Christ had indeed been raised from the dead: (1) the reality of their salvation (vv. 1,2), (2) the testimony of the Old Testament (vv. 3,4), and (3) living witnesses to Christ's resurrection (vv. 5–11). On the cross, Jesus was exposed to the eyes of unbelievers; but after the resurrection, he was seen by believers who could be witnesses of his resurrection (Acts 1:22; 2:32; 3:15; 5:32). Peter saw him, and so did the disciples collectively. James was a half-brother of the Lord who became a believer after the Lord appeared to him (John 7:5; Acts 1:14). More than five hundred followers all saw him at the same time (1 Cor 14:6), so it could not have been a hallucination or a deception. This event may have occurred just before his ascension (Matt 28:16–20). (Wiersbe, *Wiersbe Bible Commentary*, 1693)

23. See John 16:13; 15:26; 1 John 5:6.

24. As expressed in John 14:17; 15:26; 16:8–13; 1 Cor 2:6–16; Acts 1:8; 1 John 4:6.

25. Also see Rom 2:4; John 12:32; 16:8.

accepted by faith[26] alone in Jesus Christ alone.[27] However, grace conflicts with the inclination of humans, who instinctively think in terms of merit, which is magnified by Satanic deceptive PSYOP. In society, throughout the ages, humans have had to work to achieve their goals. Therefore, the element of grace has always been problematic. From the inception of Christianity, some desired to add a form of works to grace, and this has been a systemic issue and a means of diluting the Gospel.

In Galatians, Paul faced a controversy regarding the precise content and nature of the Gospel. Concerning those who desired to deny grace, Paul writes in Gal 2:4–5, "And this [circumcision] occurred because of false brethren secretly brought in (who came in by stealth to spy out our liberty which we have in Christ Jesus, that they might bring us into bondage), to whom we did not yield submission even for an hour, that the truth of the Gospel might continue with you." Paul cautions about those who propose works for salvation rather than merely grace. Paul clarifies in Rom 4:3–4 and 11:6 that if salvation is by grace, it cannot be through works; if by works, it cannot be through grace.[28] Therefore, when the Gospel

---

26. Faith is the positive human response to what God has already provided by grace. In his letter to the Romans, Paul describes the kind of faith that can be counted as righteousness: "He did not waver at the promise of God through unbelief, but was strengthened in faith, giving glory to God, and being fully convinced that what He had promised He was also able to perform. And therefore 'it was accounted to him for righteousness.'" (Rom 4:20–22, citing Gen 15:6). Abraham believed in God (Rom 4:3,17), that is, he placed his trust in God and not in an impersonal force. His faith was in a Person, not a doctrine or a belief. Thus, Abraham was able to embrace and obey whatever the Lord commanded, even when it appeared impossible to believe that such promises could ever be fulfilled. Similarly, a contemporary Christian's trust and confidence in God's Word must be comparable to Abraham's. Abraham's faith that God could and would accomplish all that God had promised was credited as virtue. The law requires righteousness, which man cannot completely provide. But Jesus lived a righteous life on Earth and died for our lack of righteousness. Thus, the sinner is credited with Christ's righteousness (Rom 4:3, 5, 8; 3:25–26, 28).

27. See Rev 21:6; 22:17; Titus 3:4–5; Eph 2:8–9; Rom 4:4–5.

28. Rom 11:6 says, "And if by grace, then it is no longer of works; otherwise grace is no longer grace. But if it is of works, it is no longer grace; otherwise work is no longer work." Satan knows that adding works not only insults

is presented as being achieved by works, it is not the Gospel as rendered in the Bible.[29] It is artificial, deceptive, and, according to Gal 1:7, a different Gospel; in effect, it is no Gospel at all. Accepting the real Gospel based on grace inflicts a striking blow on deceptive PSYOP and conditions Christians against future PSYOP attacks because "these things I have written to you who believe in the name of the Son of God, *that you may know that you have eternal life*, and that you may continue to believe in the name of the Son of God" (1 John 5:13, emphasis added).[30]

Furthermore, Satan often deceives by encouraging Christians to dwell on their sins, thus provoking guilt and hindering the personal relationship God desires. However, in 1 John 2:2, the Bible states that Jesus is the atoning sacrifice for all sin. According to John 1:29, John the Baptist said, "Behold! The Lamb of God who takes away the sin of the world"; thus Jesus knew what sins you would commit and has atoned for them. Although Christians are free from the power of sin, as per Rom 6:14, and should work to abstain from sinning, sin is a manifestation of our fallen human

---

Christ and his completed work on the cross, but nullifies the only means by which Christ saves sinners.

29. Faith, not works, is necessary for salvation (Rom 1:17; 3:28). This gift is available to us regardless of who we are or what we have done (Rom 3:22).

30. According to 1 John 5:13, you can have assurance that you have eternal life. God desires for us to be certain of our salvation. We should not live our lives wondering and worrying about our salvation. This is why the Bible makes the salvation plan so crystal clear. Assurance is the absence of doubt. By internalizing God's Word, you can be confident in the actuality of your eternal salvation. Jesus himself gives assurance to those who believe in him: "I give them eternal life, and they will never perish, and no one will snatch them out of my hand. My Father, who has given them to me, is greater than all, and no one is able to snatch them out of the Father's hand" (John 10:28–29). Simply put, eternal life is eternal. No one, not even you, can take away Christ's gift of salvation from you. (MacArthur, *1–3 John*, 199–204)

CONDITIONING, INDIRECT, AND DIRECT REFUTATION

condition.[31] Through sanctification,[32] sin becomes easier to overcome; however, it is inevitable, but it has been paid for. Conditioning to this reality disarms this deceptive PSYOP.

Lastly, given the beauty of the Gospel and God's grace, why does God love us? This simple question ranks among the most profound ever posed, and no human would ever be able to respond sufficiently. However, one thing is certain: God does not love us because we are lovable or deserving of his affection. In fact, the opposite is the case. Since the fall, humanity has been characterized by rebellion and disobedience. Jer 17:9 describes the condition of the human heart: "The heart is deceitful above all things, and desperately wicked; Who can know it?" Sin has so profoundly tainted our innermost being that we are unaware of the extent of its corruption.[33] In our natural state, we do not pursue or love or desire God. Rom 3:10–12 presents plainly the condition

---

31. In Matt 12:31–32, the unpardonable sin is presented: "Therefore I say to you, every sin and blasphemy will be forgiven men, but the blasphemy *against* the Spirit will not be forgiven men. Anyone who speaks a word against the Son of Man, it will be forgiven him; but whoever speaks against the Holy Spirit, it will not be forgiven him, either in this age or in the *age* to come." The only sin that cannot be forgiven today is persistent unbelief. There is no pardon for a person who dies in rejection to Christ. John 16:8 states that the Holy Spirit is at work in the world, convicting the unsaved of sin, righteousness, and judgment. If a person resists this conviction and does not repent, he chooses hell over paradise. "Without faith it is impossible to please Him [God]" (Heb 11:6), and Jesus is the focus of faith (Acts 16:31). Without faith in Christ, there is no forgiveness. Through his Son, God has provided for our salvation (John 3:16). Jesus is the only source of forgiveness (John 14:6). Rejecting the only Redeemer leaves one without any means of salvation; rejecting the only atonement is, of course, unpardonable.

32. As per 1 Thess 4:3, sanctification is God's will for humanity. To "sanctify" something is to set it apart for special use; to "sanctify" a person is to make them holy. This is a process that begins at the moment of salvation (justification) and continues through one's life (until glorification).

33. Jer 17:9, in addition to Prov 3:5 and 28:26, informs us that our feelings (or hearts, more precisely) cannot be trusted. Why are our emotions considered so unreliable? Because of two factors: They are constantly changing and are influenced by sin. God and his Word should ultimately shape our emotions, not the other way around. The Christian's source and foundation should be the Word of God, not emotions, feelings, or instincts.

of the natural, unregenerate person: "There is none righteous, no, not one; There is none who understands; There is none who seeks after God. They have all turned aside; They have together become unprofitable; There is none who does good, no, not one." How then can a holy, just, and perfect God love such creatures? To apprehend this, we must apprehend the essence and character of God.

According to 1 John 4:8 and v. 16, "God is love." There has never been a more significant declaration than this: God is love. This is a profound statement. God does not merely love: he is love. His essence and nature are love. Love permeates every aspect of his being, including his wrath and rage. God must demonstrate love, as well as all of his other attributes, because doing so glorifies him. God's glorification is the highest, most excellent, and most noble of all actions; therefore, God must glorify himself because he is the highest and the best and deserves all glory.

Since love is God's fundamental essence, he demonstrates his love by showering it on rebellious people who do not deserve it. God's love is not sentimental or romantic. Instead, it is *agape* or self-sacrificing love.[34] Through the divine act of sending his Son to the cross to pay the penalty for our sin (1 John 4:10), by graciously drawing us to himself (John 6:44), by forgiving our rebellion against him, and by sending his Holy Spirit to indwell us (Rom 8:9–11), he enables us to love in the same manner as he does. Despite the fact that we did not deserve it, he did this for us.

---

34. Goodwill, compassion, and deliberate delight in the object of love are the essence of *agape* love. Agape love entails commitment, faithfulness, and an act of the will. It stands out from other forms of love (e.g., *eros*, *storge*, and *philia*) due to its high moral nature and steadfast character. We are not born with the capacity for agape love. We are unable to create such a love because of our fallen nature. In order for us to love as God loves, agape must originate from its Source. This is the love that, when we became God's children, "has been poured out in our hearts by the Holy Spirit who was given to us" (Rom 5:5; see also Gal 5:22). Jesus Christ gave his life in order for us to have the ability to understand what love is. According to 1 John 3:16, "because He laid down His life for us. And we also ought to lay down our lives for the brethren." We are able to love one another because of God's love for us. (Liddell and Scott, *Greek-English Lexicon*)

CONDITIONING, INDIRECT, AND DIRECT REFUTATION

"But God demonstrates His own love toward us, in that while we were still sinners, Christ died for us" (Rom 5:8).

The love of God is personal. He is intimately acquainted with each of us and loves us individually. His love is mighty and without beginning or end. This experience of God's compassion is what sets Christianity apart from all other religions. How can God love us? Because of his nature, "God is love."[35] The love of God is the catalyst to his free gift of salvation by his grace, thus providing the framework to condition Christians against Satan's deceptive PSYOP.

On the other hand, God's perfect love would not be possible without his perfect holiness. The holiness of God refers to the incomparable magnificence of his incomparable being as well as his sinless, faultless, unblemished moral purity.[36]

God is preeminent, eternal, omniscient, omnipotent, and omnipresent—unlike his created beings. He was, is, and always will be prior to everything. He is faultless, ageless, and tireless. He defies all human comprehension. Indeed, our language lacks the requisite superlatives to adequately describe him. As a result of his incomparable goodness and majesty, the psalmist wrote in Ps 42:1, "As the deer pants for the water brooks, So pants my soul for You, O God." God is the only one who truly satisfies, as he is utterly lovely to behold. Josh 13:33 says that the Lord is our great reward and inheritance, whereas earthly treasures will perish.

---

35. According to 2 Pet 3:9, God's longing is that humankind repents and is saved. God does not desire that anyone perish or die. The central message of the Bible is that God does not desire the damnation of anyone. That is, he prefers that everyone be saved. However, in his sovereignty, omnipotence, and love, God chose not to demand or compel everyone to be saved. If God is truly sovereign, he can sovereignly allow us to choose things he does not prefer, for his own reasons. Here, Peter reveals God's heart for the people he created: he desires for all of them to be saved, but he will not force them to be so. (Wiersbe, *Wiersbe Bible Commentary*, 1833)

36. See Isa 6:1–5 and Rev 4:1–8. In Christian theology, "holy" has two distinct meanings. The meaning that is described in this paragraph and Holy also refers to something or someone that has been set apart for God's use or separated from the common.

However, the holiness of God presents mortals with a dilemma in their hearts and minds. We are drawn to him because he created us,[37] but as inherently flawed beings, we tremble in the presence of his majestic glory. As the Israelites trembled in dread when God appeared to Moses on Mount Sinai, so do we prefer to keep God at a safe distance.[38]

God's holiness should inspire us to continually offer praise and devotion. We take pleasure in him because he is our ultimate purpose and raison d'être.[39] Nobody who lives apart from God is genuinely complete. To those who have faith, he offers himself. God is more than a means of achieving a transitory desire or worldly objective, for he is our greatest good. God is sufficient unto himself.

Although God is deserving of our utmost awe and reverent fear, he is neither distant nor unapproachable.[40] He desires closeness with us. God welcomes us with open arms through the atoning work of his Son, Jesus,[41] despite the sins we have committed, the frequent foolishness of our thinking, the bouts of pride that stain our character, and the shameful lapses in our faith. It is remarkable that we are permitted to approach God as a friend, but never as an equal.

God's desire for intimacy with us should not be disregarded. Those who have placed their trust in Jesus Christ as Savior (as per Eph 1:5) he adopts as sons and daughters and (as per Rom 8:15 and Gal 4:6) encourages them to call him "Father." It is almost incomprehensible that a holy and blameless God could love such filthy orphans, "children of wrath" (Eph 2:3), but through the cleansing blood of Jesus Christ, the vile and profane are

---

37. See Gen 1:27; Ps 100:3.

38. See Exod 20:18–21. Also see Exod 20:7; 1 Sam 2:2–3; Ps 71:22–23; Isa 6:1–5, 57:15; Dan 8:17; Matt 6:7–9; 1 Pet 1:13–16; Rev 1:17, 15:2–4.

39. See Jer 29:11.

40. See Jas 2:23.

41. See 2 Cor 5:21; Eph 2:8–9.

CONDITIONING, INDIRECT, AND DIRECT REFUTATION

transformed into his beloved children and the objects of his most tender affections.[42]

On this side of eternity, we will not attain sanctity or sinless perfection, but our lives should reflect God's immaculate purity. Jesus instructed us to be "the salt of the earth" (Matt 5:13). Salt is a preservative, and in these times of moral decline, may we not be conformed to the behavior and thinking of this deteriorating planet, but rather may we be Christ's ambassadors and agents of transformation and renewal.[43] By imitating God's holiness, we honor him and bring solace to others.

Holy is God. In him, not even the slightest trace of evil exists. He is flawlessly pure, completely faultless, and uncompromisingly just. God is incapable of lying. He cannot make poor choices. He is without fault, timeless, and immaculate. In contrast, we are imperfect, sinful creatures.[44] By right, a holy and righteous God must judge sinners, and (as per Rom 6:23) the wages of sin is death; mercifully, Heb 2:3 says we can escape God's wrath by trusting in Jesus Christ as our Savior. If not for the Gospel of Jesus Christ, mankind's greatest dread would be God's holiness, for no sinner can stand in the presence of his blinding glory. Those who believe in Jesus as Savior have been forgiven, however, through a simple act of faith.[45] To the lost, God's holiness is a terrible thing, but to the redeemed, God's holiness is our greatest benefit.[46]

The Simplicity of the Gospel

One may come to believe that life and creation are complicated, and perhaps from a human perspective, this may be true. However, there is simplicity and elegance in God's creation. God intended for all of his creation, including life, to be perfect. Perfection

---

42. See 1 John 1:7.
43. See 2 Cor 5:20; Rom 12:2.
44. See Isa 53:6; 1 John 1:8.
45. See Matt 9:6.
46. Got Questions Ministries, "What Does it Mean that God is a Holy God? What is the Holiness of God?"

assumes that there are no issues or problems to solve. However, sin is a complicated subject. It inflicts devastation in both minor and major, subtle and obvious, and visible and invisible ways. Sin cloaks itself in deception and leads to the destruction of relationships, suffering, and a litany of other ailments. Sin is so complex that only God can apprehend it and provide a solution. The Bible may appear to be a complicated book because it indeed deals with a complicated subject. One of its central teachings demonstrates the complexity of sin, describing what it is and how to mitigate its effects on life. It explores existence in a fallen world in need of redemption. John reported that when Jesus Christ entered the universe, "The Light shines in the darkness, and the darkness did not comprehend [overcome] it" (John 1:5). The Light was alien to the world. The world was unable to withstand or incorporate it into its corruption, despite its efforts, which continue to the present day.

The Gospel message of faith in Jesus Christ is not complicated. Matt 11:29 says that Jesus does not present himself as a complicated Savior. If we are to understand the Gospel message, God must give us the opportunity. This is not an indication that the Gospel is difficult and requires a high level of intelligence to apprehend; rather, it is a testament to the darkness of the world. As recent and past history teaches us, the temptation to complicate the Gospel message is no exception to our propensity to complicate things. Unfortunately, the efficacy of the Gospel has been diminished, and its recognition potentially compromised, due to the influence of individuals who have succumbed to the complexities associated with its dissemination and reception. Institutionalized presentations of God's will, which the Pharisees cultivated during the time of Christ, and their modern-day counterparts, pervert the Gospel to the point where it is rendered ineffective (Mark 7:13), whereas the simplicity is repeatedly emphasized in the Gospel message as it was delivered by Christ and the apostles, and this is in line with God's will for creation.

INDIRECT REFUTATION

The counter-PSYOP defense strategy called indirect refutation aims to "question the validity of some aspect of the opponent's allegations or the source of the propaganda, thus challenging its credibility."[47] As an example, in the early 2000s, the then-chairman of Microsoft Corporation, Bill Gates, used this technique in a subtle fashion by appearing in a series of television commercials following the negative outcome of the antitrust trial against his company. He appeared in a relaxed setting, seated in an armchair, and spoke of the positive impact that Microsoft had on the lives of most Americans. He spoke at length of the commitment of Microsoft to the youth of America and to American families in general. At no time did he speak of the trial itself or the court's final ruling. He did, however, attempt to damage the credibility of that ruling by highlighting the positive impact of Microsoft on Americans, and insinuating the question, "How could a company which is so dedicated to Americans be treated so badly by the courts?" While not overtly stated, this notion appeared to be the desired reaction of his indirect refutation.[48] In essence, this technique can be thought of as a courtroom trial where one side seeks to lower the credibility of "expert" witnesses. One advantage of using this technique is that indirect refutation does not bring added publicity or credibility to the deceptive PSYOP by repeating certain aspects. When using this technique, one should ensure that the facts used to damage the credibility of the deceptive PSYOP are accurate and have some importance in the minds of the target audience.

With respect to the Christian and countering Satan's PSYOP, the facts in this case are the contents of the Bible. (For information on why the Bible is true, see Appendix C.) In order to effectively utilize this counter-PSYOP technique and ensure that the facts are accurate, the Bible must be understood as being, and considered to be, absolute, infallible, and inerrant. Indirect refutation, like conditioning, can be used against *all* of Satan's deceptive PSYOP.

---

47. Department of the Army, *Psychological Operations Tactics*, 11–23.
48. Department of the Army, *Psychological Operations Tactics*, 11–23.

The word infallible means "incapable of error."[49] If something is infallible, it is never wrong and is thus absolutely trustworthy. Likewise, the word "inerrant," also applied to Scripture, means "free from error."[50] Simply stated, the Bible is perfect, absolute truth.[51]

The Bible asserts its infallibility in 2 Pet 1:19: "And so we have the prophetic word confirmed." Peter continues in 2 Pet 1:20–21 with a discussion of the origin of Scripture: "no prophecy of Scripture is of any private interpretation, for prophecy never came by the will of man, but holy men of God spoke as they were moved by the Holy Spirit."

Similarly, the infallibility of Scripture is implied in 2 Tim 3:16–17 (NIV): "All Scripture is God-breathed and is useful for teaching, rebuking, correcting and training in righteousness, so that the servant of God may be thoroughly equipped for every good work." The very fact that God "breathed" Scripture guarantees that the Bible is infallible, for God cannot do anything in error.[52] The reality that the Bible equips Christians "thoroughly" for his service confirms that it guides humanity into truth, not error.

---

49. *Merriam-Webster's Collegiate Dictionary.*

50. *Merriam-Webster's Collegiate Dictionary.*

51. As a technicality, infallibility and inerrancy are qualities that *may* be applied to other things, but that does not necessarily make those things absolute truth. The Bible is indeed absolute truth, infallible, and inerrant, but the Bible is perfect, absolute truth, not solely because it is infallible and inerrant, but because of the authority it has in being the Word of God. God, being incapable of error, is the one who gives authority to the scriptures. The scriptures are absolute truth not solely because of their qualities of infallibility and inerrancy, but because of the authority of God.

52. The Old and New Testaments are both equally authoritative. The Old Testament prepares the way for the advent of the Messiah, Jesus Christ, who would offer himself as a sacrifice for the sins of the world (1 John 2:2). The New Testament describes the ministry of Jesus Christ, then reflects on what he did and how we should respond. Both testaments depict the same holy, merciful, and righteous God who condemns sin but seeks the salvation of sinners through an atoning sacrifice. God reveals himself to us in both testaments and demonstrates to us how we are to come to him through faith (Gen 15:6; Eph 2:8). (White, *Scripture Alone*, 95–119)

CONDITIONING, INDIRECT, AND DIRECT REFUTATION

Logically, if God is infallible, then so will his Word. Scriptural infallibility is based on an understanding of God's perfection.[53] We read in Ps 19:7 that God's Word is "perfect, converting the soul," since God himself is perfect. In addition, theologically speaking, God is strongly connected with his Word. In fact, Jesus is called "the Word" in John 1:14. (For more on why the Bible is the sole authority for faith and practice, see Appendix D.)

The Bible asserts that it is complete (as opposed to partial) perfection in Ps 12:6, Ps 19:7, Prov 30:5, and numerous other places. It is true throughout and, moreover, judges us (rather than the contrary). Heb 4:12 contends that "the word of God is living and powerful, and sharper than any two-edged sword, piercing even to the division of soul and spirit, and of joints and marrow, and is a discerner of the thoughts and intents of the heart."

The Bible is the fully sufficient source of all God has revealed to us about himself and his plan for humanity.[54] We cannot pick and choose what we want and do not want to believe in the Bible. As Augustine wrote, "If you believe what you like in the gospels, and reject what you don't like, it is not the gospel you believe, but yourself." It is up to every Christian to make sure they are walking and professing according to all of Scripture and not merely following what is convenient or making excuses for the difficult

---

53. Of note, the doctrine of infallibility involves only the original documents. Printing errors, mistranslations, and typographical errors are clear human mistakes and, in most cases, are easily spotted. (Regardless of these minor errors, no theological teaching or mandate is compromised by the text in question.) However, the biblical authors' original writings were completely free from error or omission, as the Holy Spirit oversaw the penning of the scriptures. God is truthful and perfectly reliable (John 14:6; 17:3), and so is his Word (John 17:17). (White, *Scripture Alone*, 65–94)

54. As opposed to the capriciousness of Allah of the Qur'an (the central religious text of Islam, believed by Muslims to be a revelation from God), the Bible presents God as a steadfast keeper of his promises. Salvation in the Qur'an comes through an unknowable mixture of predestination, good works, and the capricious will of Allah. "In Islam, forgiveness is an impersonal act of arbitrary divine power. In Christianity, forgiveness is a personal act of purposeful and powerful yet completely just divine grace." (White, *What Every Christian Needs to Know About the Qur'an*, 158)

commands they don't want to follow.⁵⁵ Either Christians accept the entire Bible, or they accept none of it. As God's infallible Word, the Bible is complete, inerrant, authoritative, reliable, and absolutely sufficient to meet our needs. Thus, the counter-PSYOP method of indirect refutation via using the Bible further bolsters and equips Christians to thwart deception by having absolute truth to lean on in order to question the validity of Satan's PSYOP with the purpose of defying their credibility.

DIRECT REFUTATION

The counter-PSYOP defense strategy called direct refutation is a "point-for-point rebuttal of opponent propaganda allegations or themes"⁵⁶ and "is best used in a very timely manner when PSYOP personnel have complete access to factual information regarding the allegation."⁵⁷ As an example of the effectiveness of direct refutation, in 1994, the United States Information Agency submitted a report to the United Nations entitled, "The Child Organ Trafficking Rumor: A Modern Urban Legend." This report sought to counter rumors that had been circulating worldwide since 1987 that children were being kidnapped so that they could be used as unwilling donors in organ transplants. Although the report was over forty pages in length and was not published for several years after the rumor first appeared, it serves as an example of detailed direct refutation. Each version of the rumor is laboriously examined and refuted through the use of factual information.⁵⁸ In its concluding paragraph, the report stated that "this myth derives its credibility from the fact that it speaks to widespread, largely unconscious anxieties about mutilation and death that have been

---

55. See 2 Cor 13:5; Phil 2:12.
56. Department of the Army, *Psychological Operations Tactics*, 11–22.
57. Department of the Army, *Psychological Operations Tactics*, 11–22.
58. Department of the Army, *Psychological Operations Tactics*, 11–22.

CONDITIONING, INDIRECT, AND DIRECT REFUTATION

stimulated by the dramatic advances made in the field of organ transplantation in recent years."[59]

To have complete, factual information to correctly employ the counter-PSYOP defense strategy of direct refutation, one must have information that is correctly interpreted, and in a biblical sense, this requires precise hermeneutics (the branch of knowledge that deals with interpretation).[60] This counter-PSYOP practice can be used against Satan's *lies*.

Second Pet 1:19–20 says, "And so we have the prophetic word confirmed, which you do well to heed as a light that shines in a dark place, until the day dawns and the morning star rises in your hearts; knowing this first, that no prophecy of Scripture is of any private interpretation." We cannot have a "confirmed" word about the meaning of Scripture, or anything else for that matter, unless we have a sure technique to interpret the words. Hermeneutics assists Christians to learn how to understand the Bible correctly, so that misusing its truths can be prevented and direct refutation can be employed to successfully rebut deceptive PSYOP.

Hermeneutics can help Christians to approach any text of the Bible by pursuing God's purposed meaning. Hermeneutics seeks to allow the Bible to speak for itself within its original setting before interpreters draw conclusions about how it applies to their own settings and use it for direct refutation.[61] Learning and abiding by sound hermeneutics will assist Christians in the employment of direct refutation against deceptive PSYOP. These tenets, in tandem with the aid of the Holy Spirit—which, as per John 14:26, will guide Christians toward truth and sound biblical

---

59. Levanthal, "The Child Organ Trafficking Rumor: A Modern Urban Legend," 32.

60. *Hermeneutics* most often refers to how to interpret the Bible or other sacred texts from other religions. This is not to be confused with *exegesis*. Where exegesis refers to the interpretation of a specific biblical text, hermeneutics is deciding which principles one will use in order to interpret the text. (Grudem, *Systematic Theology*, 108–09)

61. Virkler and Ayayo, *Hermeneutics*, 17.

interpretation—will point Christians toward truth and dissuade them from deceit.[62]

In addition to hermeneutics, the relationship among biblical exegesis, translation, and application[63] must be understood in its proper sequence so that each of these tasks can be successfully executed. Exegesis is the assessment of Scripture from the perspective of the author of that passage.[64] It is a way of deriving meaning from the text based on the context within which it was written.[65]

---

62. Zuck, "The Role of the Holy Spirit in Hermeneutics," 120–30. Note that there is currently some debate among evangelical theologians on the Doctrine of the Illumination of the Holy Spirit as to the specific role of the Holy Spirit in biblical understanding.

63. Translation and exegetical interpretation are the foundations of theological application. It is crucial that the biblical scholar (or author of books, commentaries, etc. that one reads and uses in Bible study and/or devotion) develop a method of scriptural interpretation and a systematic theology that is consistent with biblical revelation. Theological statements can and should be derived from Scripture, but only by using a correct exegetical methodology. The relationship between biblical interpretation and context is a critical aspect of the exegetical approach. Many theological errors are also rooted in the failure of either scholars or lay readers of the Bible to place a scripturally derived theological idea in its appropriate context, which requires knowledge of systematic theology. Consequently, translation, exegesis, and application form a triangle, because each has a dependent relationship with the others. Effective biblical scholarship depends on accurate translation, competent exegesis, and the incorporation of both into a systematized theological paradigm.

64. *Eisegesis*, the opposite approach to the interpretation of Scripture from *exegesis*, is the interpretation of a text based on a subjective, non-analytical reading. The interpreter in this approach injects his or her own ideas into the text, making it mean whatever he or she wishes. Evidently, only exegesis treats the text fairly, while eisegesis is a mistreatment of the text that often results in a misinterpretation. Exegesis is concerned with determining the true meaning of a text while taking its grammar, syntax, and setting into consideration. Eisegesis is solely focused on making a point, oftentimes contrived, even at the expense of word meaning. (Grudem, *Systematic Theology*, 108–09 and *Merriam-Webster's Collegiate Dictionary*)

65. Second Tim 2:15 commands us to use exegetical methods: "Be diligent to present yourself approved to God, a worker who does not need to be ashamed, rightly dividing the word of truth." Exegesis entails (1) observation: what is the passage saying? (2) interpretation: What is the meaning of the passage? (3) correlation: how does this passage correlate to the rest of the Bible? and (4) application: what impact should this passage have on my life?

A translation that is defective will lead to incorrect exegetical conclusions. The translation should reflect the original meaning of the text in the original biblical languages to the greatest degree possible within the context of linguistic differences. When it comes to thorough biblical understanding, one must do more than simply read. An in-depth understanding of context, original language, and book type are among the many facets to consider. Arming oneself with these skills or wisely selecting Bible commentators and authors that correctly utilize these skills will aid in thwarting deception. An important caution here is to not allow one's education to become that which is trusted. Use these tools to build trust in God and "lean not on your own understanding" (Prov 3:5).[66]

(Grudem, *Systematic Theology*, 108–09)

66. In the process of translation, it is important to acknowledge that complete equivalence between the source language and the target language is not always attainable, resulting in the loss or alteration of certain aspects of the original message. Certain subtleties may not effectively be conveyed from one language to another. Consequently, it is uncommon for a translation to achieve a flawless representation of the source material. One illustration of this phenomenon can be observed in the "aspect" category of Greek verbs. English verbs have various tenses, namely past, present, and future. Greek verbs possess identical tenses, albeit encompassing a linguistic feature referred to as "aspect." Present-tense Greek verbs encompass a broader temporal scope than the mere indication of current action. In the Greek language, a verb has the capacity to convey the notion of ongoing or repetitive action. The translation in English lacks clarity until the aspect words "continually" or "repeatedly" are incorporated alongside the verb. An illustrative instance of this concept can be found in Eph 5:18, which states, ". . . be filled with the Spirit." The verse in its original Greek language instructs individuals to maintain a perpetual state of being filled with the Spirit. The process in question is not a singular occurrence, but rather a continuous and enduring journey that spans an individual's entire lifetime. The aforementioned "aspect" is not well conveyed in the English translation. Nevertheless, the Bible explicitly states that the Holy Spirit is the author of its contents and that he will provide assistance in apprehending its message (see 2 Tim 3:16–17; John 14:26).

It is important to note that a comprehensive understanding of the Bible does not require proficiency in Hebrew and Greek languages. The intended message of God is effectively conveyed in the English language. One can possess an assurance in the ability of God to impart the interpretation of his Word, even in the absence of a knowledge of Greek and Hebrew. (Got Questions Ministries, "Is it Important to Know Greek and Hebrew when Studying the

With respect to the importance of context in sound biblical interpretation, a fighter aircraft analogy drives this point home. During World War II, fighter planes often returned from battle riddled with bullet holes. The Allies analyzed the litany of data and mapped the areas that were most commonly struck by enemy fire. In an effort to bolster resiliency for flying combat missions, engineers sought to reinforce the most commonly damaged areas of the planes to reduce the number being shot down. Dr. Abraham Wald (1902–1950)—a mathematician whose work contributed to the disciplines of decision theory, geometry, and econometrics, as well as to the foundation of the field of statistical sequential analysis[67]—noted that an alternate perspective could perhaps make more sense of the data. Contrary to prior opinion, he recognized that the reason certain areas of the planes weren't damaged was that the planes that were damaged in those areas didn't return. This insight led to the armor being reinforced on the areas of the plane with no bullet holes.[68] In this example, the context surrounding the data was highly important for its interpretation. It was necessary to consider that context in order to find and apply the proper solution to the problem of fighter aircraft survivability. Likewise, to interpret the Bible, the context surrounding biblical data is of vital importance to ascertain the intended meaning.

Unfortunately, in modern times, whether intentionally or inadvertently, it has become increasingly common for biblical data to become skewed, with the result that the associated meaning doesn't match what God intended. God emphasizes the proper interpretation of his Word, and this includes placing every word in its correct context. Accordingly, several Bible passages warn against distorting the Gospel (Gal 1:8–9); going beyond what is written (2 John 1:9); twisting the scriptures (2 Pet 3:16); and adding or subtracting from the Word of God (Rev 22:18–19).

Bible?" and Gignac, *An Introductory New Testament Greek Course*, 48–49)

67. Morgenstern, "Abraham Wald, 1902–1950," 361–67.

68. Mangel and Samaniego, "Abraham Wald's Work on Aircraft Survivability," 259–67.

CONDITIONING, INDIRECT, AND DIRECT REFUTATION

Despite these warnings, some derive meaning based on context that is misrepresented or not even present, thus preventing proper application. The dangers of taking the Bible's statements out of context are (1) that, most obviously, we end up with the wrong message, (2) that we often remove "we" and insert "me," making verses about ourselves, when the Bible was written for us but not to us, and (3) that we miss the original meaning, thus reading the Bible for what we can get out of it and not what God wants for us.[69] Proper contextualized interpretation of the Bible is

---

69. Christians should take the Bible literally. The literal, or normal, sense is the grammatical-historical sense, that is, the meaning which the writer expressed (as conveyed in Article XV of the *Chicago Statement on Biblical Hermeneutics*). This is the only method to discern what God is actually striving to convey to us. When reading any work of literature, but particularly the Bible, we must determine the author's message. Many today read a Bible verse or passage and then give their own interpretations of the words, phrases, or paragraphs, disregarding the context and the author's intent. However, this is not what God intended, which is why he instructs us to handle the Word of truth correctly (2 Tim 2:15). When the Lord Jesus quoted the Old Testament, it was always clear that he held to a literal interpretation. In Luke 4, when Jesus was tempted by Satan, he responded by quoting from the Old Testament. If God's commands in Deut 8:3, 6:13, and 6:16 had not been literal, Jesus would not have used them, and they would not have had the power to stop Satan's mouth, which they did. Additionally, the disciples took Christ's (Bible-based) directives literally. In Matt 28:19–20, Jesus commanded his disciples to go and make more disciples. In Acts 2 and subsequent chapters, we find that the disciples took Jesus' command literally and preached the gospel of Christ throughout the then-known world, telling people to "believe on the Lord Jesus Christ, and you will be saved" (Acts 16:31). We must interpret Jesus' words literally, just as the disciples did. How else can we be certain of our salvation if we do not believe Jesus when he says he came to pursue and save the lost (Luke 19:10), pay the price for our sin (Matt 26:28), and provide eternal life (John 17:3)? Although we interpret the Bible literally, there are figures of speech that are not to be taken literally, but these are readily apparent (e.g., see Ps 17:8). In fact, according to E.W. Bullinger (1837–1913) in his book *Figures of Speech in the Bible*, 217 different figures of speech are used in the scriptures. For example, in John 10:9, Jesus says, "I am the door." Does Jesus have hinges and a knob? Of course not. Jesus is using a metaphor to convey his message.

When we make ourselves the final arbiters of which portions of the Bible are to be taken literally, we exalt ourselves above God. Who, then, can claim that one person's interpretation of a biblical event or truth is more or less valid than that of another? Due to the inevitable confusion and distortions that

therefore of the utmost importance in preventing the misuse and misapplication of its truths.[70]

Interpretation in context seeks to allow the Bible to speak for itself within its original setting before drawing conclusions about how it applies to our modern setting.[71] In tandem with the aid of the Holy Spirit—who will guide Christians toward a thorough biblical interpretation (John 14:26)—these tenets point Christians toward the truth of Scripture and dissuade them from misunderstanding and misapplication.[72]

Moreover, the Lord Jesus did not say, "The *truths* shall make you free," but rather "The *truth* shall make you free" (John 8:32). Like Dr. Wald's contextual analysis of fighter aircraft damage data and its proper application to aircraft survivability, an accurate, contextual biblical interpretation ensures that truth is conveyed correctly and, therefore, that proper application can be made. When this occurs, concepts such as *ex nihilo* creation make sense and can be applied to the larger context of the Bible's message.[73]

---

would result from such a system, the scriptures would be rendered essentially invalid. The Bible is God's Word to us, and he intended for it to be taken literally and completely. (White, *Scripture Alone*, 200–13)

70. As an aside, when the books of the Bible were originally written, they did not contain chapter or verse references. The chapter divisions commonly used today were developed by Stephen Langton, an Archbishop of Canterbury, around AD 1227. The Hebrew Old Testament was divided into verses by a Jewish rabbi by the name of Nathan in AD 1448. Robert Estienne was the first to divide the New Testament into standard numbered verses, in AD 1555. The Bible was divided into chapters and verses to help us find scriptures more quickly and easily. In a few places, however, chapter breaks are poorly placed and, as a result, divide content that should flow together. The lesson is, do not let chapter divisions be a stumbling block when developing context. (Metzger, *The Early Versions of the New Testament*, 347)

71. Virkler and Ayayo, *Hermeneutics: Principles and Processes of Biblical Interpretation*, 17.

72. Zuck, "The Role of the Holy Spirit in Hermeneutics," 120–29.

73. The Latin phrase *ex nihilo* means "from nothing." God creating everything from nothing is referred to as *creation ex nihilo*. "In the beginning God created the heavens and the earth" (Gen 1:1). Prior to that moment, there was nothing. God did not construct the universe out of pre-existing building blocks. He began from nothing.

CONDITIONING, INDIRECT, AND DIRECT REFUTATION

This larger context is conveyed in 2 Cor 4:6: "For it is the God who commanded light to shine out of darkness, who has shone in our hearts to give the light of the knowledge of the glory of God in the face of Jesus Christ." Thus, God's creative power and his redemptive power are inseparable. The God who creates is also the God who redeems, and he does both with the same power.

Given this larger context, interpreted correctly, the singular most important truth of the Bible is derived: our Creator is our Savior, and if he has the power to create the universe, he has the power to save us.[74] Thus, the counter-PSYOP method of direct refutation via sound biblical hermeneutics utilized to ensure correctly understood biblical information in order to have complete, factual information to directly refute Satan's PSYOP further bolsters and equips Christians to thwart deception.

---

74. Corrado, "The Importance of Context in Sound Biblical Interpretation."

6

Counter-PSYOP Methods to Guard against Deception

Forestalling and Restrictive Measures

US Army loudspeaker team in action in Korea, 1953.[1]

The real target in war is the mind of the enemy commander, not the bodies of his troops.

—Captain Sir Basil Liddell Hart, *Thoughts on War*, 1944

---

1. *U.S. Army Loudspeaker Team in Action in Korea*, Public Domain.

FORESTALLING AND RESTRICTIVE MEASURES

ALTHOUGH PROPAGANDA MESSAGES MAY occasionally lack truth, counterpropaganda that is generally effective exclusively disseminates the truth. In fact, counterpropaganda is frequently defined as the "honest, truthful opposition" to the propaganda of an adversary. Counterpropaganda conveys veracious messages for practical and ethical purposes. During the Cold War, the United States earned the distinction of "truth teller" due to its propensity for disseminating accurate information to counter Soviet propaganda; in contrast, the Soviet Union was regarded as a "lie teller." According to Herbert Romerstein, the United States was perceived as honest as a result of its use of truth-based counterpropaganda, whereas the Soviet Union's use of deceptive statements discredited its messages. This Cold War instance illustrates how the exposure of the truth discredits a fraudulent message. In practice, an intentionally or unintentionally false counterpropaganda message may be exposed as biased as the propaganda it intended to refute. Therefore, the dissemination of accurate information enhances the efficacy of counterpropaganda while undermining the credibility of those whose deceit is exposed.[2]

As expressed, truth prevails, and deception ultimately fails. Fundamentally, successful counter-deception relies on a foundation of truth and the reinforcement of this truth as will be discussed in the following counter-PSYOP methods.

From the foundational methods discussed in the previous chapter, we now turn to the more subtle, but equally as important, methods to further bolster the Christian's defenses against Satan's deceptive PSYOP, noting the type of deception against which each is best used. As advised in the previous chapter, despite the wide variety of practices to counter PSYOP, there is no "best fit" method. The practices must be employed based on the situation and type of deception Satan is employing, and one or more practices discussed in both chapters may be used in counter-PSYOP defense.[3] The following methods can further assist in identifying, amplifying, and reinforcing truth so that deceptive PSYOP can be detected

2. Romerstein, "Counterpropaganda: We Can't Win Without It," 137–80.
3. Department of the Army, *Psychological Operations Tactics*, 11–22.

and defeated. Additionally, as previously stated, employing these defenses takes time and discipline, and so solving immediate problems may be a lifelong armament process.

FORESTALLING

The counter-PSYOP defense strategy called forestalling is a "preemptive technique [that] anticipates the specific themes the opponent may use in their PSYOP and counters them before they reach the target audience."[4] To employ this practice correctly, Christians "must know the opponent and be able to anticipate their reactions to an event or operation."[5] Christians must have "accurate information concerning the [enemy] . . . to effectively counter hostile propaganda. A detailed knowledge of opponent propaganda techniques and themes assists greatly when using this technique. This technique differs from conditioning in that PSYOP personnel preemptively address specific themes that the opponent may use."[6] As an example of the effectiveness of forestalling, in 1997, PSYOP personnel were brought in to assist in planning an operation to detain several Bosnian-Croat indicted war criminals. The PSYOP personnel developed, pre-positioned, and disseminated large numbers of counterpropaganda products as the operation unfolded. Opponent propaganda and hostile reaction was minimal; PSYOP personnel ceased this preemptive counterpropaganda campaign ten days after it began due to lack of response, thus demonstrating the powerfulness of forestalling. Conversely, earlier that year, friendly forces attempted to detain two Bosnian-Serb indicted war criminals near the town of Prijedor, Bosnia. One individual was killed in the operation and the other was peaceably detained. Bosnian-Serb propaganda against friendly forces was immediate and intense. PSYOP personnel, however, were unaware of the operation and were, for the most

---

4. Department of the Army, *Psychological Operations Tactics*, 11–25.
5. Department of the Army, *Psychological Operations Tactics*, 11–25.
6. Department of the Army, *Psychological Operations Tactics*, 11–25.

part, unable to effectively counter the hostile propaganda, thus demonstrating the consequences of not employing the counter-PSYOP defense strategy of forestalling.[7]

This strategy of forestalling again points to learning the truth of Scripture—not bits and pieces, but the whole truth. And the whole truth is learned through expositional study. When we learn the whole truth, we not only "know the opponent" but we also know the power and splendor of our Redeemer who will ultimately overcome the opponent. Forestalling is a preemptive and anticipatory measure that can be used specifically against *lack of faith, false occult practices,* and *false doctrine.*

Everything that humans learn is learned in one of three ways: empirically (i.e., via sensory means, such as vision, taste, and feelings), rationally (i.e., something that one comes to know by reason), or by faith (i.e., trusting in something you cannot explicitly prove). Faith is how humankind learns of God, and this faith, "the evidence of things not seen" (Heb 11:1), is what saves us and gives us hope. In fact, Jesus told Thomas, "Blessed are they that have not seen and yet have believed" (John 20:29). The Lord wants true faith because he gave us clear logic in the Bible, evidence for his existence, and clear evidence of the reality and the validity of the Gospel through the resurrection of Christ.[8]

Shockingly, 70 percent of professing Christians have never read the Bible in its entirety,[9] even though the Bible is designed to be read cover to cover, from Genesis to Revelation. God gave the entire book for our learning, growing, and application, and the "whole counsel" (Acts 20:27) should be employed because "faith comes by hearing, and hearing by the word of God" (Rom 10:17). Humans cannot pray for faith; it cannot be bought, and it is not received by osmosis. Faith manifests and grows via the intake of

---

7. Department of the Army, *Psychological Operations Tactics,* 11–25.

8. Grudem, *Systematic Theology,* 710.

9. Ponce Foundation, http://poncefoundation.com/christians-dont-read-their-bible/#:~:text=Christians%20Don%E2%80%99t%20Read%20Their%20Bible%20Of%20over%202,read%20their%20Bibles%20on%20Sundays%20while%20in%20church.

Defying Deception

God's Word. Additionally, as John Piper writes, "The human heart does not replenish itself with sleep. The body does, but not the heart. The spiritual air leaks from our tires, and the gas is consumed in the day. We replenish our hearts not with sleep, but with the Word of God and prayer."[10]

In the context of false dreams, visions, "miracles," and false doctrine, forestalling can be an effective deterrent. In a warning to the Corinthian Church regarding not entertaining a false Christ or an altered Gospel, Paul writes in 2 Cor 11:3, "But I fear, lest somehow, as the serpent deceived Eve by his craftiness, so your minds may be corrupted from the simplicity that is in Christ." Satan has utilized false teaching and exploited false dreams, visions, and "miracles" to lure many away from the truth of Scripture. The groups inspired by a false gospel use the Bible out of context and claim to believe that Jesus is our Savior and God. However, in many instances, they deny the Trinity, including the deity of Christ, and reject the penal substitutionary atonement of Jesus that allows salvation by grace through faith alone.[11] This rejection inevitably leads people toward a false version of Christianity and, thus, eternal damnation. Forestalling via expositional study equips the Christian to anticipate these false doctrines that Satan may use in his PSYOP and to counter them before the deceptive seeds begin to grow.

Forestalling via expositional study also assists in the detection of false prophets. False doctrines are professed by false prophets (or false teachers). Because of the way the word "prophet" is commonly used, there is a misconception that its fundamental definition is "someone who foretells the future"; however, this definition is too narrow. A prophet is better defined as "one who speaks for

---

10. Piper, *When I Don't Desire God*, 116.

11. Martin, *The Kingdom of the Cults*, 41. Penal substitutionary atonement refers to the doctrine that Christ died on the cross as a substitute for sinners. God imputed the guilt of our sins to Christ, and he, in our place, bore the punishment that we deserve. This was a full payment for sins, which satisfied both the wrath and the righteousness of God, so that he could forgive sinners without compromising his own holy standard. (Grudem, *Systematic Theology*, 579)

another."[12] A true prophet, then, is a person who speaks for God, delivering a message that God has ordained him to give. For example, in Exod 7:1, God tells Moses that Aaron, his brother, would be Moses' prophet, even as Moses was God's prophet. Because of Moses' unbelief in God's ability to speak through him, God would speak to Moses, who would tell Aaron what to say to others—to Pharaoh in particular (v. 7:2). It is the function of speaking for another, rather than the miracles they performed or their foretelling of what would befall Egypt, which defined Moses and Aaron as prophets.

Frequently, the words a prophet spoke on God's behalf were, in fact, foretelling what would happen later. However, the prophet's essential role was to speak for God, regardless of whether he did any predicting of the future. A prophet expresses the will of God in words, and sometimes he uses signs to back up what he says and to demonstrate God's power behind it.

Similarly, a false prophet also may not be one to foretell the future. A false prophet may simply speak for another but falsely. False prophets either speak for the wrong god, or they claim to have heard from the true God but do not accurately represent him or his words. At the very least, they speak out of their own human hearts, but more likely, the "god" they are speaking for is really a demon.[13]

It is true that, if a prophet foretells something that fails to come to pass, he is a false prophet,[14] but foretelling the future correctly is not the determining factor when looking at false prophets. The real issue is whether one who claims to be representing God and speaking for him is doing so accurately or falsely. A prophet may accurately predict an event or demonstrate supernatural power, but if he is leading people away from the true worship of the true God, he is a false prophet. Deut 13:1–5 says,

> If there arises among you a prophet or a dreamer of dreams, and he gives you a sign or a wonder, and the sign or the wonder comes to pass, of which he spoke to you,

---

12. Grudem, *Systematic Theology*, 1050.
13. Grudem, *Systematic Theology*, 1050.
14. See Deut 18:20–22.

saying, "Let us go after other gods"—which you have not known—"and let us serve them," you shall not listen to the words of that prophet or that dreamer of dreams, for the Lord your God is testing you to know whether you love the Lord your God with all your heart and with all your soul.

This passage begins with the assumption that the prophet does foretell the future accurately or perform some other, humanly impossible work. Nevertheless, if that prophet's central message is to follow after a different god or to take a spiritual path that the true God has not said to take, that person is a false prophet and, as Gal 1:8 states, "but even if we, or an angel from heaven, preach any other gospel to you than what we have preached to you, let him be accursed."[15] Therefore, by applying the Deut 13 and 18 "test of a prophet," the counter-PSYOP method of forestalling is invoked, preemptively testing the claims of prophets and, if they are determined to be false, countering them before they have a chance to take root.[16]

15. *Anathema* is derived from the Greek *ana'thema*, which means "a person or thing cursed or condemned to damnation or destruction." The word anathema appears just six times in the Bible and is commonly translated as "accursed," "cursed," or "eternally condemned" in more modern translations. (Strong and Kohlenberger, *New Strong's Expanded Exhaustive Concordance*, 37 and Liddell and Scott, *Greek-English Lexicon*)

16. *Shibboleth*, a word that appears only once in the Bible (in Judg 12:6), literally means "ear of corn" or "river." However, the significance of shibboleth is not derived from its literal meaning, but rather from the cunning way in which the tribe of Gilead used it to distinguish between enemy and ally. The Gileadites at the Jordan used the password *shibboleth* to detect the escaping Ephraimites. Jephthah had just concluded a very successful campaign against the Ammonites without the assistance of the Ephraimites, according to Judg 12:1–6. The latter were enraged at being denied such an opportunity to assert leadership among the tribes, and they made extremely arrogant threats against Jephthah (compare to Judg 8:1–3). Jephthah responded that his request for assistance from the Ephraimites had gone unanswered. In the subsequent battle, Jephthah's company of Gileadites prevailed and seized control of the Jordan's fords. As the Ephraimites attempted to escape across the river, they were challenged to establish that they were not Ephraimites by pronouncing the password. Each of the fugitives failed the test and, by mispronouncing the word, gave himself away and was slain. The significance of the word shibboleth

A slightly different but important corollary is that it seems that people are increasingly claiming to be shown visions or dreams they believe to be from the Holy Spirit. Although there are differing theological opinions on prophetic dreams and visions in the modern church age,[17] the Bible describes God speaking to humankind through dreams, visions, the scriptures, prophets, his audible voice, angels, and miracles. He is known to have spoken through a burning bush and a donkey and as a voice out of the clouds. God's sovereignty allows him to speak through whatever means he chooses, and God is therefore not limited in the ways he can communicate or speak with humanity. God can speak to anyone in any way he wants, as he is God. However, should the Holy Spirit choose to reveal himself in visions or dreams, he will not contradict the Word of God.[18]

Unfortunately, there is a rise in the number of people claiming to have been shown visions by the Holy Spirit that run contrary to the Word of God. It is important to understand that there are many different voices that can speak to a human being: the

---

lies not in its meaning, but in its pronunciation. (Wiersbe, *Wiersbe Bible Commentary*, 361) Similarly, like asking the pronunciation of shibboleth, one can simply ask, where is it in the Bible? Many false teachers can easily be refuted by this simple question because they have no scriptural basis for the claims they are making.

17. *Cessationism* is the view that the "miracle gifts" of tongues, healing, and prophecy have ceased—that the end of the apostolic age brought about a cessation of the miracles associated with that age. Most cessationists believe that while God can and still does perform miracles today, the Holy Spirit no longer uses individuals to perform miraculous signs. (Grudem, *Systematic Theology*, 1031–46).

18. The Holy Spirit has many important roles, but one of the most important is to give believers wisdom by which one can understand God. "These are the things God has revealed to us by his Spirit. The Spirit searches all things, even the deep things of God. For who knows a person's thoughts except their own spirit within them? In the same way no one knows the thoughts of God except the Spirit of God" (1 Cor 2:10–11). Since Christians have been given the gift of God's Spirit, Christians can apprehend the thoughts of God, as revealed in Scripture. The Spirit helps Christians understand. This is wisdom from God, rather than wisdom from man. No amount of human knowledge can ever replace the Holy Spirit's teaching (1 Cor 2:12–13). (Grudem, *Systematic Theology*, 634–53)

Holy Spirit, demon spirits, the human spirit, and the flesh. It takes discernment to know which of these is speaking to a person at certain times. Many believers have a difficult time distinguishing between the voice of the Holy Spirit and the voice of demons or their own human spirit. Naively, some have tagged whatever voice they hear as that of the Holy Spirit. Some have even tagged whatever supernatural encounter they have had as an interaction with God—which is not always the case.[19]

It is important to understand that merely because one is a believer does not stop Satan from attempting to dissuade and deceive. However, there is a method of determining whether what one hears is the voice of the Holy Spirit or not. One can distinguish spirits not only by the gift of discernment, but also by the Word of God. First John 4:1 says, "Beloved, do not believe every spirit, but test the spirits, whether they are of God; because many false prophets have gone out into the world."

So how can one test a spirit? The simple answer is to use the Bible. The truth of the Bible is vitally important to a believer's life. The Bible is the anchor of one's soul and one's protection from deception. In the last days, gradually, people will be deceived. Matt 24:5 says, "For many will come in My name, saying, 'I am the Christ,' and will deceive many." Humanity is now living in an age of increasing deception. Not everything is as it seems. Not everyone who comes saying that they believe in Jesus actually believes in the Jesus of the Bible. Today, different religions have many different variations of Jesus. Christians need to know the Jesus of the Bible so that they are not led astray. The Holy Spirit is the author of the Bible, as he inspired the writers of Scripture, and therefore he will never speak in opposition to what is recorded therein.

Satan attempted to use the Bible to trick and tempt Jesus, but Jesus was able to answer Satan using God's Word in its correct context. The lesson here is that Christians need to study scripture and

---

19. See 1 Cor 14:36–40. This passage is in the context of speaking in tongues but conveys the same warning. Participants must beware of new revelations that go beyond the Word of God. "To the law and to the testimony! If they do not speak according to this word, it is because there is no light in them" (Isa 8:20).

understand it in its correct context. Second Pet 3:15–16 says, "and consider that the longsuffering of our Lord is salvation—as also our beloved brother Paul, according to the wisdom given to him, has written to you, as also in all his epistles, speaking in them of these things, in which are some things hard to understand, which untaught and unstable people twist to their own destruction, as they do also the rest of the Scriptures." Unto their own destruction, Peter reminds us that the scriptures can be twisted. Just because someone quotes the Bible does not mean that they teach biblical truth: they may be twisting the scriptures. Further, 2 Cor 11:14 says, "And no wonder! For Satan himself transforms himself into an angel of light." Acts 17:10–11 confirms that the Jews whom Paul and Silas encountered in Berea "were more fair-minded than those in Thessalonica, in that they received the word with all readiness, and searched the Scriptures daily to find out whether these things were so." Quite simply, one must bounce everything off the Bible to ensure one is not being led astray, thus again invoking the counter-PSYOP method of forestalling.[20]

As in the preemptive counterpropaganda campaign used in the successful Bosnian-Croat indicted war criminal detainees example, the impact of forestalling by means of expositional study of the Bible is powerful in countering Satan's deceptive PSYOP, as the zealous Christian will gain knowledge of the "opponent" and his "wiles," and thus be in a position to preemptively counter him.

RESTRICTIVE MEASURES

The counter-PSYOP defense strategy called restrictive measures aims to "deny the intended target audience access" to the opponents' PSYOP.[21] In other words, it employs measures to restrict access to and the potential impact of deceptive PSYOP. In a

---

20. Additionally, the more Christians communicate with God (i.e., prayer), the better they will be able to hear him with clarity and distinguish his voice. And when one is unsure if his voice is present in dreams or visions, one should also seek counsel in prayer.

21. Department of the Army, *Psychological Operations Tactics*, 11–24.

military context, jamming, physical destruction, and occupation of media outlets (e.g., shutting down radio stations, etc.) are some examples of this technique.[22] As a military capability illustration, the EC-130J Commando Solo, a specially modified four-engine Hercules transport flown by the 193rd Special Operations Wing, a Pennsylvania Air National Guard unit, conducts airborne information operations via digital and analog radio and television broadcasts. With its ability to control the electronic spectrum of radio, television, and military communication bands in a focused area, the Commando Solo aircraft can provide broadcasting capabilities primarily for PSYOP missions, support disaster relief operations, and perform communications jamming—the deliberate use of radio noise or signals in an attempt to disrupt communications (or prevent listening to broadcasts). As part of the broader function of information operations, the Commando Solo can jam the enemy's broadcasts to their own people, thus providing a platform for invoking restrictive measures.[23] While this practice cannot prevent all deceptive PSYOP from reaching people, it can dull the effects so the PSYOP can be more easily overcome, and this is done via reinforcement of scriptural truth, which is most commonly accomplished by involvement in a Christ-centered fellowship: the local church. A strong, biblically founded church—a body of believers—has the capability of invoking restrictive measures to thwart Satan's deceptive PSYOP by encouraging, teaching, and building one another up in the knowledge and grace of the Lord Jesus Christ—the local church is where believers can fully apply the "body" principles of 1 Corinthians 12.[24] Through the ministry of the local church, Satan's deceptive PSYOP are in effect "jammed" by the bolstering of scriptural truth. As with conditioning, restrictive measures can be used against *all* of Satan's deceptive

---

22. Department of the Army, *Psychological Operations Tactics*, 11–24.

23. Department of the Air Force, "EC-130J Commando Solo" Fact Sheet.

24. The word "church" is a translation of the Greek word *ekklesia*, which is defined as "an assembly" or "called-out ones." (Liddell and Scott, *Greek-English Lexicon*)

PSYOP, and they can be used specifically against *lies, pride, bitterness*, and *lust*.

In Col 2:2 and Eph 3:16-19, Paul links God's blessings via Christ with Christian involvement in a loving believers' fellowship. Being part of a loving and encouraging Christian community will promote biblical understanding, as truth is substantiated in practice, and practice facilitates the conversion of truth into action.[25] Living and abiding in the truth reinforces truth in the Christian, which in turn establishes restrictive measures against deceptive PSYOP.

A solid body of believers practices genuine concern for one another. Authentic Christianity revolves around one's interior rather than one's façade. Christianity is not about adherence to a set of rules but rather about how we think, live, and engage with one another. Our hearts should be stimulated and strengthened as we are interwoven in love.[26] A sturdy church is a church that prays "without ceasing," as per 1 Thess 5:16-18. In Col 4:2-3, Paul explicitly calls for the Colossian Church to pray: "Continue earnestly in prayer, being vigilant in it with thanksgiving; meanwhile praying also for us, that God would open to us a door for the word, to speak the mystery of Christ, for which I am also in chains." Prayer stimulates and strengthens our love for one another. Further, different types of prayers can be used in response to deceptive attacks. For instance, a prayer of request (or supplication) can be used to petition God for aid against a specific deception, or a prayer of intercession can be used when one group or person prays for another group or person concerning an attack.[27] To this end, "praying always" (Eph 6:18) is the heavy artillery protecting those wearing the full armor of God.[28]

25. Wright, *Colossians and Philemon*, 94-95.

26. Chester and Timmis, *Total Church*, 54.

27. We are to pray to God and God only. Deut 18:11 considers it an abomination to "call up the dead," and this includes prayers to Mary and dead persons the Roman Catholic Church considers saints.

28. There are many reasons to pray. For one thing, prayer is a form of serving and obeying God (Luke 2:36-38). We pray because the Bible instructs us to (Phil 4:6-7). Christ and the early church modeled prayer for us (see Mark

The Bible is at the center of all things, especially the church. The Bible is God's revelation to humans about the work and person of Jesus Christ. Thus, at the center of the Bible is the person of Jesus. Therefore, if a church is not centered on the Bible, then that church is not centered on Christ. If a church does not consistently teach the Bible, Christians will not be prepared to resist Satan's deceptive PSYOP, and restrictive measures cannot be established.[29]

A biblically grounded church seeks to grow in Christ and seek, as Col 2:2–3 says, "all riches of the full assurance of understanding, to the knowledge of the mystery of God, both of the Father and of Christ, in whom are hidden all the treasures of

---

1:35; Acts 1:14; 2:42; 3:1; 4:23–31; 6:4; 13:1–3, among other passages). If Jesus believed that prayer was worthwhile, so should we. God intends for prayer to be the means by which his solutions are obtained in a variety of circumstances. We pray in preparation for significant decisions (Luke 6:12–13); to surmount demonic obstacles (Matt 17:14–21); "send out laborers into His harvest" (Luke 10:2); to acquire the strength to resist temptation (Matt 26:41); and to achieve the means of edifying others spiritually (Eph 6:18–19). Even if we do not receive exactly what we have asked for, God has assured us that our petitions are not in vain (see Matt 6:6 and Rom 8:26–27). He has promised that he will grant our requests if they are consistent with his will (1 John 5:14–15). Sometimes, according to his wisdom and for our benefit, he delays his responses. In these circumstances, we are to pray with diligence and perseverance (see Matt 7:7 and Luke 18:1–8). Prayer should not be viewed as a way to get God to do our will on Earth, but as a way to accomplish God's will on Earth. God's intellect is far superior to ours. Un-prayed prayers will go unanswered (for example, see Mark 7:26–30; Luke 18:35–43). God stated in Jas 4:2 that we frequently go without simply because we do not ask. An absence of prayer demonstrates a lack of trust in God's Word and a lack of faith. We pray to exhibit our faith in God, that he will fulfill his promises in his word and bless our lives abundantly (Eph 3:20). Prayer is our primary means of observing God's presence in the lives of others. Because it is our means of "plugging into" God's power, it is also our means of defeating Satan and his demon army, which we are incapable of vanquishing on our own. Jas 5:16–18 tells us that the fervent prayer of a righteous man accomplishes much. (Grudem, *Systematic Theology*, 376–96)

Lastly, we surrender our wills to God through disciplined prayer. As we spend time in prayer, we surrender our will to God and pray, with the Lord, "Not as I will, but as You will" (Matt 26:39). We must pray about everything, and let God have his way in everything. (Wiersbe, *Wiersbe Bible Commentary*, 1664)

29. Carson, "God, the Bible and Spiritual Warfare," 259.

wisdom and knowledge." In this passage, Paul does not imply that this wisdom is reserved for the select few; rather, he counters false teachers who attract people with their "secret knowledge" (i.e., deception). "Mystery," in the context of this passage, means truth that was previously hidden but is now disclosed for all (e.g., Jesus as Christ/Messiah). Discovering the riches that are in Christ forms a defense against deceptive PSYOP.[30]

In addition to a biblical foundation, a spiritually discerning church is a must. According to John MacArthur, where the greatest physical danger to the human body is a deficient immune system because one could die from countless diseases, the greatest danger to the church is also a deficient immune system, that is, the inability to discern truth from error, thus not recognizing deception and ultimately being led astray. This deception can come in different forms. For instance, it could come in the form of psychology, pragmatism, sentimentalism, liberalism, a peculiar view of the atonement, or some aberrant view of Jesus, to name a few. Anything that is not true has the potential to cause severe damage to the church because the church is the pillar and foundation of the truth. To remedy the potential of this deficient immune system, the leadership of the church must be discerning. It must have a fully functioning immune system that fights off every heresy—and, unfortunately, there are countless heresies that can kill a church. When Paul talks about these heresies, he calls them "every lofty opinion raised against the knowledge of God" (2 Cor 10:5, ESV). These ungodly ideas are like a fortress (or *stronghold*, as expressed in 2 Cor 10:5) and people are captive within these ideological fortresses. Not coincidentally, the Greek word for *fortress* is the same word as for *tomb*.[31] These fortresses become their tombs because they are entombed in aberrant theology. Satan is a liar and he and his ministers operate predominately in false religion. Thus, the greatest threat to the church today is the inability to discern because the people who are in leadership positions do not possess

---

30. Keller, *Center Church: Doing Balanced, Gospel-Centered Ministry in Your City*, 186.

31. Liddell and Scott, *Greek-English Lexicon*.

that discernment that comes from rightly dividing the Word of truth (2 Tim 2:15).[32]

Unfortunately, in today's culture, discernment is becoming more and more politically incorrect, as those who discern from a biblical foundation are seen as judgmental or intolerant. The Bible is clear and steadfast on biblical doctrines and moral issues, leaving no room for error. The Christian church needs to cling to these truths so that "we should no longer be children, tossed to and fro and carried about with every wind of doctrine, by the trickery of men, in the cunning craftiness of deceitful plotting" (Eph 4:14).[33] The Christ-centered church is stable in its faith and disciplined in all matters. Stable churches do not pursue fads or pounce on the latest church growth techniques, self-help insights, or rapture speculations.[34] The grounded church is steadfast, disciplined, and

---

32. MacArthur, "God's Demand for Discernment." Additionally, it is not enough for a pastor to stand up and tell people what the Bible says; one must let the Bible speak. If one explains the scriptures, God speaks. If a preacher says to a congregation that "this is what the Bible says," they have to believe what the pastor is saying, thus relying on the pastor rather than the scriptures. It is imperative to let the congregation believe Scripture so that there can then be a strong unity and conviction regarding what is true and then a greater degree of discernment regarding what is full of error and even subtly false. Beware of subtle lies: they sneak in like a Trojan horse and then send out their troops. Once they obtain a foothold, errors multiply, and the church begins to disintegrate.

33. King, *Is It of God?*, 67.

34. Another matter to be cautious of in modern Christianity is that of celebrity pastors. Celebrity pastors are pastors who, in addition to shepherding a local congregation, have attained a certain level of popularity. These pastors typically use mass media to expand their reach and influence through podcasts, book deals, large social media followings, and large-venue speaking engagements. Since the Bible does not prohibit fame, being a pastor with celebrity status is not a sin. However, there are prospective issues with being a celebrity pastor that must be evaluated. For instance, shepherding a local congregation is a tremendous obligation. Keeping track of a local congregation in addition to thousands of other followers is typically beyond the capacity of one individual. To effectively pastor a local church, one must cultivate and sustain personal relationships with congregants. It is virtually impossible for a single pastor to provide the necessary level of care to both local congregants and followers. This does not mean that it is impossible or that God does not call pastors to large venues and ministries; it is just difficult. While caring for

stable in its faith in Christ and centered on the Gospel, as the Gospel is the indisputable basis to protect against deceptive PSYOP and to build restrictive measures.[35]

Additionally, one way Satan works to obscure truth is by promoting a sense-driven (empirical) venue[36] for the church setting by incorporating physical objects (e.g., relics venerated in the Roman Catholic Church)[37] and artificially eliciting emotional re-

---

a large number of people is an admirable goal, it can sometimes create a false sense of closeness with adherents and distance between a pastor and his local congregation. Fans may begin to place more faith in the celebrity pastor than in their own pastor or even the Bible.

Pride and lack of accountability are two other potential issues with celebrity pastors. Pastoral characteristics and qualifications are described in 1 Tim 3:1–7. The caution against arrogance is particularly pertinent for the modern celebrity pastor. Once pastors enter the world of fame and affluence, it can be challenging to pursue accountability and maintain a humble disposition. The temptations that come with fame are not new and can affect anyone (see 2 Sam 11 for the example of King David and 1 Kgs for that of King Solomon). Pastors who have attained celebrity status should heed 1 Cor 10:12: "Therefore, let him who thinks he stands take heed, lest he fall." Pastors should prioritize their local congregation, pursue daily accountability, and recognize meekly that their platform is a gift from God that exists solely for his glory. (Got Questions Ministries, "What are the potential issues with celebrity pastors?")

35. Chester and Timmis, *Total Church*, 87.

36. "Empirical" means originating in or based on observation or experience; relying on experience or observation alone often without due regard for system and theory. (*Merriam-Webster's Collegiate Dictionary*) Using the words "faith" and the "Word of God" instead of "system" and "theory," respectively, in this definition provides a theological characterization.

37. A fragment of Jesus' cross has been discovered in Turkey. Jesus' baby blanket has been discovered in Germany. John the Baptist's index finger is currently on exhibit in a reliquary in a Missouri museum. Relics, which are revered religious artifacts that have been meticulously preserved, have long played an important role in many religions, including Christianity. By the Middle Ages, hundreds of alleged burial sites for the twelve apostles existed. It has been said that one could construct a sizable ship out of all the alleged pieces of Jesus' cross. The Shroud of Turin, the most famous Christian relic, attracts hundreds of thousands of visitors annually. (Wall, *Relics from the Crucifixion—Where They Went and How They Got There*, 32–54)

One of the inherent dangers of relic veneration is the temptation of engaging in idolatry. This was precisely the case in ancient Israel. God instructed Moses to fashion a bronze serpent to protect the Hebrews from a plague of

sponses. The church need not be a place that has the correct lighting or the perfect temperature to set the mood so that all will feel like God is moving among them. As 1 Cor 3:16 says, if you are a believer, God is resident in you. He does not have to be beckoned to be in church. Satan, on the other hand, has to undo that truth to deceive Christians. Things of the spirit that are not seen are out of his league, and he has little influence over them, but he has a great deal of influence over physically, emotionally, and sensorially driven objects of worship. Therefore, he wants to persuade professing Christians to take an empirical, sensory-rich venue. To avoid this deception, one cannot allow a sensory experience or feeling to be an authority.[38] Consider the following excerpt from Hitler's *Mein Kampf*:

> The superior oratorical art of a dominating preacher will succeed more easily in winning to the new will people who have themselves experienced a weakening of their force of resistance in the most natural way than those who are still in full possession of their mental tension

---

venomous snakes (see Num 21:8-9). The Israelites retained the bronze serpent as a reminder of God's goodness and salvation; however, by the time of King Hezekiah, the "relic" had been transformed into an object of worship. Hezekiah's reforms included shattering the bronze serpent Moses had made, to which the Israelites had previously offered incense (2 Kgs 18:4). If not commanded by God, physical aides to faith are unnecessary and inevitably lead to superstition and idolatry.

There is no power whatsoever in Christian relics. Even if the entire cross of Jesus were to be found, it would be devoid of spiritual significance. Relics do not in any way facilitate a closer relationship with God. The saint's humerus has no effect on your spirit. Relics should not be prayed to, worshipped, or used in any manner to strengthen one's relationship with God. Such talismanic use of relics is flagrant idolatry (Exod 20:3; Isa 42:8). A church filled with relics is no more valid as a place of worship than a tent in the jungle. We worship the Lord in spirit and truth (John 4:24), not with genuine or counterfeit idols, icons, or relics. (Got Questions Ministries, "How should a Christian view relics?")

38. Throughout the Gospel of John, Jesus uses physical things to point to spiritual reality; the reverse never occurs. He does not use a spiritual truth to point to a physical reality. He focuses on the spiritual, unseen, and immaterial. For instance, Jesus uses a door (physical item) to refer to the path to eternal life in Jesus (spiritual truth) in John 10:1-9. (Hodge and Patterson, *World Religions and Cults*, 36)

and will. The same purpose, after all, is served by the artificially made and yet mysterious twilight in Catholic churches, the burning lamps, incense, censers, etc.[39]

Hitler's point is that empiricism can be used to manipulate people, and this can be done simply through sensory means, by invoking an emotional response that does not originate with Christ. If the church is centered on Christ and built on a foundation of the Bible, this deception will be avoided.

Next, the Christ-centered church embraces the following: "In essentials, unity. In non-essentials, liberty. In all things, love" (Augustine of Hippo (354–430 AD), a theologian and early church father).[40] The Bible unambiguously and accurately expresses fundamental Christian doctrine that we must understand without error and in unity. Compromising these truths is a denial of the Gospel of Jesus Christ. There are other subjects of practice and doctrine on which Christians diverge; however, they do not endanger the Gospel. For instance, the timing or reality of the rapture, young-earth creationism versus old-earth creationism,

39. Hitler, *Mein Kampf*, 475.

40. 1 Cor 1:10 says "Now I plead with you, brethren, by the name of our Lord Jesus Christ, that you all speak the same thing, and that there be no divisions among you, but that you be perfectly joined together in the same mind and in the same judgment." Paul stated in the previous verse that each of these believers has been summoned into the fellowship of Christ. This requires that, as Christians, they have fellowship with one another. Now Paul addresses the first of many concerns within the Corinthian Church. The Corinthians are not unified because they are all in Christ; rather, they are divided. In the name of Christ, Paul urges them to agree with one another. He has a high standard for this church and for all Christian churches: no divisions. Paul insists that because they are all in Christ, they can live in unity. This unity can and must reach the level of cooperative thinking and judgment regarding matters of vital importance. As in other passages (Romans 14 for instance), Paul clarifies: he is not requiring all members of the church to concur with whoever is in authority. Neither does he teach that Christians cannot debate about anything. The only requirement here is for them to achieve unity, not perfect conformity. Disagreement does not necessarily necessitate division. Paul establishes Christ as the benchmark for all thoughts and judgments. As each individual conforms to Christ, they will align with one another. Through Christ, disagreements will be subordinate to fundamental agreement and brotherhood. When Christians use mere human beings as their standard, division is always the result.

charismatic versus non-charismatic, premillennialism versus amillennialism, etc. These Christian doctrines are important, as every Christian doctrine holds some degree of importance. However, these doctrines may not merit dividing or separating over. On both sides of these issues, there are committed, Christ-loving believers. Christians should not allow non-essential issues to divide the church, at least not to the extent of doubting the veracity of another person's faith.[41] We may dispute these items, but we must regard each other as fellow Christians and treat each other with love and respect.[42] Satan would like nothing more than to employ his deceptive PSYOP to divide the church over non-doctrinal, secondary matters.

Lastly, beware of a lukewarm church. In Rev 3:14–21, the Lord describes the "lukewarm" attitude of the Laodicean Church, as demonstrated by their actions. In their relationship with God, the Laodiceans were neither cold nor hot, but rather lukewarm. Hot water cleanses and purifies; cold water refreshes and enlivens. However, lukewarm water has no comparable utility. The Laodiceans grasped the Lord's comparison since their city's drinking water flowed from a spring six miles to the south via an aqueduct,

---

41. There are, however, appropriate degrees of division even with regard to non-essential Christian doctrine. Concerning focus, priorities, and ministry, a church must be unified and of one mind. If there is a doctrinal issue that prevents a church from focusing on a unified ministry, it is preferable for a person to find a different church than to cause conflict and division within a church. These types of divisions have led to the formation of many Christian denominations and divisions.

If everyone abandoned their preconceived notions, biases, and presuppositions and simply accepted the Christian doctrines taught in the Bible, division would not be an issue. We are all, however, corrupted and infected with sin (Eccl 7:20; Rom 3:23). Sin prevents us from apprehending and applying God's Word flawlessly. The failure to apprehend and submit to Christian doctrine is the source of division, not doctrine itself. Disagreements over the central tenets of the Christian faith should unquestionably lead to division. Occasionally, division over non-essential matters is also required, albeit to a lesser degree. However, doctrine should never be blamed for division. In reality, Christian doctrine is the only path to genuine, complete, and biblical unity within the Body of Christ.

42. Keller, *Center Church*, 192.

and it was disgustingly lukewarm. The water in Laodicea was neither hot nor cold, as in the adjacent hot springs where people bathed. It was lukewarm and useless. In fact, it was disgusting, and the Lord's reaction to the Laodiceans was to say, "I will vomit you out of My mouth" (Rev 3:16).

The epistle to the Church in Laodicea is the harshest of the seven letters to Asia Minor churches in Revelation 2 and 3. Jesus makes it apparent that this is a dead church by indicting their "works" (Rev 3:15). This church considers itself "rich" and self-sufficient, but the Lord views them as "wretched, pitiful, poor, blind, and naked" (Rev 3:17). Their apathetic faith was dishonest, and their church was filled with unconverted, counterfeit Christians.[43]

Jesus regularly associates actions with one's genuine spiritual status. "You will know them by their fruits," he adds, and "Every

---

43. Acts 2:42 could be regarded as a mission statement for the church: "They continued steadfastly in the apostles' doctrine and fellowship, in the breaking of bread, and in prayers." The purposes/activities of the church, according to this verse, are (1) teaching biblical doctrine, (2) providing a place for believers to fellowship, (3) observing the Lord's Supper, and (4) praying.

The church is also commanded to proclaim the gospel of salvation through Jesus Christ (Matt 28:18–20; Acts 1:8) and to faithfully proclaim the gospel through both word and deed. The church is to serve as a "lighthouse" in the community, directing people to Jesus Christ, our Lord and Savior (1 Pet 3:15). The church must both promote the gospel and educate its members to proclaim the gospel.

Jas 1:27 outlines the church's final objectives: "Pure and undefiled religion before God and the Father is this: to visit orphans and widows in their trouble, and to keep oneself unspotted from the world." The church is to minister to those in need. This encompasses not only sharing the gospel, but also providing for physical needs (food, clothing, shelter) as necessary and appropriate. The church must also equip Christians with the tools they need to overcome immorality and remain uncontaminated by the world. This is achieved through biblical instruction and Christian fellowship.

Therefore, what is the function of the church? Paul provided an illustrative example to the believers in Corinth. The church, the body of Christ, is the hands, mouth, and feet of God in the world (1 Cor 12:12–27). We are to conduct ourselves as Jesus Christ would were he tangibly present on Earth. The church should be "Christian," "Christ-like," and Christ-centered. If these church characteristics are absent, as they were in the Laodicean (lukewarm) Church, then change must occur to realign the church with the scriptural commission of Christ's church.

good tree bears good fruit" (Matt 7:16-17). The Laodiceans' lukewarm actions were clearly incompatible with true salvation. True believers' actions will be "hot" or "cold"—that is, they will benefit the world in some way and reflect the spiritual zeal of a life transformed. Lukewarm deeds, on the other hand—those done without pleasure, love, or the fire of the Spirit—do harm to the watching world. Those who claim to know God but behave as if he doesn't exist are considered lukewarm. They may attend church and engage in religious activities, but their inner posture is one of self-righteous complacency. They claim to be Christians, yet their souls remain unchanged, and their hypocrisy sickens God.

The image of Jesus standing outside the church (Rev 3:20) demonstrates that the lukewarm individuals to whom Christ speaks are not saved. He has yet to be embraced into their midst. The Lord rebukes and punishes them in love, telling them to repent (Rev 3:19). He sees their lukewarm attitudes as "the shame of your nakedness" that needs to be clothed in the white clothes of true righteousness (Rev 3:18). He exhorts them to be sincere or enthusiastic in their devotion to him. Our Lord is gracious and patient, giving the lukewarm time to repent.

The worldly affluence of the Laodiceans, combined with a semblance of pure faith, led to a false sense of security and independence.[44] According to Rev 3:17, "I am rich, have become wealthy, and have need of nothing," although they had significant spiritual needs. When people enjoy lives of luxury and prosperity, they are constantly threatened by a self-sufficient attitude and a lukewarm faith.[45] Unfortunately, the majority of prosperous Westerners today reside in modern-day Laodicea. Their faith is not threatened by persecution, but by incessant temptations to compromise with the world. Jesus, the "faithful and true witness" (Rev 3:14), admonished the Laodiceans for becoming "lukewarm" (v.16) in unfaithfulness and urged them to "buy from [Him] . . . salve to anoint [their] eyes" (v. 18) in order to heal their cataracts of compromise.

---

44. See Mark 10:23.

45. Got Questions Ministries, "Why did Jesus speak so strongly against lukewarm faith?" and MacArthur, *The MacArthur Bible Commentary*, 1989–90.

FORESTALLING AND RESTRICTIVE MEASURES

If fever is a symptom of disease in the body, then lukewarmness is a symptom of the disease of unfaithfulness in the soul. And just as we all experience bodily fevers and fight disease, we all experience lukewarmness to varying degrees and must combat the disease of unfaithfulness. How can we combat the illness if we feel lukewarm? Our trustworthy and genuine Physician prescribes the antidote: "Be zealous and repent" (Rev 3:19). But how can a lukewarm individual simply "be zealous"? Isn't this the very issue: a lack of zeal? No! The issue is not recognizing the disease whose symptom is lukewarmness. If you believe you only have a virus, you may not give a fever much thought. If you discover that cancer is the cause of your fever, however, zeal is no longer an issue. Lukewarmness is a symptom of soul disease caused by unfaithful unbelief. Jesus will vomit you out of his mouth (Rev 3:16) if left untreated. The eternal recompense is not bestowed upon the unfaithful. The recompense is for "him who overcomes" (Rev 3:21): the victorious combatant who fights and overcomes.

How does a lukewarm person repent? Do not wait for emotional inspiration. Repent immediately! Reverse course and proceed in the right direction. Take one step, then another. Rarely, when it comes to repentance, we struggle with not knowing what to do. The Holy Spirit instructs us on how to repent. Our dilemma is the desire to repent.

Grace accompanied Jesus' harsh words of warning to the Laodiceans. He was not telling them that their faithfulness would earn them salvation. He was suggesting that their lukewarm unfaithfulness could indicate that they lacked saving faith. It was a moment of "you have cancer" news. He also clearly conveyed the treatment. He was telling them to repent and return to him for healing. This is the grace he extends to the majority of his followers who, like Peter, lapse into unfaithfulness at some point.[46] Repentance is evidence of genuine faith.

Remaining faithful is not merely a struggle: it is a war. To be faithful to God, our spouse, our children, our church, and our vocation, we must fight daily against the sin that compels us to

---

46. See Luke 22:60–62.

compromise. Do not coddle minor compromises. Slay them. Fight fiercely for fidelity by fighting the fight for faith.[47]

Repentance becomes a habit for the faithful fighter. The sin of compromise is always at our doorstep, and we must exercise authority over it.[48] This is accomplished by cultivating the ability to bring every thought captive to the obedience of Christ.[49] In the end, a congregation that resists being lukewarm bolsters their restrictive measures, thus thwarting Satan's deceptive PSYOP.

Accordingly, as the EC-130J Commando Solo invokes restrictive measures by jamming enemy communication, the counter-PSYOP method of restrictive measures via involvement in a Christ-centered, biblically founded local church "jams" Satan's deceptive PSYOP, thus further bolstering and equipping Christians to thwart deception.

"Experiencing God"

As a modern corollary to a sense-driven (empirical) church venue, the current growing trend in some churches of "experiencing God" is beginning to supplant the biblically defined human relationship with God. The concept of "experiencing God" is not explicitly mentioned in the Bible, despite its popularity in Christian circles. There are many commands in the Bible concerning our relationship with God, but experiencing him is not one of them. We are to trust God (John 14:1), love God with all our hearts (Deut 6:5), fear God (Eccl 12:13 and 1 Pet 2:17), and obey God (Deut 27:10 and 1 John 5:2), among other commands. However, the Bible nowhere instructs us to "experience God." We can, however, (1) participate in the nature of God, (2) be moved by him, and (3) learn of him by personal relationship—in a sense, this is the biblical formula to experience God.

---

47. See 1 Tim 6:12.
48. See Gen 4:7.
49. See 2 Cor 10:5; Bloom, "How to Fight Lukewarmness."

FORESTALLING AND RESTRICTIVE MEASURES

Before we can participate in any way with God, we must resolve two inner conflicts. First, we are all hopeless sinners trapped in a pit from which we cannot escape through our own endeavors (Rom 3:12). Second, nothing we do in our own strength is acceptable to God (Isa 64:6). According to the Bible, in order to resolve these conflicts, we must accept Jesus Christ as our Lord and Savior and submit our lives to him. Our words and deeds are only then acceptable to God (2 Cor 12:9–10). Therefore, the first key to biblically experiencing God is to be "partakers of the divine nature" (2 Pet 1:4), which is only possible through faith in Christ's sacrifice on the cross for our sins.

The second component of biblically experiencing God is being moved by him. God's movement within the human soul is one of the Holy Spirit's functions. From the beginning of creation, when the Spirit of God "moved upon the face of the waters" (Gen 1:2, KJV), to the Spirit's movement in the souls of unbelievers, drawing them to Jesus, the Spirit is passionately involved in moving us. As per John 6:44, God moves us in his drawing us to faith; as per John 16:7–9, the Spirit moves in our hearts to convict us of sin and our necessity for the Savior; and as per Gal 5:22–23, within believers, he guides, directs, influences, and comforts us, as well as produces the fruit of the Spirit in us. Moreover, as per 2 Pet 1:21, the Spirit moved the authors of all sixty-six books of the Bible to record precisely what he inspired in their hearts and minds, and via the scriptures, he moves within us to bear witness to our spirits that we are his children (Rom 8:16).

The third aspect of biblically experiencing God is the lifelong process of learning about him and becoming so intimately acquainted with him that we joyously surrender our lives to him because we have come to know and trust him completely. This requires realizing that he is good, faithful, holy, unchanging, just, omnipotent, and sovereign over all circumstances. The intimate knowledge of God's love is a remarkably joyful aspect of experiencing God. According to 1 John 4:8, "God is love." As we experience his love, we can share our Christian love with others, regardless of the circumstances, and as others experience his love through us, this will produce more and more love.

Therefore, the key to experiencing God is to not the anticipation of an "experience" or an emotional boost. Rather, it is a lifelong process of belonging to him through Christ, being moved by the Holy Spirit who sanctifies us, and growing in knowledge of him.[50]

---

50. Got Questions Ministries, "What is the key to truly experiencing God?"

7

A Final Word on Satan's Tactic of Deception

Viewed through the Lens of Military PSYOP

World War I Australian troops carrying a dummy tank that was intended to deceive German forces during the following day's assault (September 1918).[1]

As the salt flavors every drop in the Atlantic, so does sin affect every atom of our nature. It is so sadly there, so abundantly there, that if you cannot detect it, you are deceived.

—CHARLES SPURGEON, *HONEST DEALING WITH GOD*, 1875

---

1. *E04934*, Public Domain.

DEFYING DECEPTION

A NEUTRALIZING FORCE

As the clocks continue to tick and the world creeps ever-closer to the end times, how will deceptive PSYOP affect Christians? In what is often referred to as his Olivet Discourse,[2] Jesus describes to his disciples the events that will take place before his second coming.[3] One of the warnings Christ gives is this: "For false christs and false prophets will rise and show great signs and wonders to deceive, if possible, even the elect" (Matt 24:24).[4] Will the false miracles performed by the false messiahs and prophets in the end times be so compelling that even born-again believers will be convinced?

There are two reasons that the answer to this question is "No." First, virtually all Bible commentators agree that the grammatical construction of the verse and its statement "if possible" firmly point to such a thing being improbable. The verse implies that the deception will be strong, the miracles will seem real, and Satan's deceptive PSYOP intent will be to mislead everyone, to include the elect; however, God's grace will prevail. His chosen ones will not be drawn away into this deception.

Second, the Bible strongly speaks to the fact that the elect are protected by God from deceptions that would result in eternal separation from Christ. Paul tells us in Eph 1:4 that God "chose us

---

2. See Matt 24–25; Mark 13; Luke 21.

3. Believers anticipate the second coming of Jesus Christ as evidence that God is sovereign over all things and keeps his Word's promises and prophecies (Acts 1:11; Zech 14:4; Matt 24:30). As predicted, Jesus Christ arrived on earth in Bethlehem as an infant in a manger during his first coming. A significant number of the Messianic prophecies were realized throughout the life, ministry, death, and resurrection of Jesus. Nevertheless, certain prophecies concerning the Messiah remain unfulfilled in relation to Jesus. At his second coming, Christ will return to accomplish the remainder of the prophecies (Zech 12:10 and Rev 1:7). Jesus, during his first coming, assumed the role of the suffering Servant. Jesus, upon his second coming, shall come as the conquering King. Jesus arrived in the humblest of circumstances during his first coming. During his second coming, Jesus will be accompanied by heavenly armies (Rev 19:11–16).

4. The Greek word translated as "elect" is *eklektós*, or "chosen ones," a term used a number of times in the New Testament to refer to true believers in Jesus. See Luke 18:7; Rom 8:33; Col 3:12. (Liddell and Scott, *Greek-English Lexicon*)

A FINAL WORD ON SATAN'S TACTIC OF DECEPTION

in Him before the foundation of the world, that we should be holy and without blame before Him"; Peter says in 1 Pet 1:5 that the chosen "are kept by the power of God through faith for salvation ready to be revealed in the last time"; and Jude says in Jude 1:1 that the chosen are "sanctified by God the Father, and preserved in Jesus Christ." As these verses indicate, the elect will endure in God's strength.

With respect to following false christs, Jesus says in John 10:2–5,

> He who enters by the door is the shepherd of the sheep. To him the doorkeeper opens, and the sheep hear his voice; and he calls his own sheep by name and leads them out. And when he brings out his own sheep, he goes before them; and the sheep follow him, for they know his voice. Yet they will by no means follow a stranger, but will flee from him, for they do not know the voice of strangers.

In other words, the sheep know their Shepherd.

Being deceived is an indicator of the unregenerate. According to Titus 3:3, "For we ourselves were also once foolish, disobedient, deceived, serving various lusts and pleasures, living in malice and envy, hateful and hating one another." After salvation, we may stray from the truth at times, but the Bible makes it clear that the elect of God cannot be deceived to the extent of being lost.[5] If God's chosen ones could be deceived in such a way, God's choice of them would be thwarted, and that is not possible. All who are in Christ have been predestined, called, and justified, and will eventually be glorified.[6] They have been given to Christ; and of all those who have been given to him, he will lose none.[7] However, regardless of

---

5. John 10:28–29 says, "And I give them eternal life, and they shall never perish; neither shall anyone snatch them out of My hand. My Father, who has given them to Me, is greater than all; and no one is able to snatch them out of My Father's hand." Notice there are two hands discussed: that of God the Son and God the Father. This strongly implies that a Christian's salvation is secure.

6. See Rom 8:30.

7. See John 10:28. The predestination versus free will debate is one that has consumed theologians for centuries. However, predestination versus free will should be discussed as predestination versus not-entirely-free will. Rom 8:29–30

Satan's futile deceptive PSYOP attempts against Christians, he can influence and neutralize Christians to the point of ineffectiveness and the battleground resides in the mind.

THE CHRISTIAN'S MIND

The counter-PSYOP methods to guard against deception discussed in Chapters 5 and 6 offer a front-line defense to thwart deceptive PSYOP that provide a catalyst to guarding a Christian's mind. As conveyed throughout the Bible, God wants our minds

---

and Eph 1:5–11 teach unequivocally that God predestines some to salvation. God's sovereignty, unchanging character (Mal 3:6), foreknowledge (Rom 8:29, 11:2), love (Eph 1:4–5), and purpose and pleasure (Eph 1:5) determine who will be saved. God's desire is for everyone to be saved and to confess (2 Pet 3:9). He proposes salvation to all (Titus 2:11), but we know that not all will accept it. How this all functions together can be debated, but predestination is a biblical doctrine without question. Numerous other New Testament passages refer to believers' election to salvation (Matt 24:22, 31; Mark 13:20, 27; Rom 8:33; 9:11; 11:5–7, 28; Eph 1:11; Col 3:12; 1 Thess 1:4; 1 Tim 5:21; 2 Tim 2:10; Titus 1:1; 1 Pet 1:1–2; 2:9; 2 Pet 1:10). Nevertheless, the Bible also teaches that individuals are responsible for their decisions (Josh 24:14–15, Luke 10:42, Heb 11:24–25). Our freedom is perpetually constrained by our circumstances and our temperament. Without Christ, the Bible teaches that we are "dead in our trespasses and sins" (Eph 2:1). If we are spiritually dead, logically our decision-making must be affected. John 6:44 states that no one can come to Christ for salvation unless God draws them. If deciding to trust in Christ is impossible without God's "interference," then our will is not completely "free." Nevertheless, God offers salvation to all (Titus 2:11) and has revealed himself to all, leaving no room for excuse (Rom 1:19–20). We possess free will in the sense that we can make moral decisions. Numerous factors influence our decision-making, including our sin nature, upbringing, intelligence, training/education, biology, psychology, etc. Therefore, humans do not possess true free will, as commonly defined. We have a will and we're able to make decisions. According to the Bible, it is our duty to respond to what God has revealed to us, including his call to believe the Gospel (John 1:12; 3:16; Acts 16:31; Rom 10:9–10; Rev 22:17). However, our will is not genuinely "free" because our decisions are influenced by constraints. The doctrine of predestination is explicitly biblical. God has absolute control over everything, including salvation. Concurrently, we are sincerely accountable for our salvation-related decisions. These truths are not mutually exclusive or incompatible. God implores us repeatedly in the Bible to exercise our free will and place our salvation in Christ, and we should obey these commands. (Got Questions Ministries, "What does the Bible say about predestination vs. free will?")

A FINAL WORD ON SATAN'S TACTIC OF DECEPTION

to be focused on him. He wants minds that are reverently his.[8] In Prov 4:23, God tells us that our minds are to be his dwelling place—and for this to be the case, Christians must resist the deceptive PSYOP strategy of Satan. Grace-energized Christians think and live reverently as they walk through each day of their lives. They are Christians who try by choice and conviction to worship nothing but God. Reverent Christians understand that nothing in life is neutral or harmless. Everything is either for God or against him. Everything either promotes or opposes God's Glory.[9]

Rom 12 teaches that the secret to glorifying God in our mind is to constantly be renewing our mind, giving it back to God. A mind given to God is reverent, and God wants reverent Christians. He wants Christians to regard him with awe, devoted to honoring and obeying him while living in a sin-energized world. Reverent Christians think much and often about God, remembering what God's Word says: "as he thinks . . . so is he" (Prov 23:7). And since everything starts and ends with our minds, these reverent Christians start by keeping their minds under God's influence, and that involves a life-long response to God's call to guard your mind. Reverent minds are guarded minds. If your mind is committed to God, it can't be under the control of Satan or fleshly desires that ultimately leads to destruction. Whatever controls your mind, controls you. The battle each day is for our minds. At salvation, Christ begins to dwell in the minds of Christians, and Christians are given the duty to guard, protect, and properly nourish their minds. The world, flesh, and Satan, via deceptive PSYOP, all seek to neutralize Godly minds. Grace-energized Christians of reverence know that Christ wants to inhabit their thoughts; and they never forget him as they assess the daily patterns and habits of life.

How does Satan, via his deceptive PSYOP, neutralize believers? He attacks their unguarded minds, and never before has

---

8. Reverence is profoundly felt and visibly displayed honor and worship. Due to his awe-inspiring power and majesty, the Lord deserves the utmost level of reverence (Lev 19:30). Everyone who encounters the awe-inspiring majesty of the Lord God Almighty automatically responds with reverence, according to the Bible (Num 20:6; Judg 13:20; 1 Chr 21:16).

9. See Eph 5:1–9.

he had so many ways to do so. In today's entertainment-crazed society, there is television, the internet, social media, movies, magazines, and so on. First Pet 5:8–9 says, "Be sober, be vigilant; because your adversary the devil walks about like a roaring lion, seeking whom he may devour. Resist him, steadfast in the faith, knowing that the same sufferings are experienced by your brotherhood in the world." Getting serious about God-honoring, reverent thinking means a mind that is guarded and purged of anything that invites Satan's devouring powers to be at work. Accordingly, here is a test to see what happens when every part of our life is not reverently God's.

Have You Lost Your Spiritual Appetite?

When a believer is feeding their mind with spoiled, tainted, or poisoned food, they begin to show these symptoms: Is it hard to read the Word after you watch certain movies?[10] Has your music collection become more precious than your Bible? Do you feel unable to stop thinking, imagining, and replaying thoughts that displease God?[11] As individuals who have been given the responsibility of safeguarding the presence of Christ within our minds, it is imperative that we experience a sense of unease in the presence of horror, sensual, and occult imagery. Furthermore, we should refrain from engaging in the long-term retention of entertainment that is characterized by foolishness, coarseness, filthiness, and a lack of reverence for the divine sanctity of our Almighty God who

---

10. Brain researchers conclude that we have stored three trillion "videotape" images in our brains by the time we are thirty years old. Sadly, there is no delete button for our minds, and once the images are stored there, we must then live with their spiritual consequences. Given the content of much of the media that is being irrevocably loaded into the memory banks of the minds of Americans, we need to do whatever it takes to renew and purify our minds. (Ted Baehr, "Miracle on Main Street?," 2)

11. Isa 33:15: "He who walks righteously and speaks uprightly, He who despises the gain of oppressions, Who gestures with his hands, refusing bribes, Who stops his ears from hearing of bloodshed, And shuts his eyes from seeing evil."

resides within us. If you believe you've lost your spiritual appetite, repent of any polluted or spiritually harmful pictures in your mind and seek God to rekindle your hunger and thirst for his Word.

Have You Lost Your Conviction Over Sin?

The following are some signs of spiritual insensitivity: Have you started to wonder if some sins aren't really that bad? Do words that previously upset you no longer upset you? Do images that used to bother you as displeasing to God no longer bother you? Is there a never-ending list of things you wish you could have that others have? Idolatry is defined as anything that takes God's proper place in the lives of his children. Idolatry occurs when job, entertainment, money-making, pleasure-seeking, collection-gathering, bodybuilding, or beauty-enhancing begin to erode God's role in your life. If you believe you have lost your conviction about sin, repent of allowing yourself to become insensitive to God and mourn the loss of his Spirit. Request a new cleaning and filling of his Spirit.

Have You Lost Your Longing for God's presence?

Here are some signs that you are spiritually lukewarm: Have immoral entertainers in music and cinema become idols you seek out and admire?[12] Are you gradually admitting defeat in some areas of your life because it is simply too difficult to obey the Lord, escape evil, and seek to discipline your body, mind, and emotions in the face of the flood of sin that surrounds us every day? If we think God's Word is the ultimate truth, we are led closer to what he loves with each passing day; if we are strangers to his truth, we are drawn further away from what pleases, honors, and magnifies him. According to James 3, there are only two sources of wisdom: above and below. What is the source of your wisdom? Do

---

12. If so, God says you are corrupting you mind. 1 Cor 15:33 says, "Do not be deceived: 'Evil company corrupts good habits.'"

you understand how to test, verify, and confirm truth? Only God's Word is the dependable source of all truth required to please God. If you are not being filled with God's truth through his Word, you are being filled with counterfeit truth, which is neither from God nor pleasing to him. Loving the world (everything that does not satisfy God) is an unavoidable path to confusion, corruption, and emptiness.[13] If you've lost your longing for God's presence, love him with all your heart, with all you do, and tell him that loving him is the most essential thing to you.

Personal Sanctification

Personal sanctification is the only way to recover from a corroded mind, a mind that has become neutralized, where evil seeps in a little more each day. Grace-energized Christians abstain from lust-promoting activities.[14] If there are specific areas you know right now are sin, you must repent of them and stop![15] Satan's deceptive PSYOP aim to neutralize Christians so that they are no longer engaged in the spiritual fight. Do not let Satan take you out of the fight. As Christians, we must understand that we are engaged in spiritual warfare merely by virtue of being in Christ. To meaningfully participate in this fight, we must "move toward the enemy." On June 6, 1944, Operation Overlord (commonly referred to as D-Day), the largest seaborne invasion in history, launched as Allied forces landed on Normandy beach and confronted the until-then impenetrable German military. In that moment, the only way to survive, obtain a foothold for succeeding forces, and win the war was to—contrary to intuition—move

---

13. 1 John 2:15–17: "Do not love the world or the things in the world. If anyone loves the world, the love of the Father is not in him. For all that is in the world—the lust of the flesh, the lust of the eyes, and the pride of life—is not of the Father but is of the world. And the world is passing away, and the lust of it; but he who does the will of God abides forever."

14. Barnett, "Sober Minded—Choosing Restrained Living In An Unrestrained Culture."

15. 1 Pet 2:11: "Beloved, I beg you as sojourners and pilgrims, abstain from fleshly lusts which war against the soul."

A FINAL WORD ON SATAN'S TACTIC OF DECEPTION

toward the enemy. In a spiritual context, this means championing truth. This entails holding and defending the inerrancy of the biblical text. Lastly, and most importantly, this means "not [being] ashamed of the gospel of Christ, for it is the power of God to salvation for everyone who believes" (Rom 1:16). War has been declared, and we are engaged in pitched battle. However, unlike in human wars, the ultimate victor is known. Let us all join in the fight, move toward the enemy, and, ultimately, stand for truth. As Jesus encourages us, "And you shall know the truth, and the truth shall make you free" (John 8:32).[16]

HOT WASH

On May 13, 1940, Winston Churchill, the then Prime Minister of the United Kingdom, delivered his famous "blood, toil, tears, and sweat" speech to the House of Commons of the Parliament of the United Kingdom, which stated, in part: "What is our aim? I can answer in one word: Victory. Victory at all costs—Victory in spite of all terror—Victory, however long and hard the road may be, for without victory there is no survival." By virtue of being in Christ, Christians will have victory (1 Cor 15:57), but, as in every war, the road to victory will be turbulent.

Eph 6:12 states that "we wrestle not against flesh and blood, but against principalities, against powers, against the rulers of the darkness of this world, against spiritual wickedness in high places." While they are not as powerful as God, Satan and his demon army are a formidable opposing evil force, and they are engaged in spiritual warfare with God and humanity—a warfare that manifests, in part, by deception. As this guide has discussed, Satan's deception continues to create confusion worldwide. Deception is his greatest

---

16. Corrado, "Move Toward the Enemy." Allen Dulles, the fifth and longest-serving Director of the Central Intelligence Agency, took a personal interest in the construction of the CIA's Original Headquarters Building. At the dedication ceremony, Dulles included a quotation in his speech: "And Ye Shall Know the Truth and the Truth Shall Make You Free" (John 8:32, KJV). Additionally, Dulles insisted that these words be fixed in stone in the building's lobby.

armament, and humanity will continue to combat this weapon of spiritual mass destruction until God ultimately banishes Satan, as per Rev 20:10.

A parallel was established between Satan's deceptive tactics and military PSYOP, "planned operations to convey selected [false] information and indicators to . . . audiences to influence their emotions, motives, [and] objective reasoning,"[17] because both seek to lead people into falsehood. PSYOP are designed to convey a biased notion of reality to an audience so that they will react as the aggressor wishes. PSYOP tactics and employment in a terrestrial, human sense shed light on Satanic deceptive tactics in a spiritual sense and help humankind to construct defenses to avoid its harmful effects. As this guide has conveyed, military PSYOP can define how Satan wages his deception campaign, and with this understanding, Christians can be better equipped to deter deception. The defenses derived from understanding Satan's deceptive tactics in the context of PSYOP were the counter-PSYOP methods of conditioning, forestalling, direct refutation, restrictive measures, and indirect refutation. Via these means, the Christian can engage in spiritual combat and "be able to stand against the wiles of the devil" (Eph 6:11).

---

17. Joint Chiefs of Staff, *Military Deception*, I-8–I-9.

Appendix A
Absolute (or Universal) Truth

A man may imagine things that are false, but he can only understand things that are true, for if the things be false, the apprehension of them is not understanding.

—Isaac Newton

This appendix touches on the concept of absolute (or universal) truth and its necessity in the context of the truth of Scripture.

"TRUTH WITHOUT LOVE IS BRUTALITY, AND LOVE WITHOUT TRUTH IS HYPOCRISY"[1]

The concept of truth is hotly debated. The difficulty we face is not whether individuals desire to know the answer to the question, "What is truth?" but rather, as our culture becomes more "enlightened," the growing divergence from our conventional understanding and definition of truth. Consequently, the significance of this question is heightened in modern society. In order to provide context for the counter-PSYOP method of *Indirect Refutation* and the truth of the Bible, it is important to grasp the existence of and necessity for absolute (or universal) truth.[2]

---

1. Wiersbe, *On Being a Leader for God*, 39.
2. Drawn from Got Questions Ministries, "Is there such a thing as absolute truth/universal truth?" and Geisler, *The Big Book of Christian Apologetics*, 562–66.

APPENDIX A

To apprehend absolute or universal truth, it is necessary to first define truth. *Merriam-Webster's Collegiate Dictionary* defines it as "the property (as of a statement) of being in accord with fact or reality; a judgment, proposition, or idea that is true or accepted as true." According to some, there is no objective reality, only perceptions and opinions. Others would contend that there must be an absolute truth or reality.

According to one viewpoint, there are no absolutes that define reality. Those who hold this view believe that since everything is relative to something else, there is no objective reality.[3] They believe that (1) truth is invented, not discovered; (2) truth is relative, and each culture or individual defines what is truth for themselves; and (3) since truth is invented, there is no universal transcultural truth. Depending on their background and perspective, each culture or individual will define truth differently; (4) the nature of the truth is subject to change. Since it is inextricably linked to individuals and cultures that constantly change, truth is ever-changing; (5) since truth is a matter of group or individual perspective, one's beliefs can alter a truth statement; (6) since an individual determines truth, truth is affected by the attitude of the one professing it; (7) there is no such thing as absolute truth; (8) absolute truth cannot be known. Absolute and objective truth cannot be known because it is based on the ever-changing perceptions of humans. Since each person's perception is different, the truth cannot be known.[4] Therefore, there are no moral absolutes and no authority to determine whether an action is positive or negative, right or wrong. This perspective leads to "situational ethics," the belief that right and wrong depend on circumstances.[5] Since

---

3. Cultural relativism maintains there is objective reality because all systems of truth are culturally constructed, at least according to the postmoderns of our day. This leads to extreme distrust in any kind of objective or absolute claim. So according to postmodern thinking, ethics are conceived within communities through consensus/coercion (power).

4. McCallum, *The Death of Truth*, 31.

5. For clarity, situational ethics are not necessarily postmodern because even non-postmoderns will employ situational ethics. For example, is it wrong to kill a person? It depends on the situation (e.g., a soldier in combat, etc.).

there is no right or wrong, whatever feels or seems right at the time and in the given circumstance is right. Obviously, situational ethics leads to a subjective "whatever feels good" mentality and lifestyle, which has devastating consequences for society and individuals. This is postmodernism, which is in essence building a society that regards all beliefs, values, lifestyles, and truth claims as equally valid.[6] Further, postmodernism is a rejection of reality and implies that our perceptions of reality are cultural/communal constructions. It is important to understand that a worldview like postmodernism is complex and comprises many parts.[7]

The opposing viewpoint asserts that there are, in fact, absolute realities and standards that characterize what is true and what is false. Therefore, actions can be judged as right or wrong based on their conformance to these absolute standards. Chaos ensues if there are no absolutes and no actuality. Consider the law of gravity, for example. If it were not an absolute, we could not be certain that we would remain standing or seated until we decided to move. Or, if two plus two did not always equal four, the results would be catastrophic for civilization. There would be no relevance for the laws of science and physics, and commerce would be impossible. Fortunately, two plus two equals four. Absolute truth exists and can be discovered and apprehended.

Although it is illogical to assert that there is no absolute truth, many individuals today embrace a cultural relativism that denies its existence. In addition to the problem of self-contradiction, there are

---

Additionally, situational ethics are not necessarily "feel good" ethics. "Feel good" ethics would be more akin to non-cognitive theories of ethics, such as emotivism or expressivism. These types of ethics imply that an ethical sentence like "stealing is wrong" is neither true nor false but only expresses linguistic emotion within a sentence: it expresses how I feel (emotivisim).

6. Postmodernism is a late-twentieth-century movement characterized by broad skepticism, subjectivism, or relativism; a general suspicion of reason; and an acute sensitivity to the role of ideology in asserting and maintaining political and economic power. (*Britannica*)

7. It is difficult to succinctly encapsulate this viewpoint, as there are many nuances. For a more thorough exposition on this topic, see James Sire, *The Universe Next Door: A Basic Worldview Catalog*, 5th ed. (Westmont, IL: IVP Academic, 2009).

a number of additional logical obstacles that must be surmounted in order to accept that there are no absolute or universal truths. One is that because all humans have limited knowledge and finite minds, it is logically impossible for them to make absolute negative statements. A person cannot logically assert "There is no God" (although many do so) because to do so would require absolute knowledge of the entirety of the universe's existence, spanning from its beginning to its end. Since this is impossible, the most anyone can logically assert is, "Based on my limited knowledge, I do not believe in God."

Another issue with the denial of absolute or universal truth is that it contradicts what we know to be true from our own consciences, experiences, and observations of the actual world. If there is no such thing as absolute truth, then nothing is right or wrong in the final analysis. What is "right" for you does not necessarily make it "right" for me. On the surface, this type of relativism is appealing, but it actually means that everyone establishes his or her own rules and does what he or she believes is right.[8] Eventually, one person's sense of justice will collide with that of another. If there is no absolute truth and no universal standard of right and wrong, then we can never be certain of anything. People would be free to do whatever they want, including murder, rape, theft, lying, and cheating—and no one could object. There would be no government, no laws, and no justice, as it would be impossible to assert that the majority has the authority to impose standards on the minority. A universe devoid of absolutes would be the most horrifying universe imaginable.

Spiritually, this type of relativism leads to religious confusion, as there is no one true religion and no way to have a proper

---

8. It is important to note that there is no neutrality—no neutral position. The Bible clearly conveys this concept in Matt 12:30, Eph 5:8, Matt 7:13–14, Matt 7:24–26, Rom 8:7, and Rom 1:17–19, among many others. People are not neutral because "all have sinned" (Rom 3:23) and "the heart is deceitful above all things, and disparately wicked; Who can know it?" (Jer 17:9). Because of this, the younger generations are succumbing to increasingly atheistic indoctrination. This opens the door for them to be conditioned into accepting moral relativism as they're propagandized to conform to the world's acceptance of the LGBTQ+ worldview, abortion, critical race theory, atheistic evolution, man-made climate change, and so on. (Ham, *Divided Nation*, 13–16)

ABSOLUTE (OR UNIVERSAL) TRUTH

relationship with God. Therefore, all religions would be false, as they all make absolute claims about the afterlife. Today, there exists a prevailing tendency among individuals to hold the belief that two religions with fundamentally opposing beliefs could be equally "true," despite the fact that both religions assert exclusivity as the sole means to get to heaven or espouse conflicting notions of "truth." People who do not believe in absolute truth disregard these assertions and embrace a more tolerant universalism that teaches that all religions are equal and that all roads lead to heaven. People who hold this worldview fiercely oppose evangelical Christians who believe that Jesus is "the way, the truth, and the life" (John 14:6) and that he is the ultimate manifestation of truth and the sole means to get to heaven.

Tolerance has become the sole cardinal virtue of postmodern society, the sole absolute, and therefore intolerance is the sole vice. Any dogmatic belief, particularly a belief in absolute truth, is regarded as the ultimate sin of intolerance. Those who deny absolute truth frequently assert that it is permissible to believe whatever you want, so long as you do not attempt to impose your beliefs on others. However, this view itself is a belief about what is right and wrong, and those who hold it do attempt to impose it on others. They set a behavior standard that they insist others adhere to, thereby violating the very principle they claim to uphold. This is yet another self-contradictory position. Those who hold this belief are merely unwilling to accept responsibility for their actions. If there is absolute truth, then there must be absolute standards of right and wrong, for which we are responsible. When individuals deny absolute truth, they are, in fact, rejecting this accountability.

The denial of absolute or universal truth and its accompanying cultural relativism are the logical consequence of a society that accepts evolution as the explanation for life. If naturalistic evolution were true, then life has no meaning and there is no absolute right or wrong. Humans are then unaccountable for their actions and free to live as they please. David Jeremiah, in Henry Morris' book *The Long War Against God: The History and Impact of the*

APPENDIX A

Creation/Evolution Conflict, unambiguously expresses the consequences of a foundation built on evolutionism:

> Many layers of error have been built on the faulty foundation of evolutionism. Humanism is the natural result. If God is not central in all our thinking, then man must be. Atheism is humanism's twin brother, and consistent evolutionists cannot logically believe in the personal God of the Bible, the God who is the Creator of all life. Abortion, infanticide, and euthanasia are logical behaviors for those who have so easily disposed of the image of God in the eternal soul of man. The concept of a resurrected body and eternal life is also a casualty of this evil philosophy. The average person neither knows nor cares much about the error of evolution, and yet his or her life is constantly being influenced by it. Pornography, adultery, divorce, homosexuality, premarital sex, the destruction of the nuclear family—all are weeds that have grown from Satan's big lie about the universe. We are now on the verge of adopting full-fledged animalism in human practice—promiscuity, vandalism, hedonism, even incipient cannibalism. Even the Holocaust is "explained" by evolution. Hitler's extermination of the Jews grew out of his desire to speed up the evolutionary process.[9]

Nevertheless, regardless of how much sinful men and women deny the existence of God and absolute truth, they will one day face his judgment.[10]

Is there evidence for the existence of absolute truth? Yes. First, there is the human conscience, that "something" within us that informs us that the world ought to be a certain way and that some things are right, and others are wrong. Our conscience convinces us that suffering, starvation, rape, agony, and evil are wrong, and it makes us aware that love, generosity, compassion, and peace are desirable qualities to pursue. This is true in all cultures and at all periods. Rom 2:14–16 describes the function of the human conscience: "For when Gentiles, who do not have the

---

9. Morris, *The Long War Against God*, 9.
10. See Rom 1:19–22.

ABSOLUTE (OR UNIVERSAL) TRUTH

law, by nature do the things in the law, these, although not having the law, are a law to themselves, who show the work of the law written in their hearts, their conscience also bearing witness, and between themselves their thoughts accusing or else excusing them in the day when God will judge the secrets of men by Jesus Christ, according to my gospel."

Science is the second piece of evidence for the existence of absolute truth. Science is merely the pursuit of knowledge, the study of what we already know, and the search for additional information. Therefore, all scientific research must be predicated on the belief that there are objective realities in the world that can be discovered and demonstrated. Without absolutes, there is nothing to investigate. How could one verify the accuracy of scientific findings? In fact, scientific laws are based on the existence of absolute truth.

Religion is the third evidence for the existence of absolute or universal truth. All of the world's religions attempt to define and lend meaning to life. They are the result of man's desire for more than a basic existence. Humans seek God, hope for the future, forgiveness of sins, peace in the midst of struggle, and answers to our most fundamental questions through religion. Religion is proof that humans are more than just highly evolved animals. It is evidence of a higher purpose and of the existence of a personal and purposeful Creator who implanted the desire to know him within man. And if there is a Creator, then he is the standard for absolute truth, and his authority establishes that truth.

Thankfully, such a Creator exists, and he has revealed his truth to us through his Word, the Bible. Absolute or universal truth can only be known through a personal relationship with Jesus Christ, who professes to be the Truth.[11] Jesus asserted in John 14:6 that

---

11. The word "truth" in Greek is *aletheia*, which denotes "divine revelation" and is related to a word that literally means "what can't be hidden." It represents the idea that truth is never concealed or disguised; rather, it is constantly present, available for everyone to see and understand. *Emeth*, which also means "firmness," "constancy," and "duration," is the Hebrew word for "truth." Such a definition suggests an enduring substance and something trustworthy. (Liddell and Scott, *Greek-English Lexicon*)

he is the only way, the only truth, the only life, and the only way to God. The existence of absolute truth indicates that there is a sovereign God who created the cosmos and the Earth and who has revealed himself to us so that we may know him personally through his Son, Jesus Christ. That is the absolute truth.

Evolution Elaborated

According to Rom 1:25 (NIV), "they exchanged the truth about God for a lie, and worshiped and served created things rather than the Creator—who is forever praised. Amen."

Motivation, Logic, and Biblical Compatibility

A key component in the ongoing debate surrounding creation versus evolution is that the majority of evolution-believing scientists are agnostics or atheists.[12] Some, on the other hand, hold a deistic view of God, in which he exists but is not engaged in the world; furthermore, they believe that everything unfolds in a seamless and organic fashion. Many individuals assess the data with sincerity and candor and conclude that evolution is a more accurate explanation than creation. Nevertheless, the prevailing viewpoint in this debate is that evolution is in some way incompatible with both faith in God and the Bible.

It is notable to recognize that some scientists who hold to evolution also hold convictions regarding God and the Bible, without perceiving any contradiction between the two. However, an overwhelming consensus among evolutionary scientists is that life developed in its entirety, devoid of any divine intervention. Practically speaking, contemporary theories of evolution are almost completely a naturalistic science.

Of course, there are spiritual motivators propelling some of these views. In order for atheism to be considered valid, an

---

12. Additionally, a subset of individuals maintain a variant of evolution, called theistic evolution.

ABSOLUTE (OR UNIVERSAL) TRUTH

alternative explanation must exist for the origin of the universe and life, one that does not involve a Creator. While the concept of evolution predates Charles Darwin, it was Darwin who initially proposed natural selection as a credible and plausible source for the evolutionary process. Darwin formerly identified as a Christian; however, subsequent to a series of unfortunate events, he renounced both the Christian faith and the existence of God.

It was not Darwin's intention to refute the existence of God, nor did he consider his theory to do so. Regrettably, his concepts have been propagated in this manner by individuals seeking to facilitate atheism.[13] Numerous contemporary Bible believers oppose modern evolutionary theory, in part, because it is frequently accompanied by an imposed atheistic worldview. It is unlikely that evolutionary scientists would acknowledge that their objective is to provide an alternative account of the inception of life, thus establishing a basis for atheism. Nevertheless, the Bible suggests that this is one reason why the theory of evolution is currently approached as it is. To further this point, Oxford evolutionist Richard Dawkins, a British evolutionary biologist and author, said: "The more you understand the significance of evolution, the more you are pushed away from an agnostic position and towards atheism. Complex, statistically improbable things are by their nature more difficult to explain than simple, statistically probable things."[14]

As expressed in the Bible in no uncertain terms, "The fool says in his heart, 'There is no God'" (Ps 14:1; 53:1, NIV). Additionally, the Bible asserts that individuals have no justification for not believing in a Creator God: "For since the creation of the world His invisible attributes are clearly seen, being understood by the things that are made, even His eternal power and Godhead, so that they are without excuse" (Rom 1:20). A fool, according to the Bible, is

---

13. As quoted in *Why I Believe* by D. James Kennedy: "It is well known that Karl Marx asked Darwin to write the introduction to *Das Kapital*, since he felt that Darwin had provided a scientific foundation for communism. Throughout this century, all over the world, those who pushed the communist conspiracy also pushed an evolutionary, imperialistic, naturalistic view of life, endeavoring to crowd the Creator right out of the cosmos." (Kennedy, *Why I Believe*, 38)

14. Fisher, *The Logic of Real Arguments*, 84.

one who rejects the existence of God. Foolishness, however, does not indicate an absence of intelligence as evolutionary scientists are intellectually bright. Conversely, foolishness signifies an improper application of acquired knowledge as Prov 1:7 declares, "The fear of the Lord is the beginning of knowledge, but fools despise wisdom and instruction."

Creation and/or intelligent design are often mocked by evolution-supporting atheists as unscientific and devoid of merit for scientific investigation. They contend that for something to be classified as a "science," it must possess "naturalistic characteristics." By definition, creation transcends the rules of the natural universe. The controversy is that since God cannot be subjected to scientific testing, then neither creation nor intelligent design can be regarded as scientific.

From a strictly scientific standpoint to the same extent, both evolution and intelligent design cannot be directly observed or tested. However, it appears that atheistic evolutionists do not consider this to be problematic. Consequently, all data are subjected to the filtering process of naturalism's preconceived, presupposed, and pre-accepted worldview, without accommodating any alternative explanations.

The investigation or firsthand observation of the origin of the universe or life is not possible. Acceptance of both creation and evolution necessitates a degree of faith. It is not possible to travel back in time in order to observe the universe's or life's origin. Individuals who vehemently oppose creation do so on the basis of arguments that would logically compel them to also reject evolution.

A Creator exists, to whom we are answerable. Evolution, in its contemporary form, facilitates an atheistic worldview. Evolution provides atheists an explanation for the development of life apart

ABSOLUTE (OR UNIVERSAL) TRUTH

from a Creator God.[15] Modern theories of evolution therefore function as an alternative "creation story" to the atheistic religion.[16]

It is unambiguously clear in the Bible that God is the Creator. Any scientific view that seeks to exclude God's involvement in the origins of the universe is incompatible with the Bible.

Scientific Perspective

While motive, logic, and biblical compatibility have been examined, how does scientific inquiry influence the debate? Scientifically, there are six significant problems with evolution:

1. The majority of contemporary scientists concur that the universe had a beginning. This implies the existence of a Creator (Heb 3:4: "For every house is built by someone, but He who built all things is God").

2. The universe is so perfectly fine-tuned for life on Earth that it must have been created by an intelligent Designer [God] (Rom 1:20 and Ps 19:1: "For since the creation of the world, His invisible attributes are clearly seen, being understood by the things that are made, even His eternal power and Godhead, so that they are without excuse . . . the heavens declare the glory of God, And the firmament [expanse of heaven] shows His handiwork").

3. If evolution were true, fossil records would reveal increasingly complex and transitional evolutionary forms. However, no transitional connections between species have been discovered in the fossil records.

---

15. William Provine (1942–2015) of Cornell University, an American historian of science and of evolutionary biology and population genetics, stated in a debate, "If Darwinism is true, he said, then there are five inescapable conclusions: there's no evidence for God, there's no life after death, there's no absolute foundation for right and wrong, there's no ultimate meaning for life, people don't really have free will." (Strobel, *The Case for a Creator*, 26)

16. Got Questions Ministries, "What Does the Bible say About Creation vs. Evolution?"

4. Evolution presupposes a lengthy series of beneficial and ascending mutations. In almost all known instances, however, mutations are detrimental to living organisms. This is a significant obstacle for evolution.

5. The Second Law of Thermodynamics, which has never been refuted by observable nature, states that in an isolated system (such as our universe), the natural progression of events is degenerate. The universe is descending rather than ascending. In a system that is closed and isolated, the quantity of usable energy decreases. In other words, matter and energy degrade progressively with time. Additionally, things tend to move from order to chaos, not vice versa.

6. Evolutionists frequently make false assertions. Some have asserted that scientific evidence proves evolution to be true. In general, they rely on the fact that mutations do occur within species (microevolution). To argue that mutations within species prove that mutations can produce entirely new species (macroevolution) requires an extraordinary leap of logic. Two dogs cannot produce a cat![17]

Critiquing Darwinism does not make one anti-science. We all possess identical scientific evidence. Which theory or interpretive framework best explains the evidence is the question. As expressed by C.K. Chesterton (1874–1936), an English writer, philosopher, Christian apologist, and literary and art critic, "It is absurd for the evolutionists to complain that it's unthinkable for an admittedly unthinkable God to make everything out of nothing and then pretend it is more thinkable that nothing should turn itself into anything."[18]

---

17. Rhodes, *5-Minute Apologetics for Today*, 58.

18. For resources on creation science, see the Institute for Creation Science (www.icr.org), Creation Ministries International (www.creation.com), and Answers in Genesis (https://answersingenesis.org), among others.

Imago Dei

One of the critical and most wonderful features of the creation is humans being made in God's image. There are numerous unbiblical interpretations of what it means to be human. For example, naturalism—which stems from evolutionary theory—sees humanity as a highly sophisticated, physical machine with no spirit at all—any feelings, ideas, or inspirations we experience are purely the result of chemical processes within our brains. This, of course, is not supported by the Bible and robs meaning and purpose from humanity. Only creation gives meaning, purpose, and hope to humanity and paves the way to eternal life. Being made in the image of God makes redemption possible.

On days one through five of the creation week, God developed and populated the originally empty ("without form and void") Earth introduced in Gen 1:2. He did so with great precision and tact to form a magnificent backdrop on which to place his crowning creative achievement, humankind. Not only did God save the best for last, but he created humans distinctly different from animals. Human life was segregated in distinct relation to God, as Gen 1:26 explains: by the divine plan ("let us make man"), by the divine pattern ("in our image"), and by the divine purpose ("let them have dominion"). Being in the image of God (imago Dei) is not simply an attribute bestowed by God and retained by humans. It is the essence of God's perfect attributes reflected in humankind, who were specifically designed to represent God on Earth and reflect these attributes. More succinctly, being an image-bearer of God is what humankind is rather than something humankind has.

As with the animals, God formed Adam from the dust, but he "breathed into his nostrils the breath of life; and man became a living soul" (Gen 2:7, KJV). Thus, humanity is unique and expressly set apart among God's creations, possessing both a material body and an immaterial soul.

The material part of humans is not to be thought to directly resemble God as having flesh and blood. Nevertheless, it echoes the life of God, as it was formed in perfect health and was not originally subject to death. The immaterial part of humans reflects the image of God (1) morally because humankind was created in righteousness and perfect innocence that reflects God's holiness, (2) mentally because humans have the ability to reason and choose, which reflects God's intellect and freedom, and (3) socially because humanity was created for fellowship, reflecting God's triune nature and his love. Hence these three attributes make a relationship between God and humans possible and endow humans with great capacity and, therefore, responsibility.

Since humans have significant capacity, they are able to make free choices; however, these choices (and their consequences) are their responsibility. Unfortunately, Adam and Eve made a fatal choice of which all humanity bears the scars and the responsibility. In so doing, they blemished the image of God within humankind. Jas 3:9 affirms that we still manifest the image of God, but we also exhibit the damage of sin. In *Systematic Theology* (444), Wayne Grudem explains this clearly:

> Since man has sinned, he is certainly not as fully like God as he was before. His moral purity has been lost and his sinful character certainly does not reflect God's holiness. His intellect is corrupted by falsehood and misunderstanding; his speech no longer continually glorifies God; his relationships are often governed by selfishness rather than love, and so forth. Though man is still in the image of God, in every aspect of life some parts of that image have been distorted or lost.

Since humankind was designed specifically to be the image-bearer of God, if that characteristic were eliminated, humans would cease to be humans. Furthermore, by virtue of retaining God's image, blemished by sin as it is, humans are redeemable and, by God's perfect love and abundant grace, are worth redeeming.

Thankfully, we have a perfect, omniscient Redeemer. He anticipated our fallenness and was therefore "slain from the foundation of the world" (Rev 13:8) to restore the original image of God in humanity. This action formed a "new man, which was created according to God, in true righteousness and holiness" (Eph 4:24). Faith in the redemptive act of Christ is the only way to restore humankind to its created imago Dei stature. As 2 Cor 5:17 states, "Therefore if anyone is in Christ, he is a new creation; old things have passed away; behold, all things have become new."[19]

---

19. Corrado, "Imago Dei: Man's Designed Role as Image-Bearer."

Appendix B
The Foundation of the Gospel

> We long to be successful Fishers for Jesus! But we are tempted to try methods which Jesus would never have tried. Shall we yield to this suggestion of the enemy? We must follow Jesus to succeed. Can we imagine the Lord Jesus using such means as are now commonly used? We must preach our Lord's Doctrine and proclaim a full gospel, for this is the net in which souls are taken. We must preach with his gentleness, boldness, and love to have success with human hearts. We must work under divine anointing, depending upon the Holy Spirit. Then we shall be fishers of men.
>
> —CHARLES SPURGEON, *FAITH'S CHECKBOOK*

UNDERSTANDING THE FOUNDATION OF the Gospel is extremely important. The Gospel is based on the following pillar: we are to "enter by the narrow gate; for wide is the gate and broad is the way that leads to destruction, and there are many who go in by it. Because narrow is the gate and difficult is the way which leads to life, and there are few who find it" (Matt 7:13–14).

Jesus says in Matt 7:21–23, "Not everyone who says to Me, 'Lord, Lord,' shall enter the kingdom of heaven, but he who does the will of My Father in heaven. Many will say to Me in that day, 'Lord, Lord, have we not prophesied in Your name, cast out demons in Your name, and done many wonders in Your name?' And then I will declare to them, 'I never knew you; depart from Me, you who practice lawlessness!'" Notice that those discussed in this verse were doing things in the Lord's name rather than trusting what Christ had done. Also, as they never departed from iniquity, there was no repentance.

While the Gospel is extremely simple,[1] a thorough understanding and biblical foundation are important, as this is a playground for Satan's deceptive PSYOP in false (non-saving) religions. This appendix discusses the foundational aspects of the Gospel, including God's Word as the supreme authority; the sufficiency of Christ; the characteristics of the Gospel, including its relationship to works and justification; the substitutionary atonement of Christ; the importance of fully trusting in Jesus for salvation; and dying to self. To completely grasp the Gospel, it is important to fully implement the counter-PSYOP method of *Conditioning*.

GOD'S WORD IS THE SUPREME AUTHORITY

Scripture has authority over us, as "all Scripture is inspired by God and profitable for teaching, for reproof, for correction, for training in righteousness" (2 Tim 3:16). As per Ps 138:2, God has exalted his name and his word above all things. Why do we need to rely on Scripture? The answer is given in Heb 4:12: "It is sharper than a two-edged sword." Therefore, we can use it to slay all the lies of the Devil. Every lie under the sun can be destroyed by the truth of God's word! It pierces and penetrates and cuts to the depths of the soul and never returns void, which simply means that when you proclaim the Word of God, it brings salvation to those who believe it and further condemnation for those who reject it—but it always accomplishes its purpose.

The Word of God judges. Before anyone can be saved, their sin must be judged by the Word of God. It is living and active. No other words can bring life to a dead soul. Human words have no authority or power to bring anyone to life in Christ. We must use the Gospel, "for it is the power of God to salvation for everyone who believes" (Rom 1:16). We need to use the law for conviction

---

1. See 1 Cor 15:1–4.

of sin. Rom 3:20 says, "Therefore by the deeds of the law no flesh will be justified in His sight, for by the law is the knowledge of sin"; thus the law brings mankind to a knowledge of their sin and condemnation under God's wrath. And Rom 3:19 says, the law was given so that every mouth may be closed and the whole world may become accountable to God. Lastly, no one is righteous.[2]

The Word of God is the truth. "If you abide in My word, you are My disciples indeed. And you shall know the truth, and the truth shall make you free" (John 8:31–32)—free from religious deception (deceptive PSYOP) and from the bondage of Satan.[3]

---

2. See Rom 3:10. Colossians 2 deals with the dangers a church faces when the sufficiency of Scripture is challenged and merged with non-biblical writings, full of ungodly theology and concepts. Paul warned the church at Colossae, "See to it that no one takes you captive through hollow and deceptive philosophy, which depends on human tradition and the basic principles of this world rather than on Christ" (Col 2:8). Jude puts it even more specifically: "Beloved, while I was very diligent to write to you concerning our common salvation, I found it necessary to write to you exhorting you to contend earnestly for the faith which was once for all delivered to the saints" (Jude 1:3). Notice the phrase "once for all." This makes it clear that no other writings, no matter how godly the pastor, theologian, or denominational church they may come from, are to be seen as equal to or completing the Word of God. The Bible is all that is necessary for the believer to understand the character of God, the nature of man, and the doctrines of sin, heaven, hell, and salvation through Jesus Christ. Paul's words to the Galatians indicate the seriousness of delivering a message outside the Bible: ". . . if we, or an angel from heaven, preach any other gospel to you than what we have preached to you, let him be accursed" (Gal 1:8).

3. Gendron, *Preparing for Eternity*, 5–18. The doctrine of biblical inerrancy is extremely important because truth matters. This issue reflects on the character of God and is foundational to our understanding of everything the Bible teaches. Christians should absolutely believe in biblical inerrancy because (1) the Bible itself claims to be perfect (Ps 12:6; 19:7; Prov 30:5). The Bible claims complete perfection, thwarting "partial perfection" theories; (2) The Bible stands or falls as a whole. It is either a trustworthy document, or it is not; (3) The Bible reflects its Author. The Bible was written by God himself via "inspiration" through human writers (2 Tim 3:16; 2 Pet 1:21; Jer 1:2); (4) The Bible judges us, not the other way around (Heb 4:12); (5) The Bible's message must be regarded as a whole. It is not an assortment of doctrines that Christians are free to select from (Ps 119:89); and (6) The Bible is our only rule for faith and practice (see Appendix D). It is important to note that biblical inerrancy does not mean that we are to accept the Bible blindly. We are commanded to study the Word (2 Tim 2:15), and those who search it out are commended (Acts 17:11).

CHRIST IS SUFFICIENT

Jesus Christ, who according to John 1:1–3 was preexistent with God the Father and created all things,[4] who is also the final prophet,[5]

Also, it is important to acknowledge that there are difficult passages in the Bible, as well as disagreements over some interpretations. Christians should approach Scripture reverently and prayerfully, and when something is found that is not understood, Christians should pray harder and study more, and if the answer still eludes, humbly acknowledge human limitations in the face of the perfect Scripture. (Grudem, *Systematic Theology*, 90–104)

4. To quote Heb 11:3, "By faith we understand that the worlds were framed by the word of God, so that the things which are seen were not made of things which are visible." Scholars take this to mean that the universe came into existence by divine command and was not assembled from preexisting matter or energy, thus *ex nihilo* (out of nothing).

5. The Old Testament teaches that God had a special and unique relationship with certain individuals who held the office of "prophet." Men like Moses, Isaiah, and Daniel had uncommon access to God due to their positions. Amos 3:7 says, "For the Lord GOD does nothing without revealing his secret to his servants the prophets." Whenever God wanted to communicate something to his people, he spoke through these prophets. So, an important question for us today is, "Do we still need prophets?" The answer, from the Bible, is an emphatic No! Here are three reasons: (1) Jesus replaces the prophets. Before Jesus' time, God's people needed mediators to stand between them and God. These priests and prophets provided a way for sinful people to communicate with and hear from God. But today, we no longer need these roles because, as per Heb 1:1, we have Jesus, the greater priest and prophet. Jesus supersedes the Old Testament Prophet. According to 1 Tim 2:5–6, in every way, he replaces our need for another man to stand between us and God. (2) Today, God's spirit is given to all Christians. Under the Old Covenant, God's Spirit was specially given to his prophets to equip them for their unique role. But this special giving of his Spirit was extremely limited. At any given time in Israel's history, only a small handful of people were gifted in this way. The rest of the people then were dependent upon these Spirit-filled men as intermediaries between them and God. But now God's Spirit is given freely to every Christian (John 14:26; Acts 2:17; Eph 1:13–14). There are no longer just a few who are Spirit-filled among God's people because now he gives the Holy Spirit to every believer. We no longer need prophets for God to speak to us because every Christian has immediate and unrestricted access to God through his Spirit who dwells within us. (3) Today, God's message is proclaimed by all Christians. The primary purpose of prophets was to receive a message from God, and then deliver it to the people. God's chosen messengers in the Old Testament were prophets, and his summary message was that people needed a Savior.

died once for all sin for all time; there are no more offerings for sin.⁶ He is able to save "to the uttermost those who come to God through Him" (Heb 7:25). He accomplished everything necessary to save sinners and then cried out in victory, "It is finished" (John 19:30).⁷ Nothing else needs to be done, as Jesus Christ did it all. Clearly, there is only one means to obtain salvation, and that is through a relationship with God the Father and his Son, Jesus.⁸

Jesus teaches us that God's message for people today is the good news (i.e., the Gospel) and that the ones charged to deliver this message are all of his disciples (Matt 28:18–20). Luke 16:16 says that the Bible teaches that the last prophet in history was John the Baptist, who concluded his ministry before Jesus' death. Today, God sends his disciples to proclaim his message rather than prophets. (Renner, *Apostles and Prophets*, 43–44)

6. See Heb 10:10, 12, 18.

7. In addition, the New Testament makes it abundantly clear that Christ is both the foundation (Acts 4:11–12; 1 Cor 3:11) and the head (Eph 5:23) of the church. It is a mistake to think that in Matt 16:18 he is giving either of those roles to Peter. There is a sense in which the apostles played a foundational role in the building of the church (Eph 2:20), but primacy is reserved for Christ alone, not assigned to Peter. So, Jesus' words in Matt 16:18 are best interpreted as a simple play on words in that a boulder-like (*petra*, "on this rock") truth came from the mouth of one who was called a small stone (*petros*, the word for "Peter"). And Christ himself is called the "chief cornerstone" (1 Pet 2:6–7). The chief cornerstone of any building was that upon which the building was anchored. If Christ declared himself to be the cornerstone, how could Peter be the rock upon which the church was built? It is more likely that the believers, of which Peter is one, are the stones which make up the church, anchored upon the Cornerstone, "and he who believes on Him will by no means be put to shame" (1 Pet 2:6). The Bible teaches us that Jesus Christ has all authority in heaven and on Earth; Jesus is the exclusive Head of the church (Matt 28:18; Col 1:18). (MacArthur, *The MacArthur Bible Commentary*, 1132–34)

8. See John 17:3. The Bible clearly teaches monotheism (that there is only one God, not a plurality of Gods). This truth is taught in Deut 6:4: "Hear O Israel: The Lord our God, the Lord is one." Isaiah writes about God, "Before me there was no god formed, nor will there be one after me" (Isa 43:10). There was no God created before or any to come, for there is only one God. Later he adds, "You are my witnesses. Is there any God besides me? No, there is no other Rock: I know not one." God knows of no other, not because God is limited in knowledge, but because there is no other like him in existence. Additionally, biblical Christianity teaches there is one God eternally coexisting in three persons—God the Father, God the Son, and God the Holy Spirit—not multiple gods. God has revealed himself in three coeternal and coequal persons of the

According to Acts 4:12, "nor is there salvation in any other, for there is no other name under heaven given among men by which we must be saved."[9]

THE COMPLETENESS OF THE GOSPEL FOR SALVATION

Below are several characteristics of the Gospel:

- *It is eternal.* The Gospel has the same message for every generation (Rev 14:6). It is the same Gospel first announced in the Garden of Eden that will go throughout the world, and then the end will come. Old Testament saints look forward to the cross to when their Messiah would die (Isa 53). New

---

same substance or essence, although distinct in subsistence. The Bible reveals that all three persons—Father, Son, and Holy Spirit—have the attributes of deity. All three took part in creation, have existed for eternity, and play a role in salvation. The whole, undivided essence of God belongs equally to each of the three persons. (Grudem, *Systematic Theology*, 226-61)

9. Gendron, *Preparing for Eternity*, 39–46. Is Jesus equal with God? Sadly, a Jehovah's Witness would answer "No." The logical follow-up question is, if Jesus were equal with God, what would that mean? In John 5:1–24, Jesus heals on the Sabbath, Jesus is confronted about it, and Jesus uses this moment to show his Deity, and this can be shown in the Jehovah's Witnesses' own translation of the Bible, the New World Translation. John 5:16–18 (NWT) says, "So on this account the Jews went persecuting Jesus, because he was doing these things during Sabbath. But he answered them, 'My Father has kept working until now, and I keep working.' On this account, indeed, the Jews began seeking all the more to kill him, because not only was he breaking the Sabbath but he was also calling God his own Father, making himself equal to God." This does not say that it was the Jews' opinion that Jesus was making himself equal with God. This is John's commentary declaring (in the NWT) that Jesus was in fact making himself equal with God. Further, in John 5:23 (NWT), "in order that all may honor the Son just as they honor the Father. He that does not honor the Son does not honor the Father who sent him." So, they are not only equal in the sense that Christ is declaring himself God, but also, he's asking that he should be worshipped as God is worshipped equally so. Note that the New World Translation is the first intentional, systematic effort at producing a complete version of the Bible that is edited and revised for the specific purpose of agreeing with a group's (false) doctrine. So, even in a false religion's manipulated Scripture, truth manifests and false religious teaching fails.

APPENDIX B

Testament saints look back to the cross, but everyone in Heaven will be there because they believe the one and only eternal Gospel of God.

- *It is exclusive.* All other faiths and religions are false (John 14:6). This is because the Gospel is about Christ alone. Jesus said in John 14:6, "I am the way, the truth, and the life. No one comes to the Father except through Me." He is the way for those who are lost; he is the truth for those who are deceived; and he is the life for those who are dead in their sins.
- *It is according to scripture alone.* The Gospel has no other source (2 Tim 3:15; 1 Cor 15:1–4).
- *It has divine power.* It has the power to save those who believe it (Rom 1:16).
- *It is of grace.* Those who add anything to it stand condemned (Gal 1:6–9; Rom 11:6).

If one adds anything to the Gospel and people believe it, they are condemned to hell, and if one takes anything away from the Gospel and people believe it, they ascend into "darkness where there's weeping and gnashing of teeth" (Matt 25:30). It is important to get the Gospel precisely correct.[10]

---

10. Gendron, *Preparing for Eternity*, 147–52. Subsequently, Roman Catholic theology holds to *extra Ecclesiam nulla salus* ("outside the church, no salvation"). They assert that salvation is only available through the Roman Catholic Church because the Roman Catholic Church is where Christ resides and where Christ's grace is distributed. One can access the necessary grace of Christ through the sacraments of the Roman Catholic Church, which are under the control of the Roman Catholic Church and administered by clerics within the Roman Catholic Church (see the dictum of Cyprian and the Fourth Lateran Council (1215), which says "Outside the [Roman Catholic] Church there is no salvation," as well as Thomas Aquinas' *Exposition Primae Decretalis ad Archidiaconum Tudertinum*, and quotes from Pope Boniface VIII, Pope Leo XIII, and Pope John Paul II). This assertion by the Roman Catholic Church cannot be true as per 1 Cor 15:1–8 (among many other verses). This passage is not exclusive to one particular religion or faith group but to all humanity. The gospel necessary for salvation is completely contained in the Bible (available to all people), thus no one religious group has the authority to be the source of salvation. In addition to this Roman Catholic assertion, many religions claim

What about Good Works?

It's not a matter of whether works are good; it's an issue of when they occur. Titus 2 says, "the grace of God that brings salvation has appeared to all men, teaching us that, denying ungodliness and worldly lusts, we should live soberly, righteously, and godly in the present age." Grace becomes our tutor, but the timing of works is vitally important. Isaiah said that all of our righteous acts are like filthy rags (Isa 64:6), but if we come to the cross with empty hands of faith, bringing nothing but our sin, at that very moment we are justified. After justification, according to Eph 2:10, we are created in Christ Jesus for good works prepared by God. We come to the cross, leaving our works behind, bringing nothing but our sin. Then, after justification, we do the works God has prepared for us to walk in. The motivation is important, as Christians do good works because they have been justified.[11]

It is important to remember that you can do nothing to save yourself. Eph 2:8-9 says, "for by grace you have been saved through faith, and that not of yourselves; it is the gift of God, not of works, lest anyone should boast." Also, Titus 3:5 says, he saved us "not by works of righteousness which we have done, but according to His mercy He saved us, through the washing of regeneration and renewing of the Holy Spirit." Any attempt to do so nullifies justifying

---

exclusivity when it comes to being the sole purveyor of salvation, thus alienating people and keeping them from true salvation as expressed in the Bible.

11. The contrast between works and fruit is important. A machine in a factory works and turns out a product, but it could never manufacture fruit. Fruit must grow out of life, and, in the case of the believer, it is the life of the Spirit as per Gal 5:21. When you think of "works" you think of effort, labor, strain, and toil; when you think of "fruit" you think of beauty, quietness, the unfolding of life. Paul began with love because all of the other fruit is really an outgrowth of love. Fruit grows in a climate blessed with an abundance of the Spirit and the Word. To live in the Spirit means to walk in the Spirit and the Word. To live in the Spirit means to walk in the Spirit, not running ahead and not lagging behind. This involves the Word, prayer, worship, praise, and fellowship with God's people. It also means "pulling out the weeds" so that the seed of the Word can take root and bear fruit.

APPENDIX B

grace and insults Jesus and his all-sufficient work.[12] What Jesus has done to save sinners gives all the glory to God and his saving grace. All boasting is in Jesus Christ and his righteousness.[13]

It is important to note that Jas 2:14–26 is sometimes taken out of context to create a works-based approach to righteousness, but this conflicts with myriad other passages of Scripture. In this passage, James is not saying that our works make us righteous before God; rather, real saving faith is displayed by good works. In other words, works are not the result of salvation; rather, they are the evidence of salvation, and faith in Christ always produces good works. A person who professes to be a Christian but actively disobeys Christ has a false or dead faith and is not saved,[14] as obedience to God is the mark of true saving faith.

Misunderstanding the relationship between faith and works comes from not understanding what the Bible teaches about salvation. In essence, there are two errors with regard to works and faith. The first error is the teaching that, as long as a person prayed

---

12. According to Scripture, works do not save, and we are not "saved, after all we can do" (2 Nephi 25:23, *Book of Mormon*). As expressed in Eph 2:8, on the part of God, salvation is by grace; on the part of man, it is through faith. Works are not part of the salvation equation.

13. Gendron, *Preparing for Eternity*, 141–46. In the early church, those who taught a combination of God's grace and human effort were called "Judaizers." A Judaizer taught that in order for a Christian to truly be right with God, they must conform to the Mosaic Law. Circumcision in particular was promoted as necessary for salvation. Gentiles had to become Jewish proselytes— a person who has converted from one religion to another—first, and then they could come to Christ. The doctrine of the Judaizers was a mixture of grace (through Christ) and works (through the keeping of the Law). This false doctrine was dealt with in Acts 15 and strongly condemned in the book of Galatians. To add anything to the work that Christ did for salvation is to negate God's grace. We are saved by grace alone, through faith alone, not by returning to the law: "I do not set aside the grace of God, for if righteousness could be gained through the law, Christ died for nothing" (Gal 2:21). The Bible is clear that the attempt to add human works to God's grace overlooks the very meaning of grace, which is "undeserved blessing." As Paul says, "If by grace, then it cannot be based on works; if it were, grace would no longer be grace" (Rom 11:6). Praise the Lord, "Christ has set us free. Stand firm, then, and do not let yourselves be burdened again by a yoke of slavery" (Gal 5:1).

14. See 1 Cor 6:9–10; Matt 7:16–23.

a prayer or said, "I believe in Jesus," at some point in his or her life, then he or she is saved, regardless of lifestyle. The idea that a profession of faith saves a person, even if he or she lives in blatant sin afterward, is, in reality, a dead faith that cannot save. The other error is to attempt to make works part of what justifies. The combination of works and faith to earn salvation is entirely contrary to what Scripture teaches.[15] The works that follow salvation do not render us righteous before God; they simply flow from the regenerated heart.

Jas 2:26 explains that faith without works reveals a spirit that has not been transformed by God. When we have been regenerated by the Holy Spirit, our lives will reflect this new existence.[16] Our actions will be distinguished by obedience to God. The manifestation of the fruit of the Spirit in our lives will make our faith visible.[17] Christians are followers of the Good Shepherd, Christ. As his sheep, we recognize his voice and respond by following him.[18] Because faith results in a new creation and not a repetition of old patterns of sinful behavior, faith without works is dead.[19]

---

15. There is no conflict between Rom 4:5 and Jas 2:26. We are justified by grace through faith, and the natural result of faith in the heart is works that all can see. Salvation is a sovereign act of God whereby an unregenerate sinner has the "washing of regeneration and renewing of the Holy Spirit" (Titus 3:5), resulting in being born again (John 3:3). When this happens, per Ezek 36:26, God gives the forgiven sinner a new heart and places a new spirit (the Holy Spirit) within him or her. Per Ezek 36:26–27, the Spirit then moves the saved person to walk in obedience to God's Word.

16. A faith declaration that fails to produce tangible changes in behavior and good works is considered to be a false declaration. John Calvin, a renowned theologian, once wrote, "It is faith alone that justifies, but faith that justifies can never be alone." When James characterizes false faith as dead, he is implying that it lacks utility, efficacy, and potency.

17. See Gal 5:22.

18. See John 10:26–30. Got Questions Ministries, "Why is Faith Without Works Dead?"

19. See 2 Cor 5:17. Eph 2:10 states, "For we are His workmanship, created in Christ Jesus for good works, which God prepared beforehand that we should walk in them." God's purpose in rescuing us was not only to rescue us from hell, but also so that we would reflect his goodness and character to the world. God is pleased when we grow more like his Son (Rom 8:29). We were

APPENDIX B

Justification is at the Heart of the Gospel

Justification declares the inflexible righteousness of God as the judge who must punish every sin that has ever been committed by everyone who has ever lived.[20] Because God is a holy and righteous judge,[21] he cannot let the guilty go free. Someone must satisfy divine justice. The only way condemned sinners can be justified is through faith and the sin-bearing substitutionary death and resurrection of Christ alone who satisfies divine justice.[22] Christ died as a substitute for those who repent and believe the Gospel—by

---

created in the image of God (Gen 1:27). This image was marred by sin. When God redeemed us, he did so in order to restore his image in us and set us free to become all we were created to be. When the Holy Spirit resides within us, he leads us to do things that bring glory to God (John 14:26). Our desire to satisfy God increases as our knowledge of him increases. This desire to please God motivates virtuous deeds. It is inconsistent with the Bible to assert that a person has been redeemed but has not changed. Numerous individuals go through the formalities of committing their lives to Christ, but no change in lifestyle ensues. That is not true redemption, but a faith that is "dead" (Jas 2:26). The heart is illuminated when it receives the light of salvation (John 12:46). Priorities shift. Desires transform. Outlooks alter. Life is perceived for the first time with clarity. If the darkness of sin persists, it is reasonable to infer that no light appeared. To use another biblical analogy, God desires for our lives to bear fruit (see Gal 5:22–23). We are the branches. The branches are naturally connected to the vine, which provides them with support, the capacity to produce fruit, and their very existence. Jesus declared, "I am the vine, you are the branches. He who abides in Me, and I in him, bears much fruit; for without Me you can do nothing" (John 15:5). The objective of the vineyard is to generate "much fruit." After salvation, good deeds ensue. Therefore, although we cannot be saved by our good works, once we are saved, we will produce good works. After salvation, we mature and begin to resemble our Heavenly Father more and more. This is only possible as long as we "abide in him" and permit him to reproduce his character within us (John 15:4). Good works do not result in salvation. Good works are the result of being saved. Jesus told his disciples, "Let your light so shine before men, that they may see your good works and glorify your Father in heaven" (Matt 5:16).

20. Simply stated, to justify is to declare righteous. Justification is an act by which God declares a sinner to be righteous on account of his or her faith in Christ.

21. See Ps 119:137; 145:17; Isa 46:13; John 5:30; 1 Pet 1:17, among others.

22. For "the wages of sin is death" (Rom 6:23).

THE FOUNDATION OF THE GOSPEL

faith in what God has accomplished in Christ (Rom 5:1)—so they won't have to suffer eternal death.[23] The Bible teaches that justification is an instantaneous (Rom 4:3) change in one's legal status before God whereby a condemned sinner has been acquitted and declared righteous.[24] Justification is permanent and is never lost by sin. The legal status of a justified person is as unchangeable as the righteousness of Christ as per Heb 10:14. God justifies the ungodly (Rom 4:5). Justification is the imputation (or the crediting) of Christ's completed righteousness to the justified.[25] Justification is by grace aside from works.[26] Christ's righteousness is given as a

---

23. To be clear, the living individual has to repent and believe the Gospel to be saved. In contrast, *baptism for the dead*, or *vicarious baptism*, where a living person is baptized in lieu of a person who has passed away, is an unscriptural Mormon practice with roots in Marcionism, a heresy that emerged in the mid-second century AD. By means of the rite of baptism, living individuals demonstrate their commitment and faith in Jesus Christ. It is not to impart the prospect of salvation or merit grace upon those who have died.

24. We require the imputation (the legal crediting of Jesus' perfect righteousness to believers by faith for justification) of Christ's righteousness because we have no righteousness of our own. We are by nature sinners, and we cannot make ourselves righteous; we cannot put ourselves in a proper relationship with God. We require Christ's righteousness to be imputed to us, or his holiness before God to be credited to our accounts. In his Sermon on the Mount, Jesus emphasizes the importance of imputed righteousness: "You therefore must be perfect, as your heavenly Father is perfect" (Matt 5:48). This follows Jesus' correction of his audience's misunderstanding of the law. Jesus says in Matt 5:20 that if his listeners wish to access the kingdom of heaven, their righteousness must exceed that of the Pharisees, who were experts in the law. Infused righteousness, in Roman Catholic theology, is that which comes gradually to the believer through obedience, confession, penance, and the other sacraments. There is no biblical basis for the idea of infused righteousness, which contradicts the scriptural teaching that justification comes through faith alone and not through the series of works (Rom 3:28).

25. See 2 Cor 5:21; Rom 4:5.

26. The core teaching of every false religion is identical: one must obey certain commands to be made right with God. Some accentuate Old Testament commands; some accentuate New Testament commands; some accentuate church commands; some emphasize the humanitarian principles of general morality, goodness, and kindness. Regardless of the particulars, the necessity of obedience to be right with God is a false gospel. According to Eph 2:8-9, it is not through obedience but by grace through faith that salvation is possible.

gift.²⁷ After justification, all sins are no longer taken into account or punished.²⁸ God promises to glorify everyone he justifies, because those justified can never be condemned.²⁹

THE SUBSTITUTIONARY ATONEMENT OF CHRIST

When Jesus Christ died on the cross, he died in our place. We deserved to be the ones nailed to the cross to die since we live sinful lives. However, Christ bore the penalty in our place. He was substituted for us and took what we rightly deserved. "For He made Him, who knew no sin, to be sin for us, so that we might become the righteousness of God in Him" (2 Cor 5:21). In addition, "he was pierced for our transgressions, crushed for our iniquities; the punishment that brought us peace was upon him, and by his wounds we are healed" (Isa 53:3).

He "Himself bore our sins in His own body on the tree, that we, having died to sins, might live for righteousness—by whose stripes you were healed" (1 Pet 2:24). Again, we see that Christ took our sins upon himself to pay the penalty for us. "For Christ also suffered once for sins, the just for the unjust, that He might bring us to God, being put to death in the flesh but made alive by the Spirit" (1 Pet 3:18). These verses teach us not only about Christ being a replacement for us, but also about him being the atonement, which means he satisfied the payment for humanity's sinfulness.

Sin can only be paid for on our own by being punished and condemned to hell for eternity.³⁰ But Jesus Christ, the Son of God,

---

27. Titus 3:7; Rom 4:8; 5:17; 11:6.
28. Rom 4:5; 2 Cor 5:19–21.
29. See Rom 8:1, 30. Gendron, *Preparing for Eternity*, 142–43. Jesus' motivation for justifying us is his love for us. He desires to have a personal relationship with us, as in John 14:21: "He who has My commandments and keeps them, it is he who loves Me. And he who loves Me will be loved by My Father, and I will love him and manifest Myself to him."
30. The Bible teaches that where we go after death depends on whether or not we had faith in Jesus Christ as Lord and Savior. As Christians, to be absent from our bodies means we are with the Lord (2 Cor 5:6–8). Luke 16:22–23

came to Earth to pay for our sins. Because he did this for us, we now have the opportunity to not only receive forgiveness for our transgressions, but also to spend eternity with him. To accomplish this, we must have faith in what Christ accomplished on the cross. We cannot save ourselves; a substitute must be sent in our stead. Jesus Christ's death is the substitutionary atonement.[31]

TRUST IN JESUS

The phrase "trust in Jesus" has multiple implications. In one sense, trusting in Jesus entails faith in him for salvation, as expressed in John 3:16. We believe he is God in human form, and we trust him as our Savior. In addition, we believe that he died for our sins and rose from the grave. Since we cannot save ourselves from sin and death, as per Rom 3:10-20 and John 11:25, we rely on Jesus to save us. In addition, according to Eph 1:7, we cannot receive eternal life

---

states that unbelievers are sent to hell or the place of the dead. Heaven and hell are very real, and people are destined for one or the other. When Jesus returns a second time, Christians' bodies will be resurrected and glorified (1 Cor 15:50-54) and those who do not trust in Christ will be raised to judgment. For believers, there will be a new heaven and a new Earth (Rev 21:1), while unbelievers will be cast into an eternal lake of fire (Rev 20:11-15). After death, there is no opportunity for redemption (Heb 9:27). In contrast, Mormons believe that the afterlife consists of various levels or kingdoms: the celestial kingdom, the terrestrial kingdom, the telestial kingdom, and outer darkness (Mormon Doctrine, 348). According to Mormonism, the ultimate destination of mankind is determined by their beliefs and actions in this life (2 Nephi 25:23, *Book of Mormon*; *Articles of Faith*, 79). This is contrary to the Bible.

Additionally, *annihilationism* is the teaching that those who perish apart from Christ will simply cease to exist (i.e., nonbelievers will be "wiped out" or "annihilated" after death). In other words, unbelievers will not be punished eternally in a literal hell, but will instead simply vanish (or have their souls extinguished). Many find annihilationism appealing because it spares unbelievers eternal punishment, but the Bible offers no support for this belief. On the contrary, the Bible clearly demonstrates that there are only two options after death: an eternity with God in glory or an eternity of suffering and separation from him. (See Rev 20:12-15 for a clear example)

31. Gendron, *Preparing for Eternity*, 39-46.

APPENDIX B

and spend eternity in God's presence until we have placed our faith in Jesus and accepted his forgiveness.[32]

After being saved, trusting in Jesus entails committing or devoting oneself completely to him. When we become born again, we become followers of Jesus Christ. As his followers, we have absolute confidence in him and his Word. To have trust in Jesus means to embrace as true everything he has said and accept his Word as truth. The more we know and abide in the words of Jesus, the more we will obey him, and as we experience freedom in Christ, our confidence and faith in him will grow.

According to Matt 11:28–30, one of the trustworthy promises Jesus made in his Word was that we could come to him to find rest: "Come to Me, all you who labor and are heavy laden, and I will give you rest. Take My yoke upon you and learn from Me, for I am gentle and lowly in heart, and you will find rest for your souls. For My yoke is easy and My burden is light." Rest, another way of expressing trust, is a state of learning from and relying on Jesus for strength. He shares the burden with us as we walk with him. When we grow weary and overburdened, we can find rest for our souls by coming alongside Jesus. In this way, we place our faith in Jesus by relying on him in all circumstances, particularly when we are tired and burdened.

---

32. Jas 2:19 says, "You believe that there is one God. You do well. Even the demons believe—and tremble!" This verse may be the clearest statement in the Bible regarding the distinction between "knowing about" God and "trusting in" God. This is fundamental to the idea of saving faith. Knowledge is distinct from trust, obedience, and saving faith. James contends that even demons believe that "God is one" and are terrified of him. It is not sufficient to concur that something is true. Genuine faith in God responds to this truth with personal trust and obedience. (The statement "God is one" may have been a reference to one of Judaism's core concepts. It is found in Deut 6:4 and is known as *the Shema*: "Hear, O Israel: The Lord our God, the Lord is one." Every Jewish reader of James would have grown up accepting this truth.) James's premise is that mere agreement is insufficient. This places those who profess a belief in God but fail to act accordingly in the same category as demons. It implies knowledge, but not trust. Rather than "saving faith," it means "dead faith." The peril of this condition is that self-confident "religious" individuals may spend their entire lives in simple agreement without ever crossing over into genuine, living faith.

THE FOUNDATION OF THE GOSPEL

Jesus understands our weaknesses and knows we will struggle to trust him. That is why, according to Phil 4:6-7, we are to "be anxious for nothing, but in everything by prayer and supplication, with thanksgiving, let your requests be made known to God; and the peace of God, which surpasses all understanding, will guard your hearts and minds through Christ Jesus." When we present our worries to God through prayer, he grants us peace, because his presence is peace. The passage does not state that God will always grant our requests, but it does promise that peace will protect our hearts and minds. To have faith in Jesus is to believe that he has good and trustworthy intentions for our lives and future.

According to 2 Cor 1:10, our faith in Jesus increases as we observe God working all things in our lives for his purposes. Jesus desires that we live by faith in him; therefore, the Christian existence is a training (and testing) ground in trust. Jas 1:2-4 states, "count it all joy when you fall into various trials, knowing that the testing of your faith produces patience. But let patience have its perfect work, that you may be perfect and complete, lacking nothing." In John 14:1, Jesus said, "Let not your heart be troubled; you believe in God, believe also in Me." According to Matt 28:20, we may know that Jesus loves us and promises to always be with us, but we cannot physically see him, and doubt and fear can make it difficult to apply this understanding during times of difficulty. Peter encourages us in 1 Pet 1:6-8 to trust in Jesus even when we cannot see him: "In this you greatly rejoice, though now for a little while, if need be, you have been grieved by various trials, that the genuineness of your faith, being much more precious than gold that perishes, though it is tested by fire, may be found to praise, honor, and glory at the revelation of Jesus Christ, whom having not seen you love. Though now you do not see Him, yet believing, you rejoice with joy inexpressible and full of glory."

Even though we cannot see Jesus with our physical sight, the Holy Spirit enables us to see Jesus with the eyes of our hearts.[33] In the end, our inability to see Jesus physically strengthens our faith

---

33. See Eph 1:18-20.

in him. Jesus stated as much in John 20:29: "blessed are those who have not seen and yet have believed."

Paul conveyed what it means for a believer to trust in Jesus in 2 Cor 4:17–18: "For our light affliction, which is but for a moment, is working for us a far more exceeding and eternal weight of glory, while we do not look at the things which are seen, but at the things which are not seen. For the things which are seen are temporary, but the things which are not seen are eternal."

Jesus teaches us to trust him in everything, at all times, with our entire hearts, so that our faith becomes unshakable: "Trust in the Lord forever, for the LORD, the LORD himself, is the Rock eternal" (Isa 26:4, NIV). As we grow in our trust in Jesus, we identify more with the psalmist's description of a believer at ease in God's arms as conveyed in Ps 131:2: "I have calmed and quieted myself, I am like a weaned child with its mother; like a weaned child I am content."[34]

An important note of caution regarding trust in Jesus revolves around *decisions* versus *delight* in God. In the last 200 years, Christianity in America has been distorted by the dominant teaching that decisions for God are more basic in defining a Christian than delight in God. The consequence of the dominance of this viewpoint across the Christian spectrum from Roman Catholic to fundamentalist Protestant is the emergence of many professing Christians who have made decisions about God, joined churches, etc. but have no new gladness in God, and therefore have not placed their trust in God. Unfortunately, those who merely make decisions are not necessarily Christians. The effort of this dominant viewpoint in American evangelicalism to define saving faith apart from spiritual affections is biblically futile. To define saving faith apart from feelings, affections, or emotions of glad dependence, thankful trust, fervent admiration, pleased submission, contented resting, thrilled treasuring, eager reverence, and heartfelt adoration is futile. You cannot strip those adjectives away: glad, thankful, fervent, pleased, contented, thrilled, eager, heartfelt. You cannot strip them away from the nouns: trust, admiration, submission,

---

34. Got Questions Ministries, "What does it mean to trust in Jesus?"

resting, treasuring, reverence, adoration. You cannot strip those affectional adjectives away from the nouns, which we try to make faith, and have anything left—except what Satan can do through deceptive PSYOP. Or, if you think carefully, you might have some oxymorons left over, like 'unthankful saving faith.' But there is no such thing.[35]

THE OFTENTIMES MISSING ELEMENT: DYING TO SELF

The idea of "dying to self" appears throughout the New Testament. It encapsulates the true essence of the Christian life, in which we bear our cross and follow Christ. Dying to oneself is part of being born again; according to John 3:3–7, the old self dies, and the new self is born. Christians are not only born again when they come to salvation, but they also continue to die to self as part of the sanctification process. As a result, dying to oneself is both a one-time experience and an ongoing process.

Jesus repeatedly instructed his disciples to take up their cross (a symbol of death) and follow him. He made it clear that if anyone wanted to follow him, they had to deny themselves, which meant giving up their lives spiritually, symbolically, and if necessary, physically. This was a requirement for being a follower of Christ, who declared that attempting to preserve our earthly lives would result in our losing our lives in the kingdom. Those, however, who lay down their lives for his sake will receive eternal life.[36] Jesus went so far as to assert that those hesitant to lay down their lives for him cannot be his disciples.[37]

---

35. Piper, "New God, New Gospel, New Gladness: How Is Christian Joy Distinct?"

36. See Matt 16:24–25; Mark 8:34–35.

37. See Luke 14:27. As an aside, baptism symbolizes the believer's commitment to die to the old, sinful way of life (Rom 6:4–8) and be reborn into new life in Christ (Rom 6:4–8). In Christian baptism, being submerged in water represents dying and being buried alongside Christ. Emerging from the water symbolizes Christ's resurrection. Baptism identifies us with Christ in his death and resurrection, symbolically portraying the Christian's entire life as a dying

APPENDIX B

Paul describes the process of dying to self to the Galatians as one in which he has been "crucified with Christ," and now Paul no longer lives, but Christ lives in him. The old Paul, with his proclivity to sin and following the ways of the world, is no longer alive, and the new Paul is the dwelling place of Christ, who lives in and through him. This is not to say that when we "die to self" we become passive or insensible, nor do we believe we are dead. Rather, dying to self involves rendering dead the things of the old life, particularly the sinful practices, and lifestyles we once followed, because "those who belong to Christ Jesus have crucified the sinful nature with its passions and desires" (Gal 5:24). Where we once sought selfish pleasures, we now seek with equal zeal what pleases God.

In the Bible, dying to oneself is never depicted as optional for Christians. It is the reality of the new birth; no one can come to Christ unless they are willing to see their old existence crucified with Christ and begin living a new life in submission to him. Jesus says he will spew out lukewarm followers who attempt to live partially in the old life and partially in the new life.[38] This lukewarm condition characterized both the Church of Laodicea and many congregations in the present day. Being "lukewarm" indicates a refusal to die to self and live for Christ. For Christians, death to self is not an option; it is a choice that leads to eternal life.[39]

---

to self and living for and in the one who died for us (Gal 2:20).

38. See Rev 3:15–16.

39. Got Questions Ministries, "What Does the Bible Mean by 'Dying to Self'?"

Appendix C
Why God's Word Is True

> Every one who is seriously involved in the pursuit of science becomes convinced that a spirit is manifest in the laws of the Universe—a spirit vastly superior to that of man, and one in the face of which we with our modest powers must feel humble.
>
> —ALBERT EINSTEIN

CHARLES HODGE (1797–1878), a Reformed Presbyterian theologian and principal of Princeton Theological Seminary who argued strongly for the authority of the Bible as the Word of God, says it well: "The best evidence of the Bible's being the Word of God is to be found between its covers. It proves itself." Christians should trust the Bible because it is the revelation of *all that God wants us to know* about *everything we need to know*. It's important to remember, if he hasn't revealed it in his Word, either it is a secret or it is unimportant to us now.[1] So, the more of God's Word one trusts,

---

1. The phrase "the secret things belong to the Lord" (Deut 29:29) suggests that some things are only known to God. He is all-knowing, all-powerful, and all-present. He is also eternal (Ps 90:2), sees all things (Prov 15:3), and knows the future (Jer 29:11). Humans, unlike God, have finite and limited knowledge—we cannot totally or completely understand God or his plans. So, the Lord's "secret things" are those that only he knows as the Creator and Sustainer of all creation (Col 1:16–17). However, just because the secret things belong to the Lord does not mean that mankind cannot know anything about God. In reality, Deut 29:29 mentions things revealed. We may learn a lot about who God is and what he's up to since he's revealed himself to us through "the words of this law" (Deut 29:29). (MacArthur, *The MacArthur Bible Commentary*, 193)

APPENDIX C

the more one knows about all that really matters in life. In John 17:17 (KJV), Jesus says, "Sanctify them through thy truth: thy word is truth." God says his Word is Truth; and God says that only that true Word can sanctify us (that is to set Christians apart as useful and pleasing to him). So, one's walk with God can only begin with a firm conviction of the truthfulness of the entire Bible: "So then faith comes by hearing, and hearing by the word of God" (Rom 10:17).[2] In other words, the Bible says what it means, and means what it says.[3] It is important to understand and believe this to fully implement the counter-PSYOP method of *Indirect Refutation* (and tangentially the counter-PSYOP methods of *Conditioning, Forestalling, Direct Refutation,* and *Restrictive Measures*); hence this appendix discusses why God's Word is true through the testimony of Jesus, the writers, its unity, its fulfilled prophecy, its scientific accuracy, its archeological verification, and its endurance.

---

2. Drawn from Barnett, "Your Bible Is Supernaturally-Trustworthy."

3. According to Voddie Baucham, an American pastor, author, and educator, the Bible "is a reliable collection of historical documents written down by eyewitnesses during the lifetime of other eyewitnesses. They report [of] supernatural events that took place in fulfillment of specific prophecies and claimed that their writings are Divine rather than human and origin." From 2 Pet 1:16–21: "for we did not follow cunningly devised fables when we made known to you the power and coming of our Lord Jesus Christ, but were eyewitnesses of His majesty. For He received from God the Father honor and glory when such a voice came to Him from the Excellent Glory: 'This is My beloved Son, in whom I am well pleased.' And we heard this voice which came from heaven when we were with Him on the holy mountain. And so we have the prophetic word confirmed, which you do well to heed as a light that shines in a dark place, until the day dawns and the morning star rises in your hearts; knowing this first, that no prophecy of Scripture is of any private interpretation, for prophecy never came by the will of man, but holy men of God spoke as they were moved by the Holy Spirit." Lastly, 1 John 1:1–3 says, "that which was from the beginning, which we have heard, which we have seen with our eyes, which we have looked upon, and our hands have handled, concerning the Word of life—the life was manifested, and we have seen, and bear witness, and declare to you that eternal life which was with the Father and was manifested to us—that which we have seen and heard we declare to you."

JESUS CHRIST SAID THE BIBLE WAS TRUE

Jesus believed in the verbal inspiration of the Bible.[4] That means every one of God's words is inspired by the Holy Spirit, as per Matt 5:18, and thus every word is without error.[5] Jesus affirmed that there are no errors in science, history, or the moral areas in the Bible. During Jesus' ministry, he affirmed the historical reliability of Adam and Eve as the first two humans (Matt 19:4–5), Noah and the global Flood (Matt 24:37–38), Abraham as a person who lived and who knew Christ as God the Son (John 8:56), Abel (Matt 23:35), Moses and the burning bush (Mark 12:26), David (Matt 12:3), Elijah (Luke 4:25), Daniel (Matt 4:17), and Jonah (Matt 12:40–41). Additionally, through these ratifications, Jesus confirms miracles.[6]

---

4. Jesus himself confirmed the verbal plenary inspiration of the scriptures—the view of Scripture that the Bible itself claims that every word in every part of the Bible comes from God (1 Cor 2:12–13; 2 Tim 3:16–17)—when he said, "Do not think that I came to destroy the Law or the Prophets. I did not come to destroy but to fulfill. For assuredly, I say to you, till heaven and earth pass away, one jot or one tittle will by no means pass from the law till all is fulfilled" (Matt 5:17–18). In these verses, Jesus is reinforcing the accuracy of the scriptures down to the smallest detail and the slightest punctuation mark, because it is the very Word of God. (Geisler, *The Big Book of Christian Apologetics*, 56–58)

5. There are two types of Bible translations: word-for-word and paraphrase (dynamic equivalence). It is acceptable to use a paraphrase of the Bible (e.g., the Living Bible, etc.), but it should not be used as a substitute for the word-for-word inspired scriptures because God inspired words. Paraphrasing is like a sermon: sermons are great, but don't mix a sermon up with the inspired scriptures.

6. Geisler, *The Big Book of Christian Apologetics*, 56–58. Unfortunately, liberal theology does not believe in miracles. They don't believe Jonah was actually swallowed by a fish for three days and survived, that Daniel survived the fiery furnace, that the burning bush was a real event, or that a global flood occurred; however, Jesus did. In liberal Christian teaching, which is not at all Christian, human reason is emphasized and regarded as the ultimate authority. The objective of liberal theologians is to reconcile Christianity with secular science and contemporary thought. In doing so, they consider science to be all-knowing and the Bible to be filled with myths and falsehoods.

APPENDIX C

THE WRITERS SAID THE BIBLE WAS TRUE

There is a harmony of conviction among the more than forty authors of the Bible that God spoke through them—that the words came from God, not themselves. For instance, 2 Sam 23:2, says, "the Spirit of the Lord spoke by me, and His Word was in my tongue." Thousands of times, the writers said that they were completely convinced that they were sharing words that were not originating with them—this is called inspiration.[7] Thus, the Bible

> 7. Geisler, *The Big Book of Christian Apologetics*, 51. Conversely, God did not inspire the Apocrypha (nor the Pseudepigrapha for that matter): (1) The Apocrypha itself indicates it is not Scripture. "So there was great distress in Israel, the worst since the time when prophets ceased to appear among them" (1 Macc 9:27). Additionally, these books contain theological and historical errors. For example, the Book of Wisdom states that God created the world out of pre-existing matter (11:17), which contradicts the rest of Scripture's teaching that God created the world out of nothing (*ex nihilo*). Moreover, the book of Judith incorrectly states that Nebuchadnezzar was king of Assyria, when in fact he was the king of Babylon (1:5). (2) Jews have never recognized the Apocrypha as canonical Scripture. According to the Babylonian Talmud, after the prophets Haggai, Zechariah, and Malachi perished, the Holy Spirit left Israel. Based on this text, the Jews recognized that after Malachi's death, the Spirit ceased communicating through the prophets. Thus, the Apocryphal texts, which were composed after Malachi, are not inspired by the Holy Spirit. (3) The Apocrypha are not referred to as Scripture in the New Testament. When studying the New Testament, you will encounter hundreds of Old Testament quotations. Jesus and his apostles cite various portions of the Old Testament as Scripture 295 times, according to one count. However, they never quote a text from the Apocrypha. (4) Before the Protestant Reformation, the Roman Catholic Church did not recognize the Apocrypha as Scripture. In 1546, at the Council of Trent, the Roman Catholic Church formally proclaimed the Apocrypha to be canonical. One must question why, if these texts were authoritative, it took over fifteen hundred years for their authority to be acknowledged. It appears that Rome declared these books to be canonical in direct response to Martin Luther and the Protestant Reformers, who condemned these books and their teachings. Jerome (447–420 AD) cautiously included these books in the Latin Vulgate Bible in the year 404 AD, which is perhaps the most significant reason why these books were even up for discussion. Although Jerome included these volumes in his Vulgate, he distinguished them from the remainder of the Bible. He indicated that these writings were not intended to establish the authority of church doctrines. In other words, Jerome acknowledged that these books lacked the same authority as Scripture. For instance, with respect to Judith, Tobit, and Maccabees, Jerome said, "As, then, the Church reads Judith, Tobit,

was penned by men but authored by God. In fact, writers in the Old Testament refer to their writings as the 'words of God' over 3,800 times. New Testament writers quote the Old Testament as the 'Word of God' 320 times and make reference to Old Testament passages about 1,000 times. So New Testament writers affirm the authority and divine inspiration and authorship of the Old Testament. As for the New Testament, the testimony of the writers of the New Testament about the New Testament is clear. Gal 1:11–12: "But I make known to you, brethren, that the gospel which was preached by me is not according to man. For I neither received it from man, nor was I taught it, but it came through the revelation of Jesus Christ." In 1 Tim 5:18, Paul makes two references and calls them both 'Scripture.' One is from Deut 25:4 and the other is from Luke 10:7. So Luke's writing is 'Scripture' just as is the Old Testament. In 2 Pet 3:15 and 16, Peter calls Paul's writing 'Scripture.' In Jude 17 and 18, Jude refers to the Scripture and then quotes Peter, from 2 Peter. John writes the book of Revelation and repeatedly, in chapters 2 and 3, says, "The Spirit has said this to the churches." And so it goes. One can easily trace the reality that the Bible writers knew full well they were writing the Word of God.[8]

THE BIBLE'S INCREDIBLE UNITY

The Bible's supernaturally designed unity is demonstrated in the fact that from more than forty men (most of whom never met each other), on three continents, over 1,600 years and sixty generations, comes one integrated message. In each and every word and detail, an unmistakable fabric is woven. There is only one unifying theme, one unified message, one system of doctrine, and one salvation plan. The unity of the Bible is evidence of its divine inspiration.

---

and the books of Maccabees, but does not admit them among the canonical Scriptures, so let it read these two volumes for the edification of the people, not to give authority to doctrines of the Church." Only the Bible lays out Christian doctrine. The Apocrypha lacks the authority to make such a claim. (Lumpkin, *The Encyclopedia of Lost and Rejected Scriptures*, 567–68)

8. Geisler, *The Big Book of Christian Apologetics*, 53–54.

APPENDIX C

Only the one true and holy God could have given us such a flawless Bible with such an unparalleled message: the Lord's astounding love for his creation.[9]

An example of the unity of Scripture is found in God's covenants. The Bible contains several covenants that specify the relationship between God and man. Wayne Grudem, in his *Systematic Theology*, clearly defines a covenant as "an unchangeable, divinely imposed legal agreement between God and man that stipulates the conditions of their relationship."[10]

In a human society characterized by broken promises—an unfortunate manifestation of living in a fallen, depraved world resulting in treaties violated leading to bloody wars, families fractured after married couples break their pledge "to love and to cherish till death us do part," and failure to pay what is owed as per a signed contract due to financial overextension—God always perfectly upholds his end of the agreement. He is a "covenant-keeping" God. Wholly reliable, God possesses ultimate, unwavering truth through his Word, which "cannot be broken" no matter what challenges come against it (John 10:35). The best part is that God's covenant promises are freely available to anyone.

One such covenant between God and man is the Abrahamic Covenant discussed in Gen 12:1–3 and Genesis 15. Unique to this covenant—and fortunate for mankind—is the unconditional nature of the agreement: we don't have to do anything to obtain its blessings. God binds himself alone to the covenant. In fact, six times in Genesis 12 God says, "I will." Further, this covenant applies

---

9. Geisler, *The Big Book of Christian Apologetics*, 54. As an aside, although Joseph Smith, the originator of Mormonism, was a contemporary of the Victorian era (1830–1900), he chose to not write the Book of Mormon (first printed in 1830) in the language of his time, but into a very specific type of Jacobean English (1603–1625), as used in the KJV Bible (of which was written in 1611). Although there are many speculations as to why Smith chose to style the Book of Mormon like the KJV, it is most likely he adopted this KJV biblical English in his translations because his contemporaries would not have accepted a Victorian English Book of Mormon as authentic scripture, thus, in a sense, he deceptively contrived a false unity between the Book of Mormon and the Bible by adopting an antiquated form of English.

10. Grudem, *Systematic Theology*, 515.

to all people for all time. Through this covenant God reveals his gracious love for us, the capstone of his creation, even fallen as we are. The Abrahamic Covenant includes two key components that are true today, the second being a promise of blessing and redemption.[11] Since the Abrahamic Covenant is both unconditional and everlasting, it extends to the future kingdom of Christ. All the Earth would be blessed through Abraham, and, as per John 3:16–17, all people have access to this blessing through Jesus. This promise achieves fulfillment in the New Covenant prophesied in Jer 31:31–34 and declared in Luke 22:20, and was accomplished by Jesus Christ, a descendant of Abraham and the promised Redeemer who will one day summon the "restitution of all things" (Acts 3:21). In Heb 2:16, by calling "those who are about to inherit salvation" through Christ (Heb 1:14) the "seed of Abraham" the author affirms that they are the beneficiaries of God's promise to Abraham. Jesus fulfills God's covenant faithfulness by bringing believers "to glory" (Heb 2:10), just as God brought his people to the Promised Land.[12]

---

11. For completeness, the first promise of the Abrahamic Covenant promises a specific plot of land for Abraham's descendants. (The precise dimensions are detailed in Gen 15:18–21) Not only was the land given, but this promise also had no expiration: it was declared forever. Through Abraham's son Isaac, to his son Jacob, the Children of Israel are heirs to this land despite wars, rebellion, captivities, dispossessions, and diasporas, the last of which continued for two thousand years. However, true to God's enduring promise, on May 14, 1948, then Prime Minister David Ben-Gurion (using Ezekiel 37's "dry bones" prophecy as his authority) announced the name of "Israel" as the new state and homeland for the Jews, who only a few years prior had been the target of Nazi extermination. Interestingly, at no point in history has Israel had under its control the whole Promised Land that God had defined. As prefaced by the miraculous modern reestablishment of Israel via God keeping his covenant promise, Israel will one day repent, be forgiven, and be reinstated to God's favor as anticipated in the initial giving of the Abrahamic Covenant. That favor will lead to the covenant's final fulfillment: Israel will fully occupy its God-given homeland. Subsequently, the Lord will return to establish his throne, and through his perfect rule, the world will be blessed with overflowing peace, love, happiness, and abundance. (Corrado, "God Perfectly Keeps His Promises")

12. Corrado, "God Perfectly Keeps His Promises."

APPENDIX C

THE BIBLE'S FULFILLED PROPHECY

What is the simplest yet most profound proof of the Bible's truthfulness? It is the fulfillment of prophecy: an indisputable proof found solely in the Bible.[13] All of the sacred texts of the world's religions are lacking a prophetic element. It is absent from the Qur'an, the Hindu Vedas, the Bhagavad-Gita, the Book of Mormon, and the sayings of Buddha.[14] In contrast, prophecy comprises between a quarter and a third of the Bible.[15] Isa 41:21 says, "'Present your case,' says the Lord. 'Bring forth your strong reasons.'"[16]

There are two general groupings of prophecy: fulfilled and not yet fulfilled. Examples of fulfilled prophecies are the first coming of Christ (e.g., Deut 18:15–19; Num 24:17; Dan 9:25–26; Mic 5:2) and Daniel's prophecies about the rise and fall of many kingdoms (Dan 7:2–6, 16). Examples of prophecies yet to be fulfilled are the second coming of Christ (Zech 14:3–4; Matt 24:44; Acts 1:10–11; Rev 1:7), the restoration of Israel (Jer 31:31–37; Rom

---

13. One of the most profound examples is found in Psalm 22. Psalm 22 was written 1,000 years before Jesus was born by a man that had never seen a crucifixion because crucifixion had not been invented, yet it is described in Psalm 22 in incredible detail.

14. Generally, false religions do not venture into prophecy. Why? Because if their prophecy doesn't come true, everyone will know they are lying. If it does come true, then you know God is talking (Isa 41). Prophecy is God's authenticating calling card. Only he writes the future in advance and writes history before it happens.

15. In his book *Encyclopedia of Biblical Prophecy*, J. Barton Payne contends that about 27 percent of the Bible is predictive and lists 1,1817 prophecies in the Bible. (Payne, *Encyclopedia of Biblical Prophecy*, 674–75)

16. Geisler, *The Big Book of Christian Apologetics*, 54. In his book, *Science Speaks*, Peter Stoner calculated the probability of just eight Messianic prophecies being fulfilled in the life of Jesus (Mic 5:2; Mal 3:1; Zech 9:9; 13:6; 11:12–13; Isa 53:7; Ps 22:16). The composite probability of all eight prophecies being fulfilled accidentally in the life of one person is 1 in 10^{17} or 1 in 100,000,000,000,000,000. Keep in mind that Jesus did not just fulfill eight prophecies: He fulfilled 108. The chance of fulfilling just sixteen is 1 in 10^{45}; the chance of fulfilling forty-eight increases the odds to 1 in 10^{157}. The accidental fulfillment of these prophecies is simply beyond the realm of possibility.

11:26–27), and the new heavens and new earth (Isa 65:17; 2 Pet 3:13; Rev 21:1).[17]

The Bible consistently emphasizes the role of fulfilled prophecy as compelling evidence supporting its divine authorship.[18] Considering the attribute of omniscience attributed to God, it is reasonable to expect that the Bible would have a substantial number of clear predictions, and furthermore that these predictions are literally fulfilled. Isa 46:9–10 clearly conveys God's prophetic character: "I am God, and there is no other; I am God, and there is none like me, declaring the end from the beginning and from ancient times things that are not yet done."

THE BIBLE'S SCIENTIFIC ACCURACY

Throughout the entire 1,600 years during which the Bible was written, every single scientific fact that was stated is true, and this is looking back nearly 3,500 years.[19] For example, in the book of

17. Payne, *Encyclopedia of Biblical Prophecy.*
18. See Deut 18:22; 1 Kgs 22:28; Jer 28:9.
19. Geisler, *The Big Book of Christian Apologetics*, 525–26. Science is the logical assembly of experimentally derived or observed information about the physical universe. Though the "advancement" of science and significant leaps made across the scientific disciplines over the last several centuries in and of themselves may seem substantial, in the context of the pursuit of unbiased truth they have fallen short. Those with a human-centered worldview often make science the sole basis and definer of truth rather than a tool to pursue truth. This approach is inadequate. At any given moment in history, the scientific thought or discovery at that time would be considered truth—but scientifically-acquired knowledge is ever changing. What is considered scientific fact now may not have been so a decade ago. Christians have nothing to fear. The truths of Christianity hold up to scientific interrogation. "Science" as it can be wielded loses its bearings and, subsequently, becomes a threat to Christianity only when scientists overreach its limits and begin making metaphysical claims in the name of science about reality as a whole. In his essay "Theology and Science," Carl F. H. Henry drives this point home: "The fact is that empirical science has no firm basis whatever on which to raise objections to Christianity, not because scientific and historical concerns are irrelevant to revelation and faith, but because scientists must allow for possible exceptions to every rule they affirm, and for the empirical vulnerability of the rules

APPENDIX C

Job, we learn of the Earth's positioning in space: "He stretches out the north over empty space; He hangs the earth on nothing" (Job 26:7). Scholars believe that the book of Job was written as early as the second millennium BC or perhaps later, between the sixth and fourth centuries BC. Regardless of the exact dating, this verse in Job serves as evidence that God communicated to humanity prior to the advent of Christ that our planet is suspended in space without any discernible means of support.

Throughout history, various hypotheses regarding the placement of the Earth have been proposed. Aristotle noted in the fourth century BC that the earliest theory regarding the positioning of the Earth was that it rested on water. Other ancient cultures believed that a sea turtle supported the Earth. Native Americans of North America, such as the Lenape and Iroquois, passed down creation myths in which the Earth balances on the back of a turtle. In fact, many indigenous North American communities continue to refer to the Earth or the North American continent as Turtle Island. Similarly, Hindu mythology states that the Earth balances on the backs of four elephants who, in turn, stand atop a turtle.[20]

The understanding that the Earth is maintained in orbit by the sun's gravitational force emerged following Sir Isaac Newton's discovery of gravity in 1687. Phrased differently, the sun's gravity, an invisible force, holds the Earth suspended upon nothing in space and orbiting the sun. This scientific discovery validates the Bible's teaching on the Earth's suspended position in space.[21]

---

themselves" (Olsen, *The Journey of Modern Theology*, 631). Scientifically acquired information that is confirmed to be accurate will harmonize with the Bible. In Isa 40:26 and Rom 1:20, the Bible itself petitions man to learn from God's handiwork and to observe God's incredible characteristics as revealed in scientific pursuits. As science discovers more about our world and the universe we inhabit, more evidence of creation and design is revealed. As Christians, we welcome and support science that pursues truth, but reject assertions by scientists beyond the realm of what scientific methodology can support. (Corrado, "The Role and Realm of Science")

20. Leeming, *Creation Myths of the World*, 171.
21. Phillips, *Guide to the Sun*, 226–28.

As an example of one who sought out the scientific truth of the scriptures, Matthew Fontaine Maury,[22] the "father of oceanography," a devout Christian and avid Bible student, was struck by the reference in Ps 8:8 to "the paths of the seas." As a result, throughout his career, he had a passionate desire to find the paths of the sea the psalmist spoke of—and ultimately he found them.

Amid his many successes, Maury never forgot his belief in Scripture. Physical geography is filled with references to the Bible, and Maury could not help but be fascinated by passages that mention the sea, such as Ps 8:8, Isa 43:16, Ps 107:23-24, and Eccl 1:7.[23] Maury contended that whoever studies the sea "must look upon it as a part of that exquisite machinery by which the harmonies of nature are preserved, and then will begin to perceive the developments of order and the evidences of design."[24]

When Maury observed and studied the oceans, he saw an intelligent design, the work of the Creator God whom he confidently believed had set "bars and doors to stay its proud waves; and who gave the sea His decree that its waters should not pass His command. He laid the foundations of the world so fast they should not be moved forever."[25]

---

22. Maury joined the Virginia Military Institute faculty in 1868 as a professor of physics after an internationally acclaimed career as an oceanographer, astronomer, historian, meteorologist, cartographer, geologist, writer, and commander in the United States Navy. Accordingly, he is affectionately remembered as the Pathfinder of the Seas, Father of Modern Oceanography and Naval Meteorology, and Scientist of the Seas. Maury not only enjoyed an illustrious career as a naval officer, scientist, and professor, he also was an uncompromising Christian and fervent believer in the truths of Scripture. (Corrado, "Matthew Fontaine Maury")

23. Grady, *Matthew Fontaine Maury, Father of Oceanography: A Biography, 1806–1873*. See also Major, "Honor to Whom Honor ... Matthew Fontaine Maury (1806–1873)," 82–87, and Johnson, "Matthew Maury's Paths of the Sea," 21.

24. Maury, *The Physical Geography of the Sea*, 57.

25. Maury, *The Physical Geography of the Sea*, 295–96. General revelation, God's disclosure of himself through nature or natural means, is expressed in Ps 19:1–4: "The heavens declare the glory of God; and the firmament shows His handiwork. Day unto day utters speech, and night unto night reveals knowledge. There is no speech nor language where their voice is not heard. Their line has gone out through all the earth, and their words to the end of the world."

APPENDIX C

As a testament to his convictions on creationism, thirteen years before he died, Maury delivered the following remark in a speech that fittingly embraced the whole of his professional Christian and scientific life and capped the career of one of the most outstanding creation scientists of the nineteenth century:

> I have been blamed by men of science, both in this country and in England, for quoting the Bible in confirmation of the doctrines of physical geography. The Bible, they say, was not written for scientific purposes, and is therefore of no authority in matters of science. I beg pardon! The Bible is authority for everything it touches. What would you think of the historian who should refuse to consult the historical records of the Bible, because the Bible was not written for the purposes of history? The Bible is true and science is true, and therefore each, if truly read, but proves the truth of the other. The agents in the physical economy of our planet are ministers of Him who made both it and the Bible. The records which He has chosen to make through the agency of these ministers of His upon the crust of the earth are as true as the records which by the hands of His prophets and servants,

---

In the New Testament, the Apostle Paul similarly discusses general revelation in Rom 1:20: "For since the creation of the world His invisible attributes are clearly seen, being understood by the things that are made, even His eternal power and Godhead, so that they are without excuse."

As a corollary, Matthew A. Lapine eloquently expresses the relationship between nature and Scripture in his book *The Logic of the Body: Retrieving Theological Psychology*: ". . . the book of Scripture and the book of nature. Both sources of revelation are divinely given, but the former explicitly frames how we are to understand the latter. Scripture is the *norma normans non normata*, the norming norm that is not normed; it is our magisterial authority. Nature is what saturates concepts, gives content to God's thoughts. Yet God's word is primary because his word brings into being all that is, nature included. Being (and epistemology) proceeds from his speech; what he says is. Humankind approaches nature within loving covenantal relationship with God through the regenerated gifts which we have been endowed, (embodied) reason and perception, following God's unfolding guidance through his prophets and apostles, his Son, and latterly, through the Scriptures which have been passed down and interpreted through his church and by the power of the Holy Spirit. The very words of God stand, while the ministers of his word, like our capacities and tradition, clarify and saturate the concepts." (Lapine, *The Logic of the Body*, 8)

He has been pleased to make in the Book of Life. They are both true; and when your men of science, with vain and hasty conceit, announce the discovery of disagreement between them, rely upon it, the fault is not with the witness of His records, but with the worm who essays to interpret evidence which he does not understand.[26]

THE BIBLE'S ARCHEOLOGICAL VERIFICATION

When it comes to the Bible, this amazing book names cities and their location and also names people and the dates they lived. Archaeologists have discovered time and again that every time they have unearthed an archaeological find, the biblical descriptions are accurate.[27] During the nineteenth century, Sir William Ramsay,[28] an English skeptic, embarked on a mission to dispute the historical accuracy of the Bible. Specifically, he directed his efforts toward scrutinizing the book of Acts. Ramsay initiated excavation efforts within the present-day borders of Turkey, which correspond to the historical region of Asia Minor. The discoveries made during this endeavor garnered much worldwide astonishment in the field of archaeology. The places mentioned by Paul as recorded in Acts were not only confirmed to have existed, but the terminology he employed to identify public authorities was also discovered beneath layers of archaeological remains, aligning

---

26. Lewis, *Matthew Fontaine Maury*, 99. Corrado, "Matthew Fontaine Maury."

27. Geisler, *The Big Book of Christian Apologetics*, 55.

28. Ramsay broadcast across England that he was going to disprove God's Word. His goal was to prove to England that the God that they worshiped wasn't true. He used the Book of Acts because Acts describes Paul's journeys in great detail and in the nineteenth century, when Ramsey was traveling, those cities had never been found. So Ramsey sailed to Turkey (Verga), pulled out his Bible, and followed Paul's trail. He walked three days on the Roman road to Pisidian Antioch (Acts 14:21, 26); at the end of a minor excavation, they found pieces of marble that said 'Pisidian Antioch'. Ramsey kept following Paul's trail and found Lystra (Acts 14:6, 8, 21; 16:1–2), Derbe (Acts 14:6, 20; 16:1; 20:4), Iconium (Acts 13:51; 14:1, 19, 21: 16:2), and on and on. (Ramsey and Wilson, *St. Paul: The Traveler and Roman Citizen*)

precisely with the accounts documented in the book of Acts by Luke.[29] Ramsay's resulting conversion to Christianity was influenced by the substantial historical and archaeological credibility of the biblical text.[30]

THE BIBLE HAS ENDURED THROUGH THE AGES

God's Word has endured through the ages, despite being a target of rulers and empires. The Bible was always under his custodianship: the Old Testament via the prophets and priests and the New Testament via Christ and his apostles. The closest the Bible (and Christianity) came to extinction was between 303 and 311 AD, during the rule of Roman Emperor Diocletian. He was upset by the growing detachment of Christians from society, as they would not take part in Roman society due to its paganism, bloodshed, and immodesty. In 303 AD, Diocletian decreed the return of Rome to its greatness and in doing so destroyed every church building, killed or imprisoned every pastor and church leader, and lastly, he tried to destroy every copy of the Bible. He was so effective at this eradication attempt that there is no standing church that pre-dates Diocletian and no complete Bible that predates 303 AD. How do we still have the Bible? As the news traveled of this eradication, people started to tear out pieces and parts of their Bibles so that their Bible in its entirety wasn't destroyed. That's why there exist

---

29. The word for public officials used in the Book of Acts is "Asiarch" and this term is found nowhere else. When Ramsey's crew excavated Thessalonica (Greece), the first thing they found was a sign that said "the Asiarch's welcome you." (Ramsey and Wilson, *St. Paul: The Traveler and Roman Citizen*)

30. Ramsey and Wilson, *St. Paul: The Traveler and Roman Citizen*. According to David Hunt, "Not one piece of evidence has ever been found to support the Book of Mormon—not a trace of large cities it names, no ruins, no coins, no letters or documents or monuments, nothing in writing. Not even one of the rivers or mountains or any of the topography it mentions has ever been identified" (Campbell, *Apologetics Quotes*, 57). Even the prestigious National Geographic Society commented, "Archaeologists and other scholars have long probed the hemisphere's past, and the Society does not know of anything found so far that has substantiated the Book of Mormon" (Campbell, *Apologetics Quotes*, 99).

25,000 fragmentary manuscripts of the New Testament that predate this time; however, the integrity of the Bible was not compromised, and these fragments were pulled back together following this event to ensure the Bible endured.[31]

Any objective document scholar will agree that the Bible has been astonishingly well maintained over the years. The books of the Bible from the fourteenth century AD are practically identical to those from the third century AD in content. Scholars were astounded to learn how comparable the Dead Sea Scrolls were to other ancient versions of the Old Testament, despite the fact that the Dead Sea Scrolls were hundreds of years older.[32] Even the most

---

31. Chadwick, "Diocletian," 176–89.

32. In 1947, the first Dead Sea Scrolls were discovered in Qumran, a village located about twenty miles east of Jerusalem on the northwest border of the Dead Sea. After ten years and numerous searches, eleven caves near the Dead Sea were discovered to contain tens of thousands of scroll fragments dating from the third century BC to 68 AD and representing an estimated eight hundred distinct works.

The Dead Sea Scrolls are a large collection of Jewish documents written in Hebrew, Aramaic, and Greek that cover a wide range of topics and literary styles. They include manuscripts or fragments of every book of the Hebrew Bible besides the book of Esther, all of which were composed nearly a thousand years earlier than any other known biblical manuscripts. The scrolls also include the earliest extant biblical commentary, on the book of Habakkuk, as well as numerous other writings, including religious works pertinent to contemporary Jewish sects.

The legends surrounding the contents of the Dead Sea Scrolls are vastly exaggerated. There were no lost books of the Bible or other works of literature for which there were no existing copies. The overwhelming majority of the Dead Sea Scrolls were simple copies of Old Testament books from between 250 and 150 BC. Qumran yielded copies or fragments of virtually every Old Testament book. Also discovered were extrabiblical and apocryphal writings, but the vast majority of the scrolls were Hebrew Old Testament copies. The Dead Sea Scrolls were such a remarkable discovery because they were in pristine condition and had been concealed for over two thousand years.

The discovery had the skeptic community excited because they believed this would disprove the steadfastness of the Bible; however, it was a 99 percent match, proving that the writings passed down over the many centuries were effective and under God's custodianship. The Dead Sea Scrolls can inspire confidence in the reliability of the Old Testament manuscripts, as there were few discrepancies between the previously discovered manuscripts and those discovered at Qumran. Undoubtedly, this is evidence of how God has preserved

APPENDIX C

adamant critics and skeptics of the Bible recognize that the Bible has been transmitted more correctly over the ages than any other ancient manuscript.[33]

There is no indication that the Bible has been systematically changed, edited, or tampered with. The sheer abundance of biblical writings makes any attempt to alter God's Word obvious. There is no important teaching of the Bible that is called into question because of minor variations across copies.

Despite human error and purposeful attacks, God has maintained his Word.[34] We can be certain that the Bible we have now is

---

his Word throughout the ages, safeguarding it from extinction and preventing significant error. (Vanderkam and Flint, "Dead Sea Scrolls," 27)

On the contrary, the Book of Mormon has undergone close to 4,000 revisions and counting (both non-substantive and substantive)—some of which are significant doctrinal changes—since its original printing in 1830 (Tanner and Tanner, *3,913 Changes in the Book of Mormon*). However, Joseph Smith said, "that the Book of Mormon was the most correct of any book on earth, and the keystone of our religion and a man would get nearer to God by abiding by its precepts, than by any other book" (*History of the Church*, vol. 4, p. 461).

33. For just the New Testament, there are approximately 6,000 manuscripts or portions of manuscripts, some of which date to earlier than AD 120, compared to only ten existing manuscripts of Julius Caesar's *Gaelic Wars* (the earliest known copy was written approximately 900 years after the original), five existing manuscripts of Aristotle's *Poetics* (the earliest known copy was written approximately 1,400 years after the original), less than ten existing manuscripts of the writings of Herodotus (the earliest known copy was written approximately 1,300 years after the original), and less than ten of each of Homer's writings (the earliest known copy was written approximately 500 years after the original). Additionally, within the first few centuries of Christ's death, the New Testament was translated from Greek into Syriac, Coptic, Latin, and Aramaic; 19,000 copies of those manuscripts exist. Lastly, the early church fathers wrote volumes of commentary on the Bible. Bruce Metzger, an American biblical scholar, Bible translator, and textual critic, argues that if all we had of the New Testament were the quotations and citations by the early church fathers, we could reproduce over 95 percent of the New Testament from their writings alone. (Turner, *Greek Manuscripts of the Ancient World*, 54)

34. The books of the Old Testament were composed between 1,400 BC and 400 BC and the New Testament was composed approximately between AD 40 and AD 90. So, it's been somewhere between 3,400 and 1,900 years since a book of the Bible was written. The original manuscripts have now been lost and they almost certainly no longer exist. Scribes have copied the books of the Bible several times since they were first penned, so there are copies of

the same Bible that was penned initially. According to 2 Tim 3:16 and Matt 5:18, we can believe the Bible because it is God's Word.

"I PITY THE FOOL!"[35]

One can approach the question of why one should believe the Bible as God's Word in a number of different ways, as discussed above. One can prove it via archeology, science, prophecy, etc. This is all meaningful and it matters to Christians who have a coherent worldview and wish to make sense of this discussion.

Ps 14:1 and Ps 53:1 both state that "the fool has said in his heart, 'There is no God.'" The Hebrew word for "fool" in these texts is *nabal*, which often refers to an impious individual with no sense of ethical or religious reality.[36] As a result, the implication of these passages is not that "unintelligent people do not believe in God." Instead, these verses mean that "sinful people do not believe in God." In other words, denying God is a wicked act, and denying God often coincides with a wicked lifestyle. When God calls someone a fool, it's not just a dig; it's a moral, spiritual, and intellectual evaluation of someone who knows the truth but refuses to accept it.

---

copies of copies. The question asked by skeptics and false religions is, in light of all this, can we still trust the Bible? The answer is "Yes." The Bible is inerrant because it was inspired by God, as per 2 Tim 3:16–17 and John 17:17. Of course, copies of the manuscripts cannot claim inerrancy; only the original manuscripts can. No one is flawless, no matter how meticulously the scribes copied the scriptures. The many manuscripts of the scriptures changed little over the years. Inverted words (one manuscript reads "Christ Jesus" while another reads "Jesus Christ"), simple spelling changes (like American neighbor vs. British neighbour), or readily recognizable missing words account for the great bulk of these discrepancies. In short, more than 99 percent of the biblical text is unquestionable. No theological teaching or mandate is compromised by the less than 1 percent of the text in question. In other words, the Bible copies we have now are pure. The Bible has not been tampered with, altered, edited, or rewritten. (Geisler, *The Big Book of Christian Apologetics*, 51–56)

35. Mr. T (Laurence Tureaud), known for his acting roles as B. A. Baracus in the 1980s television series *The A-Team* and as boxer Clubber Lang in the 1982 film *Rocky III*, often used catchphrase "I pity the fool!"

36. Liddell and Scott, *Greek-English Lexicon*.

APPENDIX C

Many atheists are exceptionally bright. A person's refusal to believe in God is not due to his or her intelligence, or absence thereof. A person's lack of righteousness causes them to reject faith in God. Many people do not object to the concept of a Creator—as long as he stays out of their way and minds his own business. People oppose the concept of a Creator who expects moral behavior from his creation. Rather than struggling against a guilty conscience, some individuals reject the concept of God. Ps 14:1 calls such a person a "fool."

A sense of accountability to a divine Being is accompanied by belief in this Being. Some deny God's existence in order to avoid the condemnation of their own conscience, which was created by God. They say to themselves, "There is no global overseer. There is no Day of Judgment. I am free to live as I wish." Thus, the moral draw of the conscience is easier to ignore.

Attempting to persuade oneself that God does not exist is unwise. The meaning of "The fool has said in his heart, 'There is no God'" is that a heart of impiety and sin will deny the existence of God. The atheist's denial is antithetical to overwhelming evidence, including his own conscience and the universe he inhabits.

The absence of evidence for God's existence is not the actual reason atheists reject God's existence. Their rejection is a result of their desire to live free of the moral constraints God requires and to avoid the remorse associated with violating those constraints.[37] To this point, Rom 1:18–25 sums this up well:

> The wrath of God is revealed from heaven against all ungodliness and unrighteousness of men, who suppress the truth in unrighteousness, because what may be known of God is manifest in them, for God has shown it to them. For since the creation of the world His invisible attributes are clearly seen, being understood by the things that are made, even His eternal power and Godhead, so that they are without excuse, because, although they knew God,

---

37. In his book, *The Great Divorce*, C. S. Lewis wrote, "There are only two kinds of people in the end: those who say to God, 'Thy will be done,' and those to whom God says, in the end, '*Thy* will be done.' All that are in Hell, choose it. Without that self-choice, there could be no Hell."

they did not glorify Him as God, nor were thankful, but became futile in their thoughts, and their foolish hearts were darkened. Professing to be wise, they became fools . . . Therefore God also gave them up to uncleanness, in the lusts of their hearts, to dishonor their bodies among themselves, who exchanged the truth of God for the lie, and worshiped and served the creature rather than the Creator.

Appendix D
The Bible: The Sole Authority for Faith and Practice

> There is, brethren, one God, the knowledge of whom we gain from the Holy Scriptures, and from no other source . . . so all of us who wish to practice piety will be unable to learn its practice from any other quarter than the oracles of God. Whatever things, then, the Holy Scriptures declare, at these let us look; and whatever things they teach, these let us learn.
>
> —St. Hippolytus of Rome, *Against the Heresy of One Noetus*

WHERE DOES AUTHORITY LIE? Does it reside with a person, a group of people, traditions, or the Bible? Depending on the religion or faith group in which one resides, the answer could be any of those choices, and Satan confuses the issue via his deceptive PSYOP by aligning authority with the wrong source. The purpose of this appendix is to discuss why the Bible is the sole authority for faith and practice.[1] It is important to understand this to fully implement the counter-PSYOP method of *Indirect Refutation* (and tangentially the counter-PSYOP methods of *Conditioning*, *Forestalling*, *Direct Refutation*, and *Restrictive Measures*).

---

1. Drawn from Cloud, "Is the Bible the Sole Authority for Faith and Practice?"

SCRIPTURE IS SUFFICIENT FOR FAITH AND PRACTICE

Second Timothy 3:16-17 reads, "All Scripture is given by inspiration of God, and is profitable for doctrine, for reproof, for correction, for instruction in righteousness, that the man of God may be complete, thoroughly equipped for every good work." The Scripture alone is given by inspiration from God and can make the man of God perfect. The word of men, on the other hand, falls significantly short.

Paul contrasts the word of men with the Word of God in 1 Thess 2:13: "For this reason we also thank God without ceasing, because when you received the word of God which you heard from us, you welcomed it not as the word of men, but as it is in truth, the word of God, which also effectively works in you who believe." Today, we must continue to make this essential distinction. If a teaching is not from God's Word, it is the word of man. The only thing a believer needs is the Word of God, the Bible, because it has the power to make him perfect. Therefore, nothing else is necessary beyond the Bible.

THE FAITH WAS ONCE DELIVERED TO THE SAINTS

The Bible is the complete Word of God. Jude 3 reads, "Beloved, while I was very diligent to write to you concerning our common salvation, I found it necessary to write to you exhorting you to contend earnestly for the faith which was once for all delivered to the saints." "The faith" refers to the body of New Testament truths that the apostles communicated under the guidance of the Holy Spirit. The phrase "once delivered" indicates that this body of truth was given during a single time period and was completed. It refers to the scriptures of the New Testament, which were concluded during the time of the apostles. Jude 3 ultimately refutes the notion that the Christian faith was progressively transmitted by any individual, organization, or religion.[2]

THE LAST CHAPTER OF THE LAST BOOK OF THE BIBLE WAS SEALED

Not only is the Bible complete, but God has also warned against adding to or subtracting from it. Rev 22:18–19 reads as follows: "For I testify to everyone who hears the words of the prophecy of this book: If anyone adds to these things, God will add to him the plagues that are written in this book; and if anyone takes away from the words of the book of this prophecy, God shall take away his part from the Book of Life, from the holy city, and from the things which are written in this book." Those who claim to possess a new revelation or a tradition on equal footing with the Bible are subject to the judgment described in this passage. The book of Revelation closes and completes the Holy Scripture; nothing may be added or taken away.

THE SECOND CENTURY RECOGNIZED THE COMPLETED CANON OF SCRIPTURE

During the second century, Christian leaders demonstrated their acknowledgment of the canon of the New Testament and their acceptance of the apostolic writings as Holy Scripture, attributing to them an authority equal to that of the Old Testament. God provided them with wisdom through the Holy Spirit during this process, and they did not need to wait for council declarations some decades later.[3]

For instance, in his extant writings, Irenaeus (125–192 AD) quoted the New Testament books over 1,800 times and used them

---

2. Christianity is solely defined by the Bible. Christianity is not defined by tradition that has not been passed down and continues to deepen and mature over time.

3. See John 16:13; 17:8; 1 Thess 2:13; 1 John 2:20.

"in such a way as to imply that they had for some time been considered as of unquestioned authority."[4] Irenaeus accepted the four Gospels as Scripture, and only those four. Clement of Alexandria (150–217 AD) cited and acknowledged the four Gospels and the majority of the other books of the New Testament, referring to them as "divine Scriptures." Tertullian (150–220 AD) extensively referenced the New Testament books in his writings, with a total of over 7,200 citations. Moreover, he regarded these books as authoritative Scripture. The Latin translation known as *Itala*, believed to have been produced during the second century, "contained all the books that now make up the New Testament."[5] In 1740, a collection of New Testament Scriptures dating from the latter half of the second century was unearthed in the Ambrosian Library located in Milan, Italy. The list from the second century encompasses the complete collection of twenty seven books that comprise the canon of the New Testament.[6]

Under the guidance of the Holy Spirit, God's people circulated and accepted the completed New Testament Scriptures. Numerous modern textual scholars who write about these early centuries either deny or completely disregard the Holy Spirit's role in the inspiration and canonicity of the New Testament. The apostles were not left to their own devices to transcribe the account of Christ, nor were the early Christians left to their own devices to determine which writings were inspired.[7] The New Testament contains the inspired words of the Lord Jesus Christ, and the Lord's sheep recognize the voice of their Good Shepherd and can distinguish it from that of false shepherds.[8]

---

4. Miller, *General Biblical Introduction*, 140.
5. Hentz, *History of the Lutheran Version*, 59.
6. Hentz, *History of the Lutheran Version*, 60.
7. See 1 Thess 2:13.
8. See John 10:4, 5, 27.

APPENDIX D

NOT TO THE UNINSPIRED TRADITIONS OF MEN, BUT THE INSPIRED TRADITION GIVEN BY THE APOSTLES

The passages that exhort Christians to adhere to tradition refer to the inspired tradition handed down by the apostles, not to the uninspired traditions of men who came after them. In the New Testament, "tradition" is used in two different contexts. First, it refers to divinely inspired apostolic doctrine.[9] This tradition is binding on the churches because it is supernaturally recorded in the New Testament. Second, the term refers to the uninspired teachings that religious teachers attempt to add to the Bible in order to govern the lives of men.[10] In this sense, tradition is condemned, as the following references demonstrate:

- "Making the word of God of no effect through your tradition which you have handed down. And many such things you do" (Mark 7:13).
- "And in vain they worship Me, Teaching as doctrines the commandments of men" (Matt 15:9).
- "Beware lest anyone cheat you through philosophy and empty deceit, according to the tradition of men, according to the basic principles of the world, and not according to Christ" (Col 2:8).

We are grateful that the Lord has provided us with a complete and sufficient Revelation and that we do not rely on extra-biblical prophecies, visions, voices, speech, or traditions. The Bible contains everything necessary for faith and practice for the church.

As a result, while "the Bible itself is a sort of tradition," this does not imply that it is only one among many authoritative traditions. Only the Bible is a God-inspired tradition. That is what distinguishes it from other written works. The Bible claims to be God's inspired Word. The Bible has almost two thousand instances

---

9. See 2 Thess 2:15; 3:6.
10. See Matt 15:1–6; Mark 7:9–13; Col 2:8.

of sentences such as "thus saith the Lord." Thus, the traditions that Christians are encouraged to follow are God's inspired tradition as established in the biblical text.

A CASE FOR CONTRADICTION

The Scripture always upholds itself as the absolute and sole standard for truth. For example, Isa 8:20 states, "To the law and to the testimony! If they do not speak according to this word, it is because there is no light in them." Those who speak contrary to the scriptures are in darkness. The Lord Jesus Christ severely rebuked the Pharisees because they added their manmade tradition as an authority alongside the Scriptures *and thereby contradicted them*:

> Then the scribes and Pharisees who were from Jerusalem came to Jesus, saying, "Why do Your disciples transgress the tradition of the elders? For they do not wash their hands when they eat bread." He answered and said to them, "Why do you also transgress the commandment of God because of your tradition? For God commanded, saying, 'Honor your father and your mother'; and, 'He who curses father or mother, let him be put to death.' But you say, 'Whoever says to his father or mother, "Whatever profit you might have received from me is a gift to God"—then he need not honor his father or mother.' Thus you have made the commandment of God of no effect by your tradition. Hypocrites! Well did Isaiah prophesy about you, saying: 'These people draw near to Me with their mouth, And honor Me with their lips, But their heart is far from Me. And in vain they worship Me, Teaching as doctrines the commandments of men'" (Matt 15:1–9).

Many false religions' doctrine and practice are not based on the Bible, and in many cases, they contradict the Bible, so clearly they cannot be its source.[11]

---

11. The papacy, Mariolatry (excessive veneration or worship of Mary, the mother of Jesus), saints, the priesthood, the Mass, and Purgatory are not only not contained in the New Testament, but they also contradict basic New

APPENDIX D

Each person has a choice of trusting the Bible as God's authoritative and complete Word or trusting a person, a group of people, a tradition, or a religion. They cannot both be correct because they frequently contradict each other. Innumerable ways demonstrate that the Bible is the inspired and infallible Word of God: fulfilled prophecy; scientific accuracy; cohesive unity, despite being written over hundreds of years; the power to change lives; universal appeal; the testimony of Jesus Christ; and the testimony of the apostles.[12]

Testament doctrine and practice. Among many other texts, the papacy opposes 1 Pet 5:1–4. Meanwhile, Mariolatry and the saints contradict 1 Tim 2:5, and the Mass contradicts 1 Cor 11:23–26. Purgatory contradicts 2 Cor 5:1–8 and Phil 1:23, and the priesthood contradicts the New Testament in that Christ alone is a priest after the order of Melchizedek (Heb 7:21–27), and Christ established no priesthood other than the priesthood of all believers for the New Testament churches (1 Pet 2:5, 9). There is no mention of a priest being ordained and set apart in the New Testament, nor of him practicing the type of ministry that we see in the Roman Catholic Church. There are criteria for pastors and deacons in the New Testament, but none for priests. Additionally, if one obeys 2 Thess 2:15 and 3:6 and conducts a comparative analysis between Roman Catholic tradition and the teachings of the apostles, it becomes necessary to repudiate Roman Catholicism due to its deviation from this established framework. The apostles did not espouse the notion of a special priesthood within the community of believers, nor did they advocate for the establishment of a papal authority. The apostles did not espouse the notion that the Lord's Supper should be seen as a form of sacrificial offering. Moreover, they did not impart the doctrine that Mary is sinless or that she is a perpetual virgin. Additionally, they did not teach that she ascended bodily to Heaven, holds the title of Queen of Heaven, or advocate for Christians to engage in prayer directed toward her. The apostles did not teach that their position should be passed down when they died, and they made no mention of "apostolic succession." The apostles did not espouse the notion of sacraments within the teachings of the churches. The concept of intercessory prayer toward specific saints was not included in their teachings. Regrettably, the aforementioned Roman Catholic traditions represent only a limited selection of practices that deviate from the teachings of the apostles as documented in the New Testament Scriptures. It is important to note that there exist several additional instances of such deviations. (Gendron, *Preparing for Eternity*, 81–132)

12. Study the book of Acts, for example, to appreciate what the apostles thought of Scripture.

Bibliography

Baehr, Ted. "Miracle on Main Street?" *Focus on the Family*, April 1995.
Barnett, John. "Sober Minded—Choosing Restrained Living in an Unrestrained Culture." DTBM. 2018. https://dtbm.org/sober-minded-choosing-restrained-living-in-an-un-restrained-culture/.
———. "Your Bible Is Supernaturally-Trustworthy—Seven Ways to Know that the Bible Is True." DTBM. 2023. https://dtbm.org/your-bible-is-supernaturally-trustworthy-seven-ways-to-know-that-the-bible-is-true/.
Bellshaw, William G. "The New Testament Doctrine of Satan." *Grace Theological Journal* 9, no. 3 (1968) 24–39.
Bloom, Jon. "How to Fight Lukewarmness." https://www.desiringgod.org/articles/how-to-fight-lukewarmness.
Boyd, Gerald M. "Raze Berlin Wall, Reagan Urges Soviets." *New York Times*, 1987. https://www.nytimes.com/1987/06/13/world/raze-berlin-wall-reagan-urges-soviet.html.
Bracher, Karl. *The German Dictatorship*. New York: Holt, Rinehart, and Winston, 1970.
Brierly, Peter. *UK Church Statistics, Number 2, 2010 to 2020*. Tonbridge: ADBC, 2014. https://faithsurvey.co.uk/download/csintro2.pdf.
Bruntz, George G. "Allied Propaganda and the Collapse of German Morale in 1918." *Public Opinion Quarterly* 2, no. 1 (1938) 61–76.
Bubeck, Mark. *Preparing for Battle: A Spiritual Warfare Workbook*. Chicago: Moody, 1999.
———. *The Adversary: The Christian Versus Demon Activity*. Chicago: Moody, 2013.
Bullinger, E.W. *Figures of Speech Used in the Bible: Explained and Illustrated*. New York: Messrs, E. & J. B. Young & Co., 1898.
Campbell, Charlie H. *Apologetics Quotes*. Carlsbad, CA: The Always Be Ready Apologetics Ministry, 2020.
Carlyle, Thomas. "The Hero as Man of Letters." In *On Heroes, Hero Worship, and the Heroic in History*, edited by David R. Sorensen and Brent E. Kinser, 132–61. New Haven, CT: Yale University Press, 2013.

BIBLIOGRAPHY

Carson, D. A. "God, the Bible and Spiritual Warfare: A Review Article." *Journal of Evangelical Theology* 42, no. 2 (June 1999) 251–69.

Chadwick, Henry. "Diocletian and the Great Persecution; Rise of Constantine." In *The Church in Ancient Society: From Galilee to Gregory the Great*, 176–89. Oxford: Oxford University Press, 2001.

Chester, Tim, and Steve Timmis. *Total Church*. Downers Grove, IL: InterVarsity, 2007.

The Church of Jesus Christ of Latter-day Saints. *2022 Statistical Report for the April 2023 Conference*. https://newsroom.churchofjesuschrist.org/article/2022-statistical-report-april-2023-conference.

Cloud, David. "Is the Bible the Sole Authority for Faith and Practice?" https://www.wayoflife.org/database/is_the_bible_sole_authority.html.

Corrado, Jonathan K. "Be Not Deceived: Spiritually Train to Overcome Secular Science Obstacles." Institute for Creation Research Creation Science Update, July 25, 2022. https://www.icr.org/article/Be-not-deceived.

———. "God Perfectly Keeps His Promises." *The Baptist Bulletin*, Spring 2023.

———. "Imago Dei: Man's Designed Role as Image-Bearer." Institute for Creation Research Creation Science Update, April 25, 2022. https://www.icr.org/article/mans-designed-role.

———. "The Importance of Context in Sound Biblical Interpretation." Institute for Creation Research Creation Science Update, January 9, 2023. https://www.icr.org/article/importance-of-context-in-sound.

———. "Matthew Fontaine Maury: The Father of Oceanography." Institute for Creation Research Creation Science Update, October 27, 2022. https://www.icr.org/article/Matthew-F-Maury.

———. "Move Toward the Enemy: Fighting for Truth in Science." Institute for Creation Research Creation Science Update, November 10, 2022. https://www.icr.org/article/move-toward-enemy.

———. "The Role and Realm of Science." Institute for Creation Research Creation Science Update, January 17, 2022. https://www.icr.org/article/role-and-realm-of-science.

Crumm, Robin. "Information Warfare: An Air Force Policy for the Role of Public Affairs." Master's Thesis, Air University Press, 1996.

Cuerden, Adam. *Centreville, VA, Quaker Guns in the Fort on the Heights*. March 1862. Photograph. Wikimedia. https://commons.wikimedia.org/wiki/File:Centreville,_VA,_Quaker_Guns_in_the_fort_on_the_heights.jpg#mw-jump-to-license.

Department of the Air Force. "EC-130J Commando Solo" Fact Sheet. https://www.af.mil/About-Us/Fact-Sheets/Display/Article/104535/ec-130j-commando-solo/.

Department of the Army. *FM 3–05.301/MCRP 3–40.6A Psychological Operations Tactics, Techniques, and Procedures*. Washington, DC: Department of the Army, 2003.

———. *FM 3–13.4 Army Support to Military Deception*. Washington, DC: Department of the Army, 2019.

BIBLIOGRAPHY

Dummy Sherman Tank. Photograph. Wikimedia. https://commons.wikimedia. org/wiki/File:DummyShermanTank.jpg#mw-jump-to-license.

E04934. September 17, 1918. Photograph. Wikimedia. https://commons. wikimedia.org/wiki/File:E04934.jpg#mw-jump-to-license.

F-16 Mockups on Fake Runway Spangdahlem AB 1985. April 29, 1985. Photograph. Wikimedia. https://commons.wikimedia.org/wiki/File:F-16_ mockups_on_fake_runway_Spangdahlem_AB_1985.JPEG#mw-jump-to-license.

Fassler, Barbara. "Theories of Homosexuality as Sources of Bloomsbury's Androgyny." *Signs* 5, no. 2 (1979) 237–51. http://www.jstor.org/stable/3173559.

Federal Research Division. *An Overview of Psychological Operations (PSYOP).* Washington, DC: Library of Congress, 1989. https://apps.dtic.mil/sti/pdfs/ADA302389.pdf.

Field, Clive. "Counting Religion in Britain, December 2016." January 1, 2017. http://www.brin.ac.uk/counting-religion-in-britain-december-2016/.

Fisher, Alec. *The Logic of Real Arguments.* 2nd ed. Cambridge: Cambridge University Press, 2004.

Gathercole, Simon. *Jesus' Eschatological Vision of the Fall of Satan: Luke 10, 18 Reconsidered.* Cambridge: Cambridge University Press, 2003.

Geisler, Norman. *The Big Book of Christian Apologetics.* Grand Rapids, MI: Baker, 2012.

Gendron, Mike. *Preparing for Eternity: Should We Trust God's Word or Religious Traditions?* Southlake, TX: PTG, 2011.

Gignac, Francis T. *An Introductory New Testament Greek Course.* Revised edition. Washington, DC: The Catholic University of America Press, 2015.

Got Questions Ministries. "How Should a Christian View Relics?" https://www.gotquestions.org/Christian-relics.html.

———. "Is it Important to Know Greek and Hebrew when Studying the Bible?" https://www.gotquestions.org/Greek-Hebrew-Bible.html.

———. "Is There Such a Thing as Absolute Truth / Universal Truth?" https://www.gotquestions.org/absolute-truth.html.

———. "What are the Potential Issues with Celebrity Pastors?" https://www.gotquestions.org/celebrity-pastors.html.

———. "What Does it Mean that God is a Holy God? What is the Holiness of God? https://www.gotquestions.org/holy-God-holiness-of-God.html.

———. "What Does it Mean to Trust in Jesus?" https://www.gotquestions.org/trust-in-Jesus.html.

———. "What Does the Bible Mean by 'Dying to Self'?" https://www.gotquestions.org/dying-to-self.html.

———. "What Does the Bible say About Creation vs. Evolution?" https://www.gotquestions.org/creation-evolution.html.

———. "What Does the Bible say About Predestination vs. Free Will?" https://www.gotquestions.org/predestination-vs-free-will.html.

BIBLIOGRAPHY

———. "What Does the Bible Teach About the Trinity?" https://www.gotquestions.org/Trinity-Bible.html.

———. "What is Mormonism?" https://www.gotquestions.org/Mormons.html.

———. "What is the Key to Truly Experiencing God?" https://www.gotquestions.org/experiencing-God.html.

———. "Why did Jesus Speak so Strongly Against Lukewarm Faith?" https://www.gotquestions.org/Jesus-lukewarm-faith.html.

———. "Why is Faith Without Works Dead?" https://www.gotquestions.org/faith-without-works-dead.html.

———. "What is Progressive Christianity, and is it Biblical?" https://www.gotquestions.org/Progressive-Christianity.html.

Grady J., *Matthew Fontaine Maury, Father of Oceanography: A Biography, 1806–1873*. Jefferson, NC: McFarland & Company, 2015.

Gregor, Neil. *How to Read Hitler*. London: Granta, 2005.

Grudem, Wayne A. *Systematic Theology: An Introduction to Biblical Doctrine*. Leicester, UK: Inter-Varsity, 2004.

Ham, Ken. *Divided Nation: Cultures in Chaos & A Conflicted Church*. Green Forest, AR: Master Books, 2021.

Henry, Matthew. "Commentary on Ezekiel 28." *Matthew Henry's Commentary*, Vol. 4. Peabody, MA: Hendrickson, 2018.

———. "Commentary on Isaiah 14." *Matthew Henry's Commentary*, Vol. 4. Peabody, MA: Hendrickson, 2018.

Hentz, John. *History of the Lutheran Version*. Columbus, OH: The F.J. Heer Printing Co., 1910.

Herz, Martin. "Some Psychological Lessons from Leaflet Propaganda in World War II." *Public Opinion Quarterly* 13, no. 3 (1949) 471–86.

Hitler, Adolf. *Mein Kampf*. Boston: Houghton Mifflin, 1999.

Hodge, Bodie, and Roger Patterson, eds. *World Religions and Cults: Moralistic, Mythical and Mysticism Religions*, Vol. 2. Green Forest, AR: New Leaf, 2016.

Howard, Michael. *Strategic Deception in the Second World War*. New York: W.W. Norton & Company, 1990.

Hunt, Dave. *A Woman Rides the Beast*. Eugene, OR: Harvest House, 1994.

Ingram, Chip. *The Invisible War: What Every Believer Needs to Know about Satan, Demons, and Spiritual Warfare*. Grand Rapids, MI: Baker, 2015.

Johnson, James J. S. "Matthew Maury's Paths of the Sea." *Acts & Facts* 49, no. 9 (2020).

Joint Chiefs of Staff. *Joint Publication 3-0: Joint Operations*. Washington, DC: Department of Defense, 2011.

———. *Joint Publication 3-13.2: Psychological Operations*. Washington, DC: Department of Defense, 2010.

———. *Joint Publication 3-13.4: Military Deception*. Washington, DC: Department of Defense, 2012.

Kallis, Aristotle A. *Nazi Propaganda and the Second World War*. New York: Palgrave Macmillan, 2008.

BIBLIOGRAPHY

Keller, Timothy. *Center Church: Doing Balanced, Gospel-Centered Ministry in Your City*. Grand Rapids, MI: Zondervan, 2012.

Kennedy, D. James. *Why I Believe*. Nashville, TN: Word, 1999.

King, Paul. *Is It of God? A Biblical Guidebook for Spiritual Discernment*. Newberry, FL: Bridge-Logos, 2019.

Lapine, Matthew A. *The Logic of the Body: Retrieving Theological Psychology*. Bellingham, WA: Lexham, 2020.

Leeming, David A. *Creation Myths of the World: An Encyclopedia*. Santa Barbara, CA: ABC-CLIO, 2010.

Leventhal, Todd. "The Child Organ Trafficking Rumor: A Modern 'Urban Legen.'" Washington, DC: United States Information Agency, 1994. http://pascalfroissart.online.fr/3-cache/1994-leventhal.pdf.

Lewis, C.S. *The Great Divorce*. San Fransico, CA: HarperOne, 2001.

Lewis, Charles L. *Matthew Fontaine Maury: The Pathfinder of the Seas*. Annapolis, MD: United States Naval Institute, 1969 reprint by AMS, New York, 1927.

Liddell, Henry G., and Robert Scott. *Greek-English Lexicon*. 9th ed. Oxford: Clarendon, 1996.

Löfstedt, Torsten. "Satan's Fall and the Mission of the Seventy-Two." *SEA* 76 (2011) 95–114.

Longman, Tremper, and David E. Garland. *The Expositor's Bible Commentary*. Grand Rapids, MI: Zondervan, 2006.

Ludwig, Dean C., and Clinton O. Longenecker. "The Bathsheba Syndrome: The Ethical Failure of Successful Leaders." *Journal of Business Ethics* 12 (1993) 265–73.

Lumpkin, Joseph B. *The Encyclopedia of the Lost and Rejected Scriptures: The Pseudepigrapha and the Apocrypha*. Blountsville, AL: Fifth Estate, 2010.

MacArthur, John F. *2 Corinthians*. MacArthur New Testament Commentary. Chicago: Moody, 2003.

———. *Ephesians*. MacArthur New Testament Commentary. Chicago: Moody, 1986.

———. "God's Demand for Discernment." https://www.gty.org/library/sermons-library/TM19-11/gods-demand-for-discernment-john-macarthur.

———. *1–3 John*. MacArthur New Testament Commentary. Chicago: Moody, 2007.

———. *The MacArthur Bible Commentary*. Nashville, TN: Thomas Nelson, 2005.

———. *Mark 1–8*. MacArthur New Testament Commentary. Chicago: Moody, 2015.

———. *1 Timothy*. MacArthur New Testament Commentary. Chicago: Moody, 1995.

MacArthur, John F., and Richard Mayhue, eds. *Biblical Doctrine: A Systematic Summary of Bible Truth*. Wheaton, IL: Crossway, 2017.

BIBLIOGRAPHY

Mangel, Marc, and Francisco J. Samaniego. "Abraham Wald's Work on Aircraft Survivability." *Journal of the American Statistical Association* 79, no. 386 (1984) 259–67.

Martin, Walter. *The Kingdom of the Cults*. Bloomington, MN: Bethany House, 2019.

Maury, Maury Fontaine. *The Physical Geography of the Sea*. 6th ed. New York: Harper & Brothers, 1959.

McCallum, Dennis, ed. *The Death of Truth*. Minneapolis: Bethany House, 1996.

McIntyre, Jesse. "To Respond or Not to Respond: Addressing Adversarial Propaganda." *Military Review* (May-June 2016) 62–69. https://www.armyupress.army.mil/Portals/7/military-review/Archives/English/MilitaryReview_20160630_art012.pdf.

Merriam-Webster's Collegiate Dictionary. 11th ed. Springfield, MA: Merriam-Webster, 2003.

Metzger, Bruce. *The Early Versions of the New Testament: Their Origin, Transmission, and Limitations*. Oxford: Oxford University Press, 1977.

Miller, Herbert. *General Biblical Introduction*. Houghton, NY: Word-Bearer, 1960.

Major, Trevor. "Honor to Whom Honor . . . Matthew Fontaine Maury (1806–1873)." *Creation Research Society Quarterly* 32, no. 2 (September 1995) 82–87.

Morgenstern, Oskar. "Abraham Wald, 1902–1950." *Econometrica* 19, no. 1 (1951) 361–67.

Morris, Henry. *The Long War Against God: The History and Impact of the Creation/Evolution Conflict*. Grand Rapids, MI: Baker, 1989.

Narula, Sunil. "Psychological Operations (PSYOP): A Conceptual Overview." *Strategic Analysis* 28, no. 1 (January 2004) 177–92.

Newcourt-Nowodworski, Stanley. *Black Propaganda in the Second World War*. Stroud, UK: Sutton, 2005.

Newton, John. "The Kite, or the Fall of Pride." *Thornton Family: Letters and Papers*. GBR/0012/MS Add.7674. Cambridge University Library. https://archivesearch.lib.cam.ac.uk/repositories/2/resources/7157

Olsen, Roger E. *The Journey of Modern Theology: From Reconstruction to Deconstruction*. Downers Grove, IL: InterVarsity, 2013.

O'Shaughnessy, Nicholas. *Selling Hitler: Propaganda and the Nazi Brand*. London: C. Hurst & Co., 2016.

Paxton, Robert O. *The Anatomy of Fascism*. London: Allen Lane, 2004.

Payne, J. Barton. *Encyclopedia of Biblical Prophecy*. Ada, MI: Baker, 1980.

Penn-Lewis, Jessie. *War on the Saints: A History of Satanic Deceptions in Christianity and the Conflict Between Good and Evil*. Fort Washington, PA: CLC, 1916.

Pearson, Lionel. "Propaganda in the Archidamian War." *Classical Philology* 31, no. 1 (1936) 33–52.

Pettus, David. "Reading a Protoevangelium in the Context of Genesis." *Eruditio Ardescens* 1, no. 2 (2014) 1–18.

BIBLIOGRAPHY

Pew Research Center. "Modeling the Future of Religion in America: If Recent Trends in Religious Switching Continue, Christians Could Make Up Less than Half of the US Population Within a Few Decades." September 13, 2022. https://www.pewresearch.org/religion/2022/09/13/modeling-the-future-of-religion-in-america/.

———. "Parenting in America: Outlook, Worries, Aspirations are Strongly Linked to Financial Situation." December 17, 2015. https://www.pewresearch.org/social-trends/2015/12/17/1-the-american-family-today/#:~:text=The%20declining%20share%20of%20children%20living%20in%20what,but%20so%20has%20the%20fluidity%20of%20the%20family.

Pfeiffer, Charles F. *Wycliffe Bible Encyclopedia*. Chicago: Moody, 1975.

Phillips, Kenneth J. *Guide to the Sun*. New York: Cambridge University Press, 1992.

Piper, John. "New God, New Gospel, New Gladness: How Is Christian Joy Distinct?" https://www.desiringgod.org/messages/new-god-new-gospel-new-gladness.

———. *When I Don't Desire God*. Wheaton, IL: Crossway, 2013.

Ramsey, William M., and Mark Wilson, eds. *St. Paul: The Traveler and Roman Citizen*. Grand Rapids, MI: Kregel, 2001.

Renner, Rick. *Apostles and Prophets: Their Roles in the Past, Present, and Last-Days Church*. Shippensburg, PA: Harrison House, 2022.

Ressa, Jerry F. "Satanic Influences in the American Christian Church in a Post-Modern Consumer Society." D.Min diss., George Fox University, 2018.

Rhodes, Ron. *5-Minute Apologetics for Today: 365 Quick Answers to Key Questions*. Eugene, OR: Harvest House, 2010.

Roach, Erin. "ATHEISM: Penn Jillette Urges Evangelism." *Baptist Press*, posted February 12, 2009. https://www.baptistpress.com/resource-library/news/atheism-penn-jillette-urges-evangelism.

Romerstein, Herbert. "Counterpropaganda: We Can't Win Without It." In *Strategic Influence: Public Diplomacy, Counterpropaganda, and Political Warfare*, edited by J. Michael Waller, 137–80. Washington, DC: Institute of World Politics, 2009.

Row, Thomas. "Mobilizing the Nation: Italian Propaganda in the Great War." *Journal of Decorative and Propaganda Arts* 24 (2002) 141–69.

Rutherford, Ward. *Hitler's Propaganda Machine*. London: Bison, 1978.

Shirer, William. *The Rise and Fall of the Third Reich: A History of Nazi Germany*. New York: Simon & Schuster, 1950.

Spotts, Frederic. *Hitler and the Power of Aesthetics*. New York: Overlook, 2004.

Stoner, Peter. *Science Speaks*. Chicago: Moody, 1963.

Storms, Sam. *Understanding Spiritual Warfare: A Comprehensive Guide*. Grand Rapids, MI: Zondervan Reflective, 2021.

Strobel, Lee. *A Case for the Creator: A Journalist Investigates Scientific Evidence That Points Toward God*. Grand Rapids, MI: Zondervan, 2004.

Strong, James, and John R. Kohlenberger. *The New Strong's Expanded Exhaustive Concordance of the Bible*. Nashville, TN: Thomas Nelson, 1996.

BIBLIOGRAPHY

Tanner, Jerald and Sandra Tanner. *3,913 Changes in the Book of Mormon*. Sandy, UT: Utah Lighthouse Ministry, 1996.

Thompson, Geoff. "Progressive Christianity: Testing Its Arguments." *Unifying Theology and Church* 5 (2011) 1–12.

Thurman, Chris. *The Lies We Believe: Renew Your Mind and Transform Your Life*. Nashville, TN: Thomas Nelson, 2019.

Turner, E. G. *Greek Manuscripts of the Ancient World*. Princeton, NJ: Princeton University Press, 1971.

Twibell, Simone. "Strategic-Level Spiritual Warfare: A Theological Assessment of its Premises and Practices." *Mediator* 15, no. 1 (2020) 83–110.

UH-60 PSYOP Leaflet Drop, near Hawijah, Iraq 06 March 2008. March 14, 2008. Photograph. Wikimedia. https://commons.wikimedia.org/wiki/File:UH-60_PSYOP_Leaflet_Drop,_near_Hawijah,_Iraq_06_March_2008.jpg#mw-jump-to-license.

U.S. Army Loudspeaker Team in Action in Korea. 1953. Photograph. Wikimedia. https://commons.wikimedia.org/wiki/File:U.S._Army_loudspeaker_team_in_action_in_Korea.jpg.

Vanderkam, James, and Peter Flint. *The Meaning of the Dead Sea Scrolls: Their Significance For Understanding the Bible, Judaism, Jesus, and Christianity*. New York: Harper Collins, 2002.

Virkler, Henry A., and Karelynne Gerber Ayayo. *Hermeneutics: Principles and Processes of Biblical Interpretation*. 2nd ed. Grand Rapids, MI: Baker, 2007.

Wall, James C. *Relics from the Crucifixion—Where They Went and How They Got There*. Manchester, NH: Sophia Institute, 2016.

Welch, David. *Germany, Propaganda and Total War, 1914–1918*. New Brunswick, NJ: Rutgers University Press, 2000.

White, James. *What Every Christian Needs to Know About the Qur'an*. Minneapolis, MN: Bethany House, 2013.

———. *Scripture Alone: Exploring the Bible's Accuracy, Authority and Authenticity*. Minneapolis, MN: Bethany House, 2004.

Wiersbe, Warren W. *On Being a Leader for God*. Grand Rapids, MI: Baker, 2011.

———. *The Wiersbe Bible Commentary*. Colorado Springs: David C. Cook, 2007.

Wilmington, Harold. *The Doctrine of Satan*. Lynchburg, VA: Liberty University, 2018.

Wilson, Jared C. *The Gospel According to Satan: Eight Lies about God that Sound Like the Truth*. Nashville, TN: Nelson, 2020.

Wishart, Mervyn. "The Preservation of the Messianic Line—Part 1." *Precious Seed* 76, no. 3 (2021) 18–19.

———. "The Preservation of the Messianic Line—Part 2." *Precious Seed* 76, no. 4 (2021) 14.

WO201-2841 Middle East Command Camouflage Development and Training Centre, Helwan 'Sunshield'. 1941. Photograph. Wikimedia. https://commons.wikimedia.org/wiki/File:WO201-2841_Middle_East_Command_Camouflage_Development_and_Training_Centre,_Helwan_%27Sunshield%27.jpg#mw-jump-to-license.

Wright, N. T. *Colossians and Philemon*. Downers Grove, IL: IVP Academic, 2008.
Yourman, Julius. "Propaganda Techniques Within Nazi Germany." *Journal of Educational Sociology* 13, no. 3 (1939) 148–63.
YouVersion. "When the Devil Knocks." https://www.bible.com/reading-plans/9196-when-the-devil-knocks#.
Zuck, Roy B. "The Role of the Holy Spirit in Hermeneutics." *Bibliotheca Sacra* 141, no. 562 (1984) 120–29.

Subject Index

Aaron [biblical], 54, 101
Abel [biblical], 24, 167
Abraham (Abram) [biblical], 23, 77n26, 167, 171
Abrahamic Covenant, 170–71
Adam [biblical]
  and absolute (universal) truth, 143–44
  and belief in the truth of the Bible, 167
  and deceptive PSYOP in Scripture, 41
  and the fall of man, 13, 14n33
  and Satan's ambitions, 21–23nn13–14, 22, 24
  and Satan's PSYOP strategy as religious deception, 60, 62, 66
  and understanding Satan's strategies in the context of PSYOP, 35
Adams, John, 12
Afghanistan War, 12
Against the Heresy of One Noetus (Saint Hippolytus), 184
agnosticism, 138–39
Allah, 87n54
Allies, 30–31, 70–71, 92, 128
"Amazing Grace" [hymn], 49
Ambrosian Library, 187
American Revolution, 12

Amin, Idi, 11n27
Ammonites, 102n16
Ananias [biblical], 26
Antichrist, 35, 37, 54
Apocrypha, 168–69n7
Aquinas, Thomas, 152n10
Arbeit macht frei, 7n12
Aristotle, 174, 180n33
Army, US, 17, 31, 73, 96
The Art of War (Sun Tzu), 4, 18
Aryans, 8
Asia Minor, 115, 177
Assyria [historical], 168n7
The A-Team [TV show], 181n35
atheism, ix, 53, 56n33, 134n8, 136, 138–41, 182
Athenian and Spartan Archidamian War, 70
Augustine of Hippo, Saint, 87, 113

Babylon [historical], 19–20, 168n7
Babylonian Talmud, 168n7
Baracus, B. A. [character], 181n35
Bathsheba [biblical], 44–45
Bathsheba Syndrome, 45n10
Battle of Anzio, 71
Baucham, Voddie, 166n3
Bellshaw, William G., 19
Ben-Gurion, David, 171n11
Berea [historical], 105
Berlin Wall, 71–72

201

SUBJECT INDEX

Bethlehem [historical], 25, 62, 122n3
Bhagavad-Gita, 172
bitterness, deceptive PSYOP as, 51–52
Boniface VIII, Pope, 152n10
Bosnia, 73n17, 98
Brendon, Piers, 7
Britain, 10–11
Buddha, 61, 172
Buddhism, 64n52
Bullinger, E. W., 93n69

Caesar, Julius, 180n33
Cain [biblical], 24
Calvin, John, 155n16
Canaan [historical], 31
Canterbury, England, 94n70
Carlyle, Thomas, 55n32
Cassino Front, 71
Castro, Fidel, 11n27
Catholicism, 113
Central Intelligence Agency (CIA), 12, 129n16
Cephas [biblical], 75
Chamberlain, Neville, 10–11
Chesterton, C. K., 142
Chicago Statement on Biblical Hermeneutics, 93n69
"The Child Organ Trafficking Rumor: A Modern Urban Legend" (US Information Agency), 88
Christ. *see* Jesus Christ [biblical]
Christianity
    and absolute (universal) truth, 135, 139, 142
    and archaeological verification of the Bible, 178
    and belief in the truth of the Bible, 167n6, 169n7
    and the Bible as sole authority for faith and practice, 186–89, 190n11
    and Christ as sufficient, 149n5, 150n8
    and conditioning as counter-PSYOP method to guard against deception, 74, 76–78, 79n33, 81
    and counter-PSYOP methods to guard against deception, 72, 97
    deception as Satan's way to thwart, x–xi
    and deceptive PSYOP as false doctrine, 55–56
    and deceptive PSYOP as lack of faith, 52–53
    and deceptive PSYOP as lust, 45n11, 46–48
    and deceptive PSYOP in Scripture, 41
    and defining deception, 2–3, 6
    and direct refutation as counter-PSYOP method to guard against deception, 89–90, 93n69, 94–95
    and disbelief of the Bible as foolish, 181
    and dying to self, 163–64
    and experiencing God, 118–19
    and the fall of man, 16
    and forestalling as counter-PSYOP method to guard against deception, 98–100, 103n18, 104–5
    and God's Word as supreme authority, 148–49n3
    and God's Word as true, 165–66
    and the Gospel's completeness for salvation, 153–55
    guarding Satan's deception in the minds of, 124–26
    and indirect refutation as counter-PSYOP method to guard against deception, 85–88

SUBJECT INDEX

proselytism of, ix–x
and restrictive measures as counter-PSYOP method to guard against deception, 107–8, 110, 111n37, 112–16, 118
and Satan's ambitions, 21n13, 22, 26
and Satan's deception viewed through lens of military PSYOP, 122, 123n5, 124, 128–30
and Satan's power, 27
and Satan's PSYOP strategy as religious deception, 59, 61n45, 63, 64n53, 64n55, 66–68
and scientific accuracy of the Bible, 173–74n19, 175–76
and the substitutionary atonement of Christ, 158–59n30
and trust in Jesus, 161–62
and understanding Satan's strategies in the context of PSYOP, 18, 35–37
Church of Laodicea, 164
Churchill, Winston, 129
CIA (Central Intelligence Agency), 12, 129n16
Clausewitz, Carl von, 4
Clement of Alexandria, 187
Cold War, 4, 97
Colossae [historical], 148n2
Colossians, 107
conditioning as counter-PSYOP method to guard against deception, 73–84
Confederate States of America, 29
Confucianism, 64n52
Confucius, 61
Congress, US, 21
Coniah (Jeconiah, Jehoiachin) [biblical], 24n20

Corinth [historical], 76n22, 115n43
Corinthians, 37, 100, 113n40
Council of Trent, 168n7
Crossing of the Red Sea, 53
Crusades, 64n55
Cuba, 11n27
Cyprian, 152n10
Czechoslovakia [historical], 9–10

Daniel [biblical], 28, 149n5, 167, 172
Darwin, Charles, 139
Darwinism, 141n15, 142
Das Kapital (Marx), 139n13
David, King [biblical], 24n20, 44–45, 51, 167
Davidic Covenant, 24n20
Dawkins, Richard, 139
Day of Judgment, 182
D-Day, 30–31, 128
Dead Sea, 179n32
Dead Sea Scrolls, 179
deception
   and absolute (universal) truth, 134n8
   and the Bible as sole authority for faith and practice, 184
   counter-PSYOP methods to guard against, 69–120
   and the fall of man, 11–16
   and the foundation of the Gospel, 147
   and God's Word as supreme authority, 148
   introduction to, 1–16
   military and PSYOP, 29–38
   and propaganda as optimized by Nazi Germany, 6–11
   PSYOP as bitterness, 51–52
   PSYOP as false doctrine, 55–57
   PSYOP as false occult practices, 54–55
   PSYOP as lack of faith, 52–54
   PSYOP as lies, 42–43
   PSYOP as lust, 43–49

SUBJECT INDEX

deception (continued)
    PSYOP as pride, 49–50
    of PSYOP in Scripture, 39–68
    of Satan viewed through lens of military PSYOP, 18, 121–30
    and Satan's ambitions, 26
    and Satan's fall, 21
    and Satan's power, 27–28
    Satan's PSYOP strategy as religious, 58–68
    as strategy of Satan, x
    and trust in Jesus, 163
Department of Defense, US, x
Department of the Army, US, 72
Derbe [historical], 177n28
Diocletian, Emperor, 178
direct refutation as counter-PSYOP method to guard against deception, 88–95
doctrine, deceptive PSYOP as false, 55–57
Doctrine of Eternal Functional Subordination, 60n43
Doctrine of the Illumination of the Holy Spirit, 90n62
Dulles, Allen, 129n16

EC-130J Commando Solo, 106, 118
Egypt, 53–54, 101
Einstein, Albert, 165
Eisenhower, Gen. Dwight D., 39
Elijah [biblical], 167
Encyclopedia of Biblical Prophecy (Payne), 172n15
England, 30, 64n55, 94n70, 176, 177n28
Ephraimites, 102n16
Estienne, Robert, 94n70
Europe, 9–10, 26n27, 30, 41, 71
Eve [biblical]
    and absolute (universal) truth, 144
    and belief in the truth of the Bible, 167

    and deceptive PSYOP in Scripture, 41
    and defining deception, 3
    and the fall of man, 13–15
    and forestalling as counter-PSYOP method to guard against deception, 100
    and Satan's ambitions, 22, 24
    and Satan's power, 27
    and Satan's PSYOP strategy as religious deception, 58
    and understanding Satan's strategies in the context of PSYOP, 35
evolution, 134n8, 135–43
Exposition Primae Decretalis ad Archdiaconum Tudertinum (Aquinas), 152n10
Ezekiel [biblical], 20

faith, deceptive PSYOP as lack of, 52–54
Faith's Checkbook (Spurgeon), 146
Figures of Speech in the Bible (Bullinger), 93n69
The Fine Art of Propaganda (Lee and Lee), 1
First US Army Group (FUSAG), 30
Flood, the, 167
Foreign Office, German, 70
forestalling as counter-PSYOP method to guard against deception, 98–105
Fourth British Army, 30
Fourth Lateran Council, 152n10
France, 10–11, 30–31, 128
Franklin, Benjamin, 12
Frederick the Great, 17
FUSAG (First US Army Group), 30

Gaddafi, Muammar, 11n27
Gaelic Wars (Caesar), 180n33
Galatians, 56, 148n2, 164

SUBJECT INDEX

Garden of Eden, 3, 6, 15, 21–22n13, 41–42, 58, 151
Gates, Bill, 85
Germany, 6–11, 70, 72, 111n37
Gileadites, 102n16
Global War on Terrorism, 32
God
    and absolute (universal) truth, 134–45
    and the Bible as sole authority for faith and practice, 184–90
    and Christ as sufficient, 149–50, 150–51nn8–9
    and conditioning as counter-PSYOP method to guard against deception, 74–76, 77n26, 78–84
    deception as Satan's way to thwart, x
    and deceptive PSYOP as bitterness, 51–52
    and deceptive PSYOP as false doctrine, 55n32, 56–57
    and deceptive PSYOP as false occult practices, 54–55
    and deceptive PSYOP as lack of faith, 52–54
    and deceptive PSYOP as lies, 42–43
    and deceptive PSYOP as lust, 44–49
    and deceptive PSYOP as pride, 49–50
    and deceptive PSYOP in Scripture, 41–42
    and defining deception, 3, 5–6
    and direct refutation as counter-PSYOP method to guard against deception, 89, 90n65, 91–95
    and dying to self, 164
    experiencing, 118–20
    and the fall of man, 13–15
    and forestalling as counter-PSYOP method to guard against deception, 99–105
    and the foundation of the Gospel, 146–47
    and the Gospel's completeness for salvation, 152–58
    image of. *see imago Dei* (image of God)
    and indirect refutation as counter-PSYOP method to guard against deception, 86–88
    and propaganda and deception as optimized by Nazi Germany, 11
    and restrictive measures as counter-PSYOP method to guard against deception, 106–9, 110n32, 110–11n34, 111n37, 112, 113n40, 114–17
    and Satan's ambitions, 21–26
    and Satan's deception viewed through lens of military PSYOP, 122–30
    and Satan's fall, 19–21
    and Satan's power, 27–28
    and Satan's PSYOP strategy as religious deception, 58–68
    and the substitutionary atonement of Christ, 158, 159n30
    and trust in Jesus, 159–62
    and understanding Satan's strategies in the context of PSYOP, 18, 33–36, 37n28
    Word of as supreme authority, 147–48
    Word of as true, 165
Goebbels, Joseph, 7–8, 10
Gorbachev, Mikhail, 71–72
Gospel, completeness of for salvation, 151–58

SUBJECT INDEX

Gospel, foundation of the, 146–64
Great Commission, ix, 25
The Great Divorce (Lewis), 182n37
Greece, 178n29
Gregor, Neil, 7
Grudem, Wayne, 144, 170

Haggai [biblical], 168n7
Hart, Capt. Sir Basil Liddell, 96
Hebrews [people]. *see* Israelites
Henry, Carl F. H., 173n19
Herod, King [biblical], 25, 50
Herodotus, 180n33
Hezekiah, King [biblical], 50, 112n37
Hinduism, 172, 174
Hippolytus, Saint, 184
Hitler, Adolf, 6–11, 40, 112–13, 136
Hodge, Charles, 165
Holocaust, 136
Holy Spirit
    and belief in the truth of the Bible, 167, 168n7
    and the Bible as sole authority for faith and practice, 185–87
    and Christ as sufficient, 149n5, 151n8
    and conditioning as counter-PSYOP method to guard against deception, 74nn18–19, 76, 79n31, 80
    and direct refutation as counter-PSYOP method to guard against deception, 89, 90n62, 91n66, 94
    and experiencing God, 119–20
    and forestalling as counter-PSYOP method to guard against deception, 103–4
    and the foundation of the Gospel, 146
    and God's Word as true, 166n3
    and the Gospel's completeness for salvation, 153, 155, 156n19
    and indirect refutation as counter-PSYOP method to guard against deception, 86, 87n53
    and restrictive measures as counter-PSYOP method to guard against deception, 117
    and Satan's ambitions, 25–26
    and Satan's PSYOP strategy as religious deception, 60n43, 61
    and scientific accuracy of the Bible, 176n25
    and trust in Jesus, 161
    and understanding Satan's strategies in the context of PSYOP, 37n28
Homer, 180n33
Honest Dealing with God (Spurgeon), 121
House of Commons, UK Parliament, 129
House of Representatives, U.S., 21
Hunt, David, 178n30
Hussein, Saddam, 11n27

Iconium [historical], 177n28
imago Dei (image of God), 23n14, 136, 143–45, 156n19
Implementation Force (IFOR), 73n17
indirect refutation as counter-PSYOP method to guard against deception, 85–88
Information Agency, US, 88
Instruction to His Generals (Frederick the Great), 17
Iraq, 11n27, 17
Irenaeus, 186–87
Iroquois tribe, 174

SUBJECT INDEX

Isaac [biblical], 171n11
Isaiah [biblical], 20, 149n5, 150n8,
   153, 189
Islam, 61, 64nn52–53, 87n54
Israel, land of [historical], 111n37,
   168n7, 171–72
Israelites
   and Christ as sufficient, 149n5
   and conditioning as counter-
      PSYOP method to guard
      against deception, 82
   and deceptive PSYOP as
      bitterness, 51
   and deceptive PSYOP as false
      occult practices, 54
   and deceptive PSYOP as lack of
      faith, 53
   and restrictive measures as
      counter-PSYOP method to
      guard against deception,
      111–12n37
   and Satan's ambitions, 23–24
   and Satan's fall, 19–20
   and unity of the Bible, 171n11
Itala, 187
Italy, 187

Jacob [biblical], 171n11
James [biblical], 75, 76n22, 154,
   155n16, 160n32
Japan, 21
Jeconiah (Jehoiachin, Coniah)
   [biblical], 24n20
Jehovah's Witnesses, 56, 61–62,
   64n52, 151n9
Jephthah [biblical], 102n16
Jeremiah, David, 135
Jerome, 168n7
Jerusalem [historical], 24n20, 44,
   50, 65n56, 189
Jerusalem [modern], 179n32
Jesus Christ [biblical]
   and absolute (universal) truth,
      135, 137–38, 145
   and belief in the truth of the
      Bible, 167, 168n7, 169
   and the Bible as sole authority
      for faith and practice, 187,
      189–90
   and conditioning as counter-
      PSYOP method to guard
      against deception, 73n17,
      74–75, 76n22, 77–78,
      79n31, 80n34, 81–84
   and deceptive PSYOP as false
      doctrine, 55n32, 56–57
   and deceptive PSYOP as false
      occult practices, 54
   and deceptive PSYOP as lack of
      faith, 52–53
   and deceptive PSYOP as lust,
      45–46, 48
   and deceptive PSYOP as pride,
      50
   and deceptive PSYOP in
      Scripture, 42
   and direct refutation as
      counter-PSYOP method to
      guard against deception,
      93n69, 94–95
   and dying to self, 163–64
   and endurance of the Bible,
      178, 180–81nn33–34
   and experiencing God, 119–20
   and the fall of man, 13, 15
   and forestalling as counter-
      PSYOP method to guard
      against deception, 99–100,
      104
   and the foundation of the
      Gospel, 146–47
   and God's Word as supreme
      authority, 148n2
   and God's Word as true, 166–67
   and the Gospel's completeness
      for salvation, 152–57,
      158n29

SUBJECT INDEX

Jesus Christ (continued)
    and indirect refutation as counter-PSYOP method to guard against deception, 86n52, 87
    and propaganda and deception as optimized by Nazi Germany, 7
    proselytism by, x
    and restrictive measures as counter-PSYOP method to guard against deception, 106–11, 112nn37–38, 113–18
    and Satan's ambitions, 22, 24–26
    and Satan's deception viewed through lens of military PSYOP, 122–23, 124n7, 125–26, 128–29
    and Satan's fall, 19
    and Satan's power, 27
    and Satan's PSYOP strategy as religious deception, 58–68
    and scientific accuracy of the Bible, 174
    subsitutionary atonement of, 158–59
    as sufficient, 149–51
    trust in, 159–63
    and understanding Satan's strategies in the context of PSYOP, 33, 35–37
    and unity of the Bible, 171–72
Jillette, Penn, ix–x
Joab [biblical], 45
Job [biblical], 19
John [biblical], 13, 19, 60, 84, 151n9, 169
John Paul II, Pope, 152n10
John the Baptist [biblical], 78, 111n37, 150n5
Johns Hopkins University, 69
Joint Chiefs of Staff, U.S., 4
Joint Resolution, 21

Jonah [biblical], 167
Jordan River, 102n16
Joseph [biblical], 24n20
Joshua [biblical], 31
Judah [historical], 24n20, 50
Judaism
    and absolute (universal) truth, 136
    and belief in the truth of the Bible, 168n7
    and Christ as sufficient, 151n9
    and deceptive PSYOP as lust, 47n13
    and deceptive PSYOP as pride, 50
    and direct refutation as counter-PSYOP method to guard against deception, 94n70
    and endurance of the Bible, 179n32
    and forestalling as counter-PSYOP method to guard against deception, 105
    and the Gospel's completeness for salvation, 154n13
    and propaganda and deception as optimized by Nazi Germany, 8
    and Satan's ambitions, 23
    and Satan's fall, 19
    and Satan's PSYOP strategy as religious deception, 61n45
    and trust in Jesus, 160n32
    and unity of the Bible, 171n11
Judaizers, 154n13
Judas [biblical], 22n13, 25
Jude [biblical], x, 123, 148n2, 169

Kennedy, D. James, 139n13
King Follet Discourse, 67
"The Kite, or the Fall of Pride" (Newton), 49
Korea, 96

SUBJECT INDEX

Lang, Clubber [character], 181n35
Langton, Stephen, 94n70
Laodicea [historical], 115–16
Laodiceans, 114–17
Lapine, Matthew A., 176n25
Latter-day Saints (LDS). *see* Mormonism
Lee, Alfred McClung, 1
Lee, Elizabeth Briant, 1
Lenape tribe, 174
Leo XIII, Pope, 152n10
Lewis, C. S., 182n37
LGBTQ+ movement, 48n16, 134n8, 136
Libia, 11n27
lies, deceptive PSYOP as, 42–43
The Lies We Believe: Renew Your Mind and Transform Your Life (Thurman), 43
The Logic of the Body: Retrieving Theological Psychology (Lapine), 176n25
The Long War Against God: The History and Impact of the Creation/Evolution Conflict (Morris), 135–36
Lord's Supper, 115n43, 190n11
Lucifer, 18
Luke [biblical], 169, 178
lust, deceptive PSYOP as, 43–49
Luther, Martin, 168n7
Lystra [historical], 177n28

MacArthur, John, 18, 109
Malachi [biblical], 168n7
Manassas Junction, 29
Marcionism, 157n23
Mariolatry, 189–90n11
Marx, Karl, 56n33, 139n13
Marxism, 56n33
Mary, Queen "Bloody," 64n55
Mary [biblical], 24n20, 62n48, 67, 107n27, 189–90n11
Mass, 189–90n11

Maury, Matthew Fonaine, 175–76
Mein Kampf (Hitler), 112
Melchizedek [biblical], 190n11
Merriam-Webster's Collegiate Dictionary, 2, 132
Messiah, 22n13, 24, 86n52, 109, 122n3, 151, 172n16
Metzger, Bruce, 180n33
Michael [biblical], 28, 61
Microsoft Corporation, 85
Middle Ages, 111n37
Middle East, 61n45
Milan, Italy, 187
military deception (MILDEC) and PSYOP, 29–38
Military Deception (US Joint Chiefs of Staff), 32
The Military Institutions of the Romans (Renatus), 29
Ministry of Public Enlightenment and Propaganda, 7
Missouri, 111n37
Mormonism
   and deceptive PSYOP as false doctrine, 56
   and the Gospel's completeness for salvation, 157n23
   and Satan's PSYOP strategy as religious deception, 60, 63n49, 64nn52–53, 65–68
   and the substitutionary atonement of Christ, 159n30
   and unity of the Bible, 170n9
Morris, Henry, 135
Mosaic Law, 154n13
Moses [biblical], 54, 82, 101, 111–12n37, 149n5, 167
Mr. T (Laurence Tureaud), 181n35
Muhammad, 61
Munich, Germany, 11
Muslims. *see* Islam

Napoleonic Wars, 31

SUBJECT INDEX

Narula, Sunil, 33
Nathan, Rabbi, 94n70
National Geographic Society, 178n30
Native Americans, 174
Navy, US, x, 175n22
Nazism, 6–11, 40–41, 171n11
Nebuchadnezzar, King [biblical], 168n7
New Covenant, 171
New World Translation, 62
Newton, Isaac, 131, 174
Newton, John, 49
Noah [biblical], 167
Normandy, France, 30–31, 128
North America, 174
Norway, 30
Nuremberg Tribunal, 7

occult practices, deceptive PSYOP as false, 54–55
Olivet Discourse, 122
193rd Special Operations Wing, Pennsylvania Air National Guard, 106
On War (Clausewitz), 4
Operation Fortitude North, 30
Operation Fortitude South, 30
Operation Overlord. *see* D-Day
Operations Research Office, Johns Hopkins University, 69

Parliament, UK, 129
Pas de Calais, France, 30–31
Patton, Gen. George S., 30
Paul [biblical]
 and archaeological verification of the Bible, 177
 and belief in the truth of the Bible, 169
 and the Bible as sole authority for faith and practice, 185
 and conditioning as counter-PSYOP method to guard against deception, 75–77
 and deceptive PSYOP as false doctrine, 56–57
 and deceptive PSYOP as lack of faith, 52–53
 and deceptive PSYOP as lust, 46–47
 and defining deception, 2
 and dying to self, 164
 and forestalling as counter-PSYOP method to guard against deception, 100, 105
 and God's Word as supreme authority, 148n2
 and the Gospel's completeness for salvation, 153n11, 154n13
 and restrictive measures as counter-PSYOP method to guard against deception, 107, 109, 113n40, 115n43
 and Satan's deception viewed through lens of military PSYOP, 122
 and Satan's fall, 19
 and Satan's power, 27
 and Satan's PSYOP strategy as religious deception, 58
 and scientific accuracy of the Bible, 176n25
 and trust in Jesus, 162
 and understanding Satan's strategies in the context of PSYOP, 37
Payne, J. Barton, 172n15
Pearl Harbor, 21
Peloponnesian Wars, 70
Penn and Teller, ix
Pennsylvania Air National Guard, 106
Persia [historical], 28
Peter [biblical]

SUBJECT INDEX

and belief in the truth of the Bible, 169
and Christ as sufficient, 150n7
and conditioning as counter-PSYOP method to guard against deception, 76n22, 81n35
and deceptive PSYOP as lust, 46
and forestalling as counter-PSYOP method to guard against deception, 105
and indirect refutation as counter-PSYOP method to guard against deception, 86
and restrictive measures as counter-PSYOP method to guard against deception, 117
and Satan's ambitions, 26
and Satan's deception viewed through lens of military PSYOP, 123
and Satan's power, 28n31
and trust in Jesus, 161
Pew research, 26n27
Pharaoh [biblical], 54, 101
Pharisees, 22n13, 50, 84, 157n24, 189
Pillar of Smoke and Fire, 53
Piper, John, 100
Pisidian Antioch, 177n28
Poetics (Aristotle), 180n33
Presbyterianism, 165
pride, deceptive PSYOP as, 49–50
Prijedor, Bosnia, 98
Princeton Theological Seminary, 165
Progressive Christianity, 55, 55–56n33
Promised Land. *see* Israel, land of [historical]
propaganda
and conditioning as counter-PSYOP method to guard against deception, 73

and counter-PSYOP methods to guard against deception, 69–72, 97
and deception as optimized by Nazi Germany, 6–11
and deceptive PSYOP in Scripture, 40–41
and direct refutation as counter-PSYOP method to guard against deception, 88
and the fall of man, 11–13
and forestalling as counter-PSYOP method to guard against deception, 98–99, 105
and indirect refutation as counter-PSYOP method to guard against deception, 85
as instrument of aggression, 1
proselytism, ix, 154n13
Protestant Reformation, 74n19, 168n7
Protestantism, 6n11, 55n33, 162
Provine, William, 141n15
Pseudepigrapha, 168n7
Psychological Operations Tactics (US Department of the Army), 72, 73n17
A Psychological Warfare Casebook (Johns Hopkins University), 69
PSYOP (psychological operations)
and absolute (universal) truth, 131
and the Bible as sole authority for faith and practice, 184
counteractive methods of to guard against deception, 69–120
deception as bitterness, 51–52
deception as false doctrine, 55–57
deception as false occult practices, 54–55

PSYOP (continued)
    deception as lack of faith, 52–54
    deception as lies, 42–43
    deception as lust, 43–49
    deception as pride, 49–50
    deception of in Scripture, 39–68
    and defining deception, 2–6
    and the fall of man, 16
    and the foundation of the Gospel, 147
    and God's Word as supreme authority, 148
    and God's Word as true, 166
    intention behind, 17
    and military deception, 29–38
    propaganda other than, 6n11
    Satan's deception viewed through lens of military, x, 18, 121–30
    Satan's strategy as religious deception, 58–68
    and trust in Jesus, 163
    understanding Satan's strategies in the context of, 33–38
    use of by Satan, 36–38
Purgatory, 189–90n11

Qumran [historical], 179n32
Qur'an, 87n54, 172

Ramsay, William, 177–78
Reagan, Ronald, 71–72
refutation, direct as counter-PSYOP method to guard against deception, 88–95
refutation, indirect as counter-PSYOP method to guard against deception, 85–88
Renatus, Flavius Vegetius, 29
restrictive measures as counter-PSYOP method to guard against deception, 105–18
Rocky III [movie], 181n35
Roman Catholicism
    and belief in the truth of the Bible, 168n7
    and the Bible as sole authority for faith and practice, 190n11
    and conditioning as counter-PSYOP method to guard against deception, 74n19
    and the Gospel's completeness for salvation, 152n10, 157n24
    propaganda invented in, 6n11
    and restrictive measures as counter-PSYOP method to guard against deception, 107n27, 111
    and trust in Jesus, 162
Romans, 22n13, 53, 77n26, 178
Rome [historical], 168n7, 178, 184
Romerstein, Herbert, 97
Roosevelt, Franklin D., 21n12

Sabbath, 151n9
Satan
    and absolute (universal) truth, 136
    ambitions of, 21–26
    and the Bible as sole authority for faith and practice, 184
    character of, 34–36
    and conditioning as counter-PSYOP method to guard against deception, 73, 74n17, 77–78, 81
    and counter-PSYOP methods to guard against deception, 72, 97
    deception as strategy of, x
    deception of viewed through lens of military PSYOP, 18, 121–30
    and deceptive PSYOP as bitterness, 51–52

SUBJECT INDEX

and deceptive PSYOP as false doctrine, 57
and deceptive PSYOP as false occult practices, 54–55
and deceptive PSYOP as lack of faith, 52–53
and deceptive PSYOP as lies, 42–43
and deceptive PSYOP as lust, 43–49
and deceptive PSYOP as pride, 49–50
and deceptive PSYOP in Scripture, 41–42
and defining deception, 2–3, 5–6
and direct refutation as counter-PSYOP method to guard against deception, 89, 93n69, 95
fall of, 18–21
and the fall of man, 13–16
and forestalling as counter-PSYOP method to guard against deception, 100, 104–5
and the foundation of the Gospel, 147
and God's Word as supreme authority, 148
and indirect refutation as counter-PSYOP method to guard against deception, 85, 88
power of, 27–28
and propaganda and deception as optimized by Nazi Germany, 11
PSYOP strategy of as religious deception, 58–68
and restrictive measures as counter-PSYOP method to guard against deception, 106, 108–9, 111–12, 114, 118

and trust in Jesus, 163
understanding strategies of in the context of PSYOP, 33–38
use of deceptive PSYOP by, 36–38
Saul, King [biblical], 51
Schweinehund, 8
Science Speaks (Stoner), 172n16
Scotland, 30
Second Law of Thermodynamics, 142
self, dying to, 163–64
Senate, U.S., 21
Sermon on the Mount, 157n24
Seth [biblical], 24
Shema, 160n32
Sheol, 20
Shroud of Turin, 111n37
Silas [biblical], 105
Sinai, Mount, 54, 82
Smith, Joseph, 65–67, 170n9, 180n32
Snow, Lorenzo, 67
Soviet Union, 11n27, 71–72, 97
Spanish Inquisition, 64n55
Speer, Albert, 7
Spurgeon, Charles, 121, 146
Stalin, Joseph, 11n27
Stoner, Peter, 172n16
Sudeten Mountains, 9
Sudetendeutsches Freikorps (Sudeten German Free Corps), 10
Sudetenland, 9–11, 13
Sun Tzu, 4, 18, 31
Systematic Theology (Grudem), 144, 170

Taoism, 64n52
Ten Plagues, 53
Tertullian, 187
"Theology and Science" (Henry), 173n19

SUBJECT INDEX

Thessalonica [historical], 105, 178n29
Third Reich, 7
Thomas [biblical], 99
Thoughts on War (Hart), 96
Thucydides, 70
Thurman, Chris, 43
Timothy [biblical], 2, 47, 57
Treaty of Versailles, 10
Tree of Knowledge, 42
Trinity, 46, 60n43, 61–62, 76, 100
truth, absolute (universal), 131–45
Tureaud, Laurence (Mr. T), 181n35
Turkey, 111n37, 177
Turtle Island, 174
Tyre [historical], 19–20

Uganda, 11n27
United Kingdom, 26n27, 129
United Nations, 88
Uriah the Hittite [biblical], 44–45
Uzziah, King [biblical], 50

Vedas, 172
Verga [historical]. *see* Turkey
Victorian era, 170n9
Vietnam War, 4
Virginia Military Institute, 175n22
Voice of America [news broadcaster], 12

Wald, Abraham, 92, 94
Washington, George, 12
Watchtower and Tract Society, 61
Why I Believe (Kennedy), 139n13
Wilmington, Harold, 20
World War I, 70–71, 121
World War II, 3–4, 9, 30, 69, 71, 92
The Wycliffe Bible Encyclopedia, 75

Young, Brigham, 66

Zechariah [biblical], 168n7

Scripture Index

OLD TESTAMENT

Genesis

1	23n15, 67
1:1	60n43, 94n73
1:2	119, 143
1:26	23n14, 60n43, 143
1:27	49n16, 82n37, 156n19
1:28	23n14, 56n33
1:31	23n15
2:4–25	15n34
2:7	23n14, 143
2:24	44n9
3	27, 33n9, 41
3:1–3	14n33
3:1–5	33n8
3:1–6	13
3:4	13
3:4–5	14n33
3:5	13
3:6	14n33
3:13	14n33
3:14	21n13
3:15	21, 21n13, 24, 36n23
3:22	60n43
4:7	118n48
6:5–6	23
11:7	60n43
12	170
12:1–3	23n16, 170
15	170
15:6	77n26, 86n52
15:18–21	171n11
17:8	74n17
19:1–13	47n14

Exodus

Reference	Pages
7:1	101
7:2	101
7:11	54n28
7:22	54
8:7	54n28
8:18	54n29
9:11	54n29
20:3	112n37
20:7	82n38
20:18–21	82n38
32:1–6	54

Leviticus

18:22	47n14
19:30	125n8
20:13	47n14

Numbers

20:6	125n8
21:8–9	112n37
23:19	67
24:17	172

Deuteronomy

4:1–2	61n44
6:4	60n43, 66, 150n8, 160n32
6:5	118
6:13	93n69
6:16	93n69
8:3	93n69
13	102
13:1–5	101–102
18	102
18:11	107n27
18:15–19	172
18:20–22	101n14
18:22	173n18
22:5	49n16
25:4	169
27:10	118
29:29	165n1
30:11–14	74n18
33:27	67

Joshua

13:33	81
24:14–15	124n7

Judges

8:1–3	102n16
12:1–6	102n16
12:6	102n16
13:20	125n8

1 Samuel

2:2	67
2:2–3	82n38
15:29	67
18	51
18:9–10	27n29

2 Samuel

11	111n34
11:2	44
11:5	44
11:9–11	44
11:27	45
23:2	168
23:39	44

1 Kings

22:28	173n18

2 Kings

6:17	28n34
18:4	112n37

1 Chronicles

17:11–14	24n20
21:16	125n8

2 Chronicles

26:16	50n20
32:25–26	50n21

Esther

3:12–14	23n17

Job

1	19
26:7	174

Psalms

8:8	175
12:6	87, 148n3
14:1	139, 181–182
16:10	75
17:8	93n69

19:1	141	**Isaiah**		
19:1–4	175n25	6:1–5	81n36, 82n38	
19:7	87, 148n3	6:8	60n43	
22	172n13	8:20	104n19, 189	
22:16	172n16	14	19–21	
24:1	67	14:12	18, 18n3	
42:1	81	14:13–14	20, 49	
53:1	139, 181	14:13–15	20	
71:22–23	82n38	14:14	21	
86:8	67	14:15	20	
90:2	67, 165n1	26:4	162	
91	36	33:15	126n11	
91:11–12	36	37:16	67	
91:13	36	40:25	67	
100:3	82n37	40:26	174n19	
103:20	27	41	172n14	
107:23–24	175	41:21	172	
119:89	148n3	42:8	112n37	
119:137	156n21	43:10	66, 150n8	
131:2	162	43:16	175	
138:2	147	44:6	63n49	
145:17	156n21	44:6–8	66	
		44:8	63n49	
Proverbs		45:7	28	
1:7	140	45:22	58	
3:5	79n33, 91	46:9–10	173	
4:23	125	46:13	156n21	
5:19	44n9	48:16	60n43	
15:3	165n1	53	151	
23:7	125	53:3	158	
28:26	79n33	53:6	83n44	
30:5	87, 148n3	53:7	172n16	
30:5–6	61n44	53:8–10	75	
		57:15	82n38	
Ecclesiastes		59:1–2	15n35	
1:7	175	61:1	60n43	
1:9	41	64:6	119, 153	
7:20	114n41	65:17	173	
12:13	118			
		Jeremiah		
Song of Songs		1:2	148n3	
		17:9	79, 79n33, 134n8	
1:2–4	44n9	22	24n20	

Jeremiah (continued)

22:30	24n20
28:9	173n18
29:11	82n39, 165n1
31:31–34	171
31:31–37	172

Ezekiel

28	19–21
28:13–19	20
28:15	35
36:26	155n15
36:26–27	155n15
37	74n17, 171n11

Daniel

7:2–6	172
7:16	172
8:17	82n38
9:25–26	172
10	28
10:13	28
10:14	74n17
11:41	74n17

Hosea

11:9	67

Amos

3:7	149n5

Micah

5:2	172, 172n16

Zechariah

9:9	172n16
11:12–13	172n16
12:10	122n3
13:6	172n16
14:3–4	172
14:4	122n3

Malachi

3:1	172n16
3:6	124n7

DEUTEROCANONICAL BOOKS

1 Maccabees

9:27	170n7

Book of Wisdom

11:17	168n7

Judith

1:5	168n7

NEW TESTAMENT

Matthew

1:12	24n20
3:7	22n13
3:16–17	60n43
4:1–11	36n21, 42
4:9	25n22
4:17	167
5:13	83
5:16	156n19
5:17–18	167n4
5:18	167, 181
5:20	157n24
5:48	157n24
6:6	108n28
6:7–9	82n38
6:19	55n32
6:24	55n32
7	63
7:7	108n28
7:13	58
7:13–14	62, 134n8, 146
7:15	59n41

7:15–19	62	26:41	108n28
7:16–17	115–116	28:16–20	76n22
7:16–23	154n14	28:18	150n7
7:21–23	146	28:18–20	115n43, 150n5
7:22	65n55	28:19	60n43
7:24–26	134n8	28:19–20	ix, 25, 93n69
9:6	83n45	28:20	161
11:28–30	160		
11:29	84	## Mark	
12:3	167	1:12–13	36n21
12:22	27n29	1:23–26	27n29
12:30	134n8	1:32	27n29
12:31–32	79n31	1:35	107–108n28
12:40–41	167	4:15	63
13	25n25	5:1–5	27n29
13:25	64	7:9–13	188n10
13:38	64–65	7:13	84, 188
15:1–6	188n10	7:26–30	108n28
15:1–9	189	8:34–35	163n36
15:9	188	10:23	116n44
15:22	27n29	12:26	167
16:18	25, 150n7	13	122n2
16:24–25	163n36	13:20	124n7
17:14–21	108n28	13:27	124n7
19:4–5	167	16:9	27n29
19:26	67		
23:6–12	50	## Luke	
23:35	167	2:36–38	107n28
24:4–5	57, 59n41	3:31	24n20
24:5	104	4	93n69
24:5–8	73n17	4:10–11	36
24:11	58, 59n41	4:25	167
24:22	124n7	6:12–13	108n28
24:24	37, 57, 59, 59n41, 122	10:2	108n28
24:30	122n3	10:7	169
24:31	124n7	10:18	19
24:36	73n17	10:42	124n7
24:37–38	167	12:15	55n32
24:44	172	14:27	163n37
24–25	122n2	16:16	150n5
25:30	152	16:22–23	158n30
26:28	93n69	16:31	15n38
26:39	108n28	18:1–8	108n28

Luke (continued)

18:7	122n4
18:35–43	108n28
19:10	93n69
19:13	25
21	122n2
22:3	25n23, 27n29
22:20	171
22:60–62	117n46
24:39	67

John

1	60, 62
1:1	60n43, 61
1:1–3	149
1:1–8	67
1:5	84
1:11	47n13
1:12	124n7
1:14	60n43, 61, 87
1:29	78
3:1–18	47n13
3:3	155n15
3:3–7	163
3:12	24
3:16	61, 67, 75, 79n31, 124n7, 159
3:16–17	171
4:24	67, 112n37
5:1–24	151n9
5:16–18	151n9
5:23	151n9
5:30	156n21
6:27	60n43
6:44	80, 119, 124n7
7:5	76n22
8:31–32	148
8:32	94, 129, 129n16
8:44	13, 27, 33–34, 42, 65n56
8:56	67, 167
8:58	61
10:1–9	112n38
10:2–5	123
10:4	187n8
10:5	187n8
10:9	93n69
10:26–30	155n18
10:27	187n8
10:28	123n7
10:28–29	78n30, 123n5
10:30	61
10:35	170
11:25	159
12:31	27
12:32	76n25
12:37	15n38
12:46	156n19
13:27	25n23
14:1	118, 161
14:6	62, 79n31, 87n53, 135, 137, 152
14:16–17	74n18
14:17	76n24
14:21	158n29
14:26	89, 91n66, 94, 149n5, 156n19
14:30	27
15:4	156n19
15:5	156n19
15:26	74n18, 76nn23–24
16:7–9	119
16:8	76n25, 79n31
16:8–13	76n24
16:13	74n18, 76n23, 186n3
16:13–14	74n18
17:3	62, 67n58, 87n53, 93n69, 150n8
17:8	186n3
17:17	87n53, 166, 181n34
19:30	25, 150
20:29	99, 162

SCRIPTURE INDEX

Acts

1:8	76n24, 115n43
1:10–11	172
1:11	122n3
1:14	76n22, 108n28
1:22	76n22
2	93n69
2:17	149n5
2:32	76n22
2:42	108n28, 115n43
3:1	108n28
3:15	76n22
3:21	171
4:11–12	150n7
4:12	67n58, 151
4:23–31	108n28
5:3	26
5:3–4	60n43
5:16	27n29
5:32	76n22
6:4	108n28
12:20–23	50
12:23	50
13:1–3	108n28
13:51	177n28
14:1	177n28
14:6	177n28
14:8	177n28
14:19	177n28
14:20	177n28
14:21	177n28
14:26	177n28
15	154n13
16:1	177n28
16:1–2	177n28
16:2	177n28
16:14	76
16:31	79n31, 93n69, 124n7
17:10–11	105
17:11	148n3
17:24	15n36
19:13–16	27n29
20:4	177n28
20:24	76
20:27	99

Romans

1:7	60n43
1:16	129, 147, 152
1:17	67n58, 78n29
1:17–19	134n8
1:18–25	182–183
1:19–20	124n7
1:19–22	136n10
1:20	139, 141, 174n19, 176n25
1:25	138
1:26–27	47n14
2:4	76n25
2:14–16	136–137
3:10	148n2
3:10–12	79
3:10–20	159
3:11	76
3:12	119
3:19	148
3:20	148
3:22	67n58, 78n29
3:23	114n41, 134n8
3:25–26	77n26
3:28	63n51, 67n58, 77n26, 78n29, 157n24
4:3	63n51, 77n26, 157
4:3–4	77
4:4–5	77n27
4:5	77n26, 155n15, 157, 157n25, 158n28
4:8	77n26, 158n27
4:17	77n26
4:20–22	77n26
4:22	63n51
5:1	157
5:5	80n34
5:8	81

Romans (continued)

5:8–11	75
5:12–18	13n32
5:17	158n27
6:4–8	163n37
6:6	5
6:14	78
6:16–23	15n35
6:23	67–68, 83, 156n22
6:25	42
6–7	35n18
8:1	158n29
8:3	5
8:7	134n8
8:9–11	80
8:15	82
8:16	119
8:20–23	13n31
8:23	47n13
8:26–27	108n28
8:29	124n7, 155n19
8:29–30	123n7
8:30	123n6, 158n29
8:33	122n4, 124n7
9:5	60n43
9:11	124n7
10:9–10	124n7
10:17	99, 166
11:2	124n7
11:5–7	124n7
11:6	77, 77n28, 152, 154n13, 158n27
11:26–27	172–173
11:28	124n7
12	125
12:2	83n43
12:4–5	45n11
14	113n40
16:17–18	55n31
16:20	36n23

1 Corinthians

1:2	67
1:10	113n40
1:10–11	57n36
1:20	15n38
1:26	15n38
2:6–8	28n32
2:6–16	76n24
2:10–11	103n18
2:12–13	103n18, 167n4
3:11	150n7
3:16	60n43, 112
6:9	47n14
6:9–10	2n7, 154n14
7:2	44n9
7:5	44n9
8:4	60n43
10:12	111n34
10:13	42
11:23–26	190n11
12	106
12:12–27	45n11, 115n43
14:3	37n28
14:6	76n22
14:29	37n28
14:36–40	104n19
15:1	76n22
15:1–4	147n1, 152
15:1–8	75–76, 152n10
15:2	76n22
15:3	76n22
15:4	76n22
15:5–11	76n22
15:33	127n12
15:50–54	159n30
15:57	129

2 Corinthians

1:10	161
2:11	36n20
4:2	74n18
4:4	27, 33n9
4:6	95

4:17–18	162	**Ephesians**	
5:1–8	190n11	1:3	15n36
5:6–8	158n30	1:4	122–123
5:7	53	1:4–5	124n7
5:14–19	75	1:5	47n13, 82, 124n7
5:17	145, 155n19	1:5–11	124n7
5:19–21	158n28	1:7	159
5:20	83n43	1:11	124n7
5:21	82n41, 157n25, 158	1:13–14	74n18, 149n5
		1:14	47n13
10:5	109, 118n49	1:18–20	161n33
11:3	14n33, 34, 100	1:22–23	45n11
11:3–4	37	2:1	124n7
11:13–15	37, 55n31	2:2	27, 35, 44
11:14	14n33, 35, 105	2:3	82
11:15	26	2:8	86n52, 154n12
12:9–10	119	2:8–9	61, 77n27, 82n41, 153, 157n26
13:5	65n55, 88n55		
13:14	60n43	2:10	22n14, 153, 155n19
Galatians		2:13	37
1:6–9	56, 57n34, 152	2:20	37n28, 150n7
1:7	78	3:16–19	107
1:8	102, 148n2	3:20	108n28
1:8–9	55n31, 92	4	51
1:11–12	169	4:12	45n11
2:4–5	77	4:14	110
2:20	164n37	4:24	144–145
2:21	154n13	4:31–32	51
3:6	63n51	5:1–9	125n9
3:20	60n43	5:8	134n8
3:25–26	47n13	5:11	22
3:28	15n38	5:18	91n66
4:1–7	47n13	5:23	45n11, 150n7
4:6	47n13, 82	5:30–32	45
5:1	154n13	6	52
5:16	36n22	6:11	6, 36n20, 52, 130
5:17–24	15n37	6:12	x, 3, 27, 52n24, 129
5:21	153n11		
5:22	80n34, 155n17	6:13–17	52n24
5:22–23	119, 156n19	6:14–17	52
5:24	164	6:16	52
5:25	36n22	6:18	107
6:7	2n7	6:18–19	108n28

Philippians

1:23	190n11
2:6–11	67
2:12	88n55
4:6–7	107n28, 161

Colossians

1:16–17	v, 165n1
1:18	45n11, 150n7
1:24	45n11
2	148n2
2:2	107
2:2–3	108
2:8	148n2, 188, 188n10
2:9	60n43
2:20–23	57n34
3:5	5
3:12	122n4, 124n7
3:13	51
4:2–3	107

1 Thessalonians

1:4	124n7
1:5	76
2:13	185, 186n3, 187n7
4:3	79n32
4:14–17	47n13
5:16–18	107
5:19–21	37n28

2 Thessalonians

2:3	73n17
2:3–8	37
2:8–10	42
2:9	54
2:15	188n9, 190n11
3:6	188n9, 190n11

1 Timothy

1:10	47n14
1:17	67
2:4	25
2:5	60n43, 62n48, 190n11
2:5–6	149n5
2:14	14n33
3:1–7	111n34
3:3	55n32
3:4–5	48n15
3:6	19
3:15	46
4:1	25–26, 58–59, 73n17
5:18	169
5:21	124n7
6:3–5	55n31
6:10	55n32
6:12	118n47

2 Timothy

2:10	124n7
2:15	90n65, 93n69, 110, 148n3
2:26	57
3:1–9	73n17
3:13	2
3:15	152
3:16	66, 147, 148n3, 181
3:16–17	86, 91n66, 167n4, 181n34, 185
4:2–4	57

Titus

1:1	124n7
1:10–11	57n34
2	153
2:11	124n7
2:11–14	75
3:3	123
3:4–5	77n27
3:5	61, 153, 155n15
3:7	158n27

Hebrews

1:1	149n5
1:8	60n43
1:14	171
2:3	83
2:10	171
2:11–15	62n48
2:14–15	22n13
2:16	171
3:4	141
4:12	87, 147, 148n3
7:21–27	190n11
7:25	150
7:26	67
9:27	159n30
10:10	150n6
10:12	150n6
10:14	157
10:18	150n6
10:35	52
11:1	99
11:3	149n4
11:6	79n31
11:24–25	124n7
12:14–15	51
12:15–16	51
13:4	44n9
13:5	55n32

James

1:2–4	161
1:5	56n33
1:13–15	35n18
1:13–18	2n7
1:14–15	5
1:27	56n33, 115n43
2:14–26	154
2:19	160n32
2:23	82n40
2:26	155, 155n15, 156n19
3	127
3:9	144
4:2	108n28
4:10	49
5:16–18	108n28

1 Peter

1:1–2	124n7
1:2	60n43
1:5	123
1:6–8	161
1:13–16	82n38
1:17	156n21
1:22–25	47n13
2:5	190n11
2:6	150n7
2:6–7	150n7
2:9	124n7, 190n11
2:11	128n15
2:17	118
2:24	158
3:15	xi, 115n43
3:18	158
4:17	46
5:1–4	190n11
5:8	5, 36n23
5:8–9	126

2 Peter

1:4	119
1:10	124n7
1:16–21	166n3
1:19	86
1:19–20	89
1:20–21	86
1:21	119, 148n3
2:10	28n31
2:11	27–28
3:9	81n35, 124n7
3:13	173
3:15	169
3:15–16	105
3:16	92, 169

SCRIPTURE INDEX

1 John

1:1–3	166n3
1:7	83n42
1:8	83n44
2:2	78, 86n52
2:15–17	128n13
2:16	49
2:19–21	74n18
2:20	186n3
2:27	74n18
3:1–2	47n13
3:2	47n13
3:8	22n13
3:12	24n19
3:16	80n34
4:1	55, 55n31, 104
4:1–3	60
4:1–6	60
4:4–6	60
4:6	76n24
4:8	80, 119
4:10	80
4:16	80
5:2	118
5:6	76n23
5:13	78, 78n30
5:14–15	108n28
5:20	60n43

2 John

1:7	55n31
1:7–11	59
1:9	92

Jude

1:1	123
1:3	x, 25, 148n2
3	185
17	169
18	169

Revelation

1:7	122n3, 172
1:17	82n38
2	115, 169
2:10	26
3	115, 169
3:14	116
3:14–21	114
3:15	115
3:15–16	164n38
3:16	115–117
3:17	115–116
3:18	116
3:19	116–117
3:20	116
3:21	117
4:1–8	81n36
11:8	74n17
12:4	35n15
12:9	13, 34, 35n15, 37–38
12:9–10	27
12:10	19
12:17	26n26
13:8	144
13:11–14	54
14:6	151
15:2–4	82n38
19:11–16	122n3
20:2	36n23
20:3	33n9
20:10	130
20:11–15	159n30
20:12–15	159n30
21:1	159n30, 173
21:6	77n27
22:17	77n27, 124n7
22:18	60–61
22:18–19	61n44, 92, 186

SCRIPTURE INDEX

THE CHURCH OF JESUS CHRIST OF LATTER-DAY SAINTS

Book of Mormon

1 Nephi

13:28	66
14:10	66

2 Nephi

25:23	154n12, 159n30

Doctrine and Covenants

130:22	66
130:22–23	63n49
132:20	67

Pearl of Great Price

Joseph Smith—History

1:18	66
1:19	66

Articles of Faith

8	66
35	66
79	159n30
182–185	66

LDS Bible Dictionary

697	67

www.ingramcontent.com/pod-product-compliance
Lightning Source LLC
Chambersburg PA
CBHW070311230426
43663CB00011B/2082